D0249043

RV Adventures
in the

PACIFIC NORTHWEST

A Camping Guide to
Washington, Oregon, & British Columbia

Mike and Terri
Church

ROLLING HOMES PRESS

Copyright © 2000 by Mike and Terri Church

All rights reserved. No part of this book may be reproduced in any form, except brief extracts for the purpose of review, without permission in writing from the publisher. All inquiries should be addressed to Rolling Homes Press.

Published by
Rolling Homes Press
P.O. Box 2099
Kirkland, WA 98083-2099

www.rollinghomes.com

Printed in the United States of America
First Printing 2000

Publisher's Cataloging in Publication

Church, Mike
    RV adventures in the Pacific Northwest : a camping guide to Washington, Oregon & British Columbia / Mike and Terri Church
    p.cm
    Includes index
    Preassigned LCCN: 99-97835
    ISBN 0-9652968-4-9

    1. Camping–Northwest, Pacific–Guidebooks. 2. Recreational vehicle living–Northwest, Pacific–Guidebooks. 3. Camp sites, facilities, etc.–Northwest, Pacific–Guidebooks. 4. Northwest, Pacific–Guidebooks. I. Church, Terri. II. Title.

GV191.42.N75C48 2000   796.54′09795–dc21

*This book is dedicated
to the next generation of Northwest campers–*

*Chiyo, Sophie, Emily, Miye, Ellen, Perry, Matt, Ben,
Jace, Natalya, Kelsey, Julie, Jeremy, and Jon*

Other Books by Mike and Terri Church
and
Rolling Homes Press

Traveler's Guide To European Camping
Traveler's Guide To Mexican Camping
Traveler's Guide To Alaskan Camping

A brief summary of the above books is provided on pages 221-223

WARNING, DISCLOSURE, AND COMMUNICATION WITH THE AUTHORS AND PUBLISHERS

Half the fun of travel is the unexpected, and self-guided camping travel can produce much in the way of unexpected pleasures, and alternately, complications and problems. This book is designed to increase the pleasures of camping in the Pacific Northwest and reduce the number of unexpected problems you may encounter. You can help ensure a smooth trip by doing additional advance research, planning ahead, and exercising caution as appropriate. There can be no guarantee that your trip will be trouble free.

Although the authors and publisher have done their best to ensure that the information presented in this book was correct at the time of publication they do not assume and hereby disclaim any liability to any party for any loss or damage caused by errors, omissions, or any other cause.

In a book like this it is inevitable that there will be omissions or mistakes, especially as things do change over time. If you find inaccuracies we would like to hear about them so that they can be corrected in future editions. We would also like to hear about your enjoyable experiences. If you come upon an outstanding campground or destination please let us know, those kinds of things may also find their way to future versions of the guide. You can reach us by mail at:

Rolling Homes Press
P.O. Box 2099
Kirkland, WA 98083-2099

www.rollinghomes.com

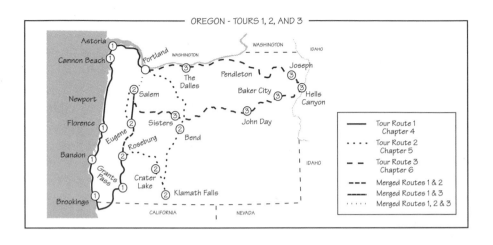

OREGON - TOURS 1, 2, AND 3

Astoria
Cannon Beach
Portland
WASHINGTON
IDAHO
Joseph
The Dalles
Pendleton
Newport
Salem
Baker City
Hells Canyon
Florence
Sisters
John Day
Eugene
Roseburg
Bend
Bandon
Grants Pass
Crater Lake
IDAHO
Klamath Falls
Brookings
CALIFORNIA
NEVADA

- —— Tour Route 1
  Chapter 4
- ···· Tour Route 2
  Chapter 5
- ─ ─ Tour Route 3
  Chapter 6
- ─ ─ Merged Routes 1 & 2
- ─── Merged Routes 1 & 3
- ···· Merged Routes 1, 2 & 3

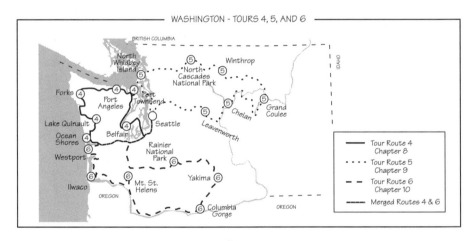

WASHINGTON - TOURS 4, 5, AND 6

BRITISH COLUMBIA
North Whidbey Island
Winthrop
North Cascades National Park
Forks
Port Angeles
Port Townsend
Chelan
Grand Coulee
Lake Quinault
Seattle
Leavenworth
Ocean Shores
Belfair
Westport
Rainier National Park
Yakima
Mt. St. Helens
Ilwaco
OREGON
Columbia Gorge
OREGON

- —— Tour Route 4
  Chapter 8
- ···· Tour Route 5
  Chapter 9
- ─ ─ Tour Route 6
  Chapter 10
- ─── Merged Routes 4 & 6

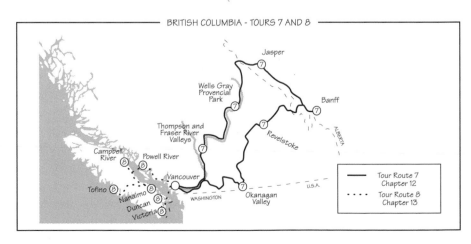

BRITISH COLUMBIA - TOURS 7 AND 8

Jasper
Wells Gray Provencial Park
Banff
Thompson and Fraser River Valleys
Revelstoke
ALBERTA
Campbell River
Powell River
Vancouver
Tofino
Nanaimo
Duncan
Victoria
WASHINGTON
Okanagan Valley
U.S.A.

- —— Tour Route 7
  Chapter 12
- ···· Tour Route 8
  Chapter 13

Table Of Contents

Preface

RV Adventures in the Pacific Northwest is our fourth guidebook. The titles of the earlier ones are *Traveler's Guide to European Camping*, *Traveler's Guide to Mexican Camping* and *Traveler's Guide to Alaskan Camping*. This new book is a departure for us because it covers an area that is easier to visit and with many more camping facilities than the places covered in our previous books. The information needed by RVers in the Continental U.S. and British Columbia is much different than that needed in more remote and unfamiliar places like Europe, Mexico, and even Alaska. Our previous books needed to include a lot of information about the culture and "how-to" aspects of travel, that's not the case in this book. We've tried to strike a balance by including enough information to be useful but not so much that the book is overwhelming.

All four books, however, are aimed at a large part of the traveling public that has been virtually ignored by travel book publishers - RVers. There are lots of travel guides out there, but few really provide the information that RVers need to make their trip fun and comfortable.

One big difference between this and previous books is that we've arranged this one into a series of tours. We recognize that many users will not really follow the tours, but a tour format provides a good way to introduce a reader with little local knowledge to the various destinations of the area. It's good to know that you can travel around the region and spend each night at a location that is interesting and that also has good camping accommodations.

Another difference from our other books is that this one provides much less in the way of detailed information about individual campgrounds. Most RVer carry, or should carry, one of the large catalog-type RV guides that list every campground in the U.S. and Canada. They're inexpensive, frequently updated, comprehensive, and do a good job of giving you the statistical bare facts about campgrounds. We've tried to give you what they don't. We give you a map so you can easily find each campground, as well as form a picture in your mind of how that campground fits into the surrounding region and the things you may want to do.

We've also limited the number of campgrounds that we show. Many campgrounds listed in the "catalogs" just aren't the best place to stay. Some have inconvenient locations, some aren't up to snuff quality-wise, some are not as customer-friendly as they might be. Some are great, it's just that there are other places nearby that are better. Actually, if we haven't listed a campground it doesn't necessarily mean that it's not good, it might just mean that we've never had occasion to use it.

We've included quite a bit of information in this book about the attractions and things you'll find to do in each area. That's something we did in the other books too, and readers seem to like it. On the other hand, we've also tried not to include too much of that information. As we mentioned above, there are other guidebooks providing pretty much the same information, often quite a bit more. Sometimes there is so much information available that you can't sort out the basic good stuff from the huge volume of chaff. It can be disappointing to find after you've returned home that you missed a great attraction just because you didn't know about it or were doing something that turned out to be much less interesting. We recommend that you use other guidebooks in addition to this one, but we've tried to include enough information for you to plan and execute a great trip without spending a ton of time on research.

Perhaps it would be a good thing to say a little here about our qualifications to write a guidebook for RVing in the Northwest. We've been RVing most of our lives (at least one of us is in his late 40s). Much of that was in Alaska, but about eight years ago we hit the road as full-time RVers. Since that time we've traveled most of the western U.S. and Canada, Alaska, Mexico and Europe. As we mentioned above, during our travels we've researched and written three other well-received RVing guides; to Europe, Mexico, and Alaska.

In the last few years we've maintained a home base in the Seattle area and done a great deal of RVing in the region. It was a great way to relax from the writing and traveling that went into the other books. We gradually realized that there was probably just as much need for an RVing guidebook to the Northwest as there was for guides to more remote and exotic locales.

To make a long story short, this is that book. We've had a lot of fun writing it, we hope you'll have just as much fun using it.

NEAR MOUNT RAINIER IN WASHINGTON STATE

Chapter 1

Introduction

The Pacific Northwest is a wonderful camping destination. It is hard to think of another place in the world with such a diverse range of natural attractions and with such good highway access to them. While it is a temptation to think of the Northwest as just two regions, the rainy west of the mountains and the dry east of the mountains, the Northwest is really much more complex. Here's a quick rundown.

Much of the Pacific coastline is easily accessible because there are highways running along almost the entire length. In the south, in Oregon, there are charming small towns and larger regional centers. Farther north, in Washington, there are fewer people and wilder beaches. In the far north Vancouver Island is really wild, the only way to visit the coast is along remote highways that stretch westward to isolated small towns. If you want to explore the coastline north and south from the towns you'll have to hike or use a boat.

Inland from the coast are a range of coastal mountains. In Washington some of this range is the Olympic National Park. In Oregon the coastal range isn't quite as spectacular, but much of it is partially protected as national forest land. Geologically speaking, Vancouver Island in British Columbia is really part of this coastal range too.

Between the coastal range and the Cascade Mountains is a flat region with most of the Northwest's people. Here you'll find the big cities: Portland, Seattle, and Vancouver. But this region isn't all cities, there's also the Willamette Valley, Puget Sound, Vancouver Island's east coast, and also B.C.'s Sunshine Coast.

Moving eastward, the next range of mountains are the Cascades. Geologically the Cascade Mountains are a young range. They're much higher than the coastal range, and have steep slopes and deep valleys. They form a barrier to moisture that creates one of the most memorable features of the Northwest–while the western part of the region is wet and lush the eastern part is dry, much is actual desert. The Cascades are full of interesting destinations. There are National Parks and Monuments: the North Cascades, Rainier, St. Helens, and Crater Lake. The mountains are cut by transportation routes that are destinations themselves including the Fraser Canyon, the Columbia Gorge, and the North Cascades Highway.

In British Columbia the Cascades get confused. Almost the entire southern part of the province is mountainous, to the traveler there's really no well-defined separation between the Cascade Range and the Rocky Mountains. But the Columbia River starts in B.C., and farther south its valley widens to form the Columbia Basin that occupies much of the dry eastern part of the state of Washington. Eastern Oregon is dry too, but here the topography is a high, dry, rugged plateau. Ranges like the Blue Mountains provide pine-covered relief from parched lower elevations.

Camping Travel

We realize that not everyone who uses this book will be an experienced camper with their own personal RV. Camping is becoming more and more popular each year as more people recognize the unique benefits of this type of travel. Traveling in your own car or RV, sleeping in your own mobile bed, visiting the great outdoors but having the comforts of home, and saving lots of money doing it–that's camping travel.

You don't need an RV to travel this way. During the summer months you can comfortably camp out of the back of your car. For just a small investment you can equip yourself with everything you need to stay in a campground. Today's camping equipment is inexpensive and usually pretty well designed. You don't need expedition-quality gear for car camping, and there is no reason to spend extra money to get something that is ultra-light weight. You're not going to be carrying this equipment on

CAMPSITE ON THE SUNSHINE COAST

your back. It is much more important to get equipment that will be comfortable. Get a big tent, they're not really expensive. You don't have to sleep on the ground–there are foam and air mattresses, not to mention cots, that are almost as comfortable as your bed at home. We spend several months in Europe most years camping with equipment; including a big tent, cots, a table, chairs, stoves, and kitchen equipment; that fits in two duffel bags, so we know what we're talking about.

If sleeping in a tent seems a little more like roughing it than you are willing accept you still can camp. Rental RVs are readily available, below you'll find information about renting RVs in Portland, Seattle, and Vancouver. When you check prices remember that the RV provides both transportation and lodging, you'll also spend less on food because you can easily cook in the RV and won't have to eat every meal in a restaurant. When you pick up your rental RV you'll get an introductory tour so that you will understand its features and systems. It won't take long to feel at home at the wheel of your rental rig, most roads aren't crowded, and you'll be surprised at the great views that you'll have from that high RV seat. When renting we recommend that you don't get a rig that is larger than you need. Big is not necessarily better with RV's, especially when you are traveling most of the time. If you have kids along, and they're old enough, consider having them sleep in a tent, they'll probably enjoy it more anyway.

This is a good place to discuss RV maneuverability. When you are comfortably parked in a campsite you want the biggest RV possible, but when you are on the road you want the smallest one possible. We've all seen the huge RVs traveling the interstate, usually pulling a tow car (often called a "toad" by RVers). Those rigs are fine when you are in an RV park but they're not really very convenient when on the road. For the type of travel outlined in this book you'll be much happier in a smaller rig. It will be easier to park when shopping, easier to fill with gas at a station, be more economical, and allow you to camp at almost any campground, not just those with really big sites.

Once you reach the destinations you're going to want to be able to drive around to see the sights, go shopping, and conveniently get around. Fortunately, most of the destinations in this book aren't crowded urban areas so you can use a pretty large rig for local access, but those with really big rigs will want to have a "toad" or, in the case of those pulling trailers, use their towing vehicle for local exploring. Rental motorhomes in the 18- to 22-foot range are not too difficult to maneuver and park so you won't need a "toad" if you have one of those. In urban areas it is probably best to just rely on public transportation. Portland, Seattle, and Vancouver all have good public transportation systems with decent service from their RV parks.

Tour Routes

In this book we outline eight tours that you can follow to enjoy much of what the Northwest has to offer. They all start at one of what we call the gateway cities: Portland, Seattle, or Vancouver, B.C. Each tour includes six or seven destinations that offer good RV facilities and things to see and do. The idea is that you can spend a week traveling and know that you will enjoy each of the stops you make. Actually, it would be easy to spend two or three weeks on each route, but that is up to you.

Tour 1–The Oregon Coast - Starts in Portland, Oregon. Travels quickly south to reach the extreme south end of Oregon's Pacific coast, then leisurely wanders north on Hwy. 101 to return to Portland.

Tour 2–Central Oregon - Starts in Portland, Oregon. Crosses the Cascade Mountains near Portland and then travels down the east side of the range as far as the California border. Returns north through Crater Lake National Park and then the length of the Willamette Valley.

Tour 3–Northern Oregon - Starts in Portland, Oregon. Heads eastward through the Columbia Gorge and then across the Blue Mountains as far as Hells Canyon, then returns westward through the John Day Country and crosses the Cascades near Sisters, Oregon.

Tour 4–The Olympic Peninsula - Starts in Seattle, Washington. After crossing Puget Sound near Tacoma this tour circles the Olympic Peninsula with visits to mountains, hot springs, ocean beaches, and resorts.

Tour 5–The North Cascades Loop - Starts in Seattle, Washington. You'll take a ferry to Whidbey, Island, then drive north and cross the North Cascades Highway to the Methow Valley. In Eastern Washington you'll visit the sunny Grand Coulee Area, then return through apple country and Stevens Pass.

Tour 6–Southern Washington - Starts in Seattle, Washington. On this tour you'll visit Rainier National Park, tour the Yakima Valley wine district, see the north side of the Columbia Gorge, view Mt. St. Helens, then circle west to Washington State's pacific coast.

Tour 7–British Columbia Mainland - Starts in Vancouver, British Columbia. Travel eastward to the Okanagan Valley, then even farther east to the Rocky Mountain national parks: Banff and Jasper. As you turn back toward Vancouver you'll visit two more parks, Mt. Robson and Wells Gray, before descending through the Fraser Canyon to the coast.

Tour 8–Vancouver Island - Starts in Vancouver, British Columbia. Hop up the Sunshine Coast to Powell River using a combination of ferries and roads, then cross to Vancouver Island. Visit the west coast of the Island at Tofino, then head southward to Victoria before returning to Vancouver, again by ferry.

Campgrounds

Campgrounds in the Northwest can be classified in many ways, but we think of them as commercial, state or provincial, or federal. When they are available we've tried to provide a range of campground types to choose from at each destination. The type you like will depend upon how you value hookups, amenities, natural settings, convenience and cost.

Commercial campgrounds provide the widest range of amenities. They are owned by companies or individuals and must at least break even to stay open. This does not necessarily mean that they are always the most expensive campground choice since the government-owned campgrounds have been raising their rates in recent years.

Commercial campgrounds almost always offer hookups for electricity, water, and sewer; dump stations; and hot showers. They also often have swimming pools, hot tubs, laundromats, cable TV hookups and other amenities. A big advantage of commercial campgrounds is that they usually will accept reservations over the phone with no additional charge. They are usually the only type of campground that is located near or inside a town. Parking sites in commercial campgrounds are almost always closer to each other than those in government campgrounds, land is a big cost to a commercial campground but is not even considered a cost by the government. Commercial campgrounds have been forced to enlarge sites to remain viable so most can deal fairly well with large rigs.

Washington and Oregon state campgrounds are similar to each other. Most are located in scenic or historic locations. Government campgrounds tend to have lots of land so parking sites are spread farther apart than in a commercial campground and landscaping is usually very nice. Sites themselves can be large enough for the largest rigs although this varies, older campgrounds were built when rigs were smaller and many have not been updated. State campgrounds in Washington and Oregon often have hookups, but not always. They also often provide showers, although there is usually a small charge in the form of a coin-operated timer. State campgrounds are much more likely to allow campfires than commercial campgrounds, usually wood can be purchased at the campground. During the summer most state campgrounds now have an on-site host. Usually the host is an experienced RVer who parks in one of the sites and helps run the campground by collecting fees, managing reservations,

CAMPGROUND IN HELLS CANYON

providing information, and helping state employees keep the facility clean, safe, and organized. Many state campgrounds in Washington and Oregon are now on a reservation system although the system is not nearly as convenient or inexpensive as the system provided by commercial campgrounds. Some state campgrounds are very popular, particularly on weekends, to use them you must either reserve a space or arrive early in the day. The reservation system is described below

British Columbia provincial campgrounds are similar to Washington and Oregon state campgrounds. They are located in scenic areas, they tend to have lots of acreage, and sites are often plenty large enough for big rigs. Provincial campgrounds, on the other hand, do not have utility hookups, and they seldom have showers. Some are on a reservation system, it is described below. Provincial campgrounds often stop collecting fees in early October because fewer amenities are available. Some are open all winter but do not begin to collect fees until May.

U.S. Forest Service campgrounds are the least-developed type of campground listed in this book. These are located in the national forests, they are usually fairly small and do not have hookups or showers. Many have pit toilets instead of flush ones. Sites are usually separated by vegetation but can be small, particularly in old campgrounds built before the advent of big rigs. On the other hand, these are the least expensive campgrounds and often the least crowded with the best natural setting. They're particularly good for tent campers and those with small maneuverable rigs. Very few can be reserved.

Other federal campgrounds are a mixed bag. The ones in this book are mostly national park campgrounds. They range from the beautiful and highly-developed sites in Canada's Banff National Park to the basic sites at most U.S. national parks. See the individual entries in this book for more details.

For many RVers camping is just not camping without a campfire. European visitors seem to particularly enjoy them, maybe because they don't find campfires in European campgrounds. We find that campfires are more popular in Canada than in the U.S.

Many commercial campgrounds do not allow campfires, probably due to burning restrictions in urban areas and the supervision and cleanup that fires require. Most state, provincial, and federal campgrounds do allow campfires.

You will not be able to find sufficient firewood on the ground in any of the campgrounds listed in this book. That means that you must either bring your own or purchase it at the campgrounds. Most campgrounds that allow fires do sell firewood (at a steep price). Many British Columbia provincial campgrounds provide free firewood although we find that it is not always dry enough for a decent fire.

Campground Reservations

The destinations in this book are popular. If you are traveling during the period from Memorial Day (end of May) to Labor Day (beginning of September), as most RV travelers do, you will find that campgrounds are sometimes full when you arrive. To avoid a late-in-the-day search for a place to stay all you have to do is take the time to reserve a space. If we list a telephone number it means that the campground accepts reservations.

It is easy to make reservations at virtually all commercial campgrounds. Almost all accept MasterCard or Visa charges and some even have toll-free numbers. Best of all, there is almost always no additional charge for making a reservation.

Federal, state, and provincial campgrounds are another story. The good news is that many do now accept reservations. The bad news is that most charge a substantial fee to make reservations and most use a sub-contractor for the reservation-taking process. Unfortunately, often the sub-contractor has limited information about the campground. Also, it is usually necessary to make reservations several days in advance. Here are the reservations details for the several systems in operation for the campgrounds covered in this book.

Most state campgrounds in Washington and Oregon use one reservation system. There are just a few exceptions and we note those in the individual campground write-ups. The system is called Reservations Northwest, you can reach it by calling 800 452-5687. It is open from 8 a.m. to 5 p.m. (local Pacific time) on weekdays, you must call at least two days in advance of the day you want to reserve but no more than 11 months in advance. You will be charged a $6 reservation fee plus the first night's charge for each site reserved. If you reserve 1 site for 2 nights that's a $6 fee. If you reserve another site, say at a second campground, that's a second $6 charge. This can be charged on a Visa or MasterCard or you can send in a check if you have called at least three weeks in advance. You can not make a reservation by mail. For general information about Oregon State parks call 800 551-6949. For general information about Washington State parks call 800 233-0321.

The British Columbia Provincial Parks have a similar system. Not all parks take reservations but many do. To make a reservation you call Discover Camping at 800 689-9025 (from Vancouver call 689-9025). The reservation service is open from March 1 to September 15, Monday to Friday from 7 a.m. to 7 p.m. (Pacific Standard Time) and Saturday and Sunday from 9 a.m. to 5 p.m. Reservations can be made from 2 days to 3 months ahead. There is a fee of $6.42 Canadian per day for a maximum of 3 days. To clarify, that means that if you make a reservation for 3 consecutive days at one campground you will have to pay the fee three times, but additional days have no reservation fee. If you then make a reservation at an additional site the fee again applies. There are a maximum of 14 days stay allowed per Provincial Park each calendar year. Further information (no reservations) is available at 250 387-4550.

Renting an RV

It is not necessary to own your own RV to enjoy the tours detailed in this book. You can easily rent an RV in Portland, Seattle, or Vancouver. Here are a few of the firms in that business. Give them a call or drop them a line for information about rigs and rates. Don't forget to ask if they will pick you up at the airport. We have not used any of these companies ourselves so we can not give personal recommendations, use care in selecting a company just as you would in any monetary transaction.

Portland

- Coast to Coast RV Rentals, Vancouver, WA 98860; 360 546-2670

- Cruise America Motorhome Rental and Sales, 2032 NW 23rd Ave., Portland, OR 97210-0233; 503 775-0538; http://www.cruiseamerica.com

- El-Mar Enterprises Inc., P.O. Box 68979, Portland, OR 97268-0097; 503 654-1002

- Golden Circle Recreation, 17985 SW Pacific Hwy., Tualatin, OR 97062; 503 692-2779

- Rent RV, 1660 SW Bertha Blvd., Portland, OR 97219; 503 245-5145; http://www.rentrv.com

Seattle

- Cruise America Motorhome Rental and Sales, 1164 Denny way, Seattle, WA 98109; 206 264-8531; http://www.cruiseamerica.com

- Motorhome America RV Rentals, 43028 SE North Bend Way, North Bend, WA 98045; 800 400-9226 or 425 888-3600; www.halcyon.com/rvrenter

- El Monte RV Rentals & Sales, 316 SW 16th Street, Renton, WA 98055; 800 367-3687 or 425 430-1133; www.elmonte.com

- NW Van & Motorhome Rentals, 16068 Ambaum Blvd., Seattle, WA 98148; 206 241-6111; www.fivecornersrv.com

- Western Motorhome Rentals, 19303 Hwy. 99, Lynwood, WA 98036; 425 775-1181; www.westernrv.com

Vancouver

- Canada Camper R.V. Rentals Ltd., 1080 Millcarch Street, Richmond, B.C. V6V 2H4; 604 327-3003; www.canada-camper.com

- Candan RV Rentals, 20257 Langley Bypass, Langley, B.C. V3A 6K9; 604 530-3645; www.candan.com

- El Monte RV Rentals & Sales; 5242 Pacific Hwy., Ferndale, WA 98248; 800 367-3687 or 360 380-3300

- Fraserway RV Rentals, 747 Cliveden Place, Delta, BC V3M 6C7; 800 661-2441 or 604 527-1102

- Go West Motorhome Rentals, 1577 Lloyd Avenue, North Vancouver, B.C. V7P 3K8; 604 987-8288; www.go-west.com

- Westcoast Mountain Campers Ltd., 150-11800 Voyageur Way, Richmond, B.C. V6X 3N8; 604 279-0550

Border Crossings

None of the tours in this book require you to cross the U.S.-Canada border but it is very possible that a border crossing will be required either en-route to a starting point or possibly during a side-trip from one of the tours. Crossing the border is nothing to fear, even in an RV the process is relatively painless.

No visa or passport is required for U.S. or Canadian citizens crossing either way but proof of citizenship must be carried. This means a passport, certified birth certificate, or voters registration card, along with a photo I.D. like your driver's license. A driver's license alone is not enough. If you have children along it is very important to have certified copies of their birth certificates and permission letters from parents if they are not yours.

For your vehicle you'll want the following: registration, up-to-date license tags and proof of insurance. Make sure you have your vehicle registration with you and if you are not the registered owner a signed statement that it is OK to take it out of the country. Check to make sure your automobile insurance is good in Canada. You can get a Canadian Non-Resident Interprovincial Motor Vehicle Liability Insurance Card from your insurance company. It is likely that you will not have to show any of these documents but having them on hand is definitely nice if you are asked for them, you could be turned back.

Guns are a problem in Canada, don't try to take one in from the U.S. unless yours is a hunting trip. If it is a hunting trip check with Canadian officials before you leave home about regulations. Never fib about weapons at the border, vehicles are often searched and penalties are steep.

Many people like to carry pepper spray for defense against bears. This can be a problem at the border going into Canada. Several different laws are involved, if your spray wasn't manufactured in Canada it probably isn't legal. Sprays designed for defense against people definitely aren't allowed. If you must have pepper spray buy it in Canada once you are there.

For more information about border crossings you can use these addresses: Canadian Customs, Connaught Building, Sussex Drive, Ottawa, Ontario, Canada K1A 0L5 or Customs Office, 333 Dunsmuir Street, Suite 503, Vancouver, B.C., Canada V6B 5R4 (604 666-0545); United States Customs, P.O. Box 7407, Washington, D.C. 20044, U.S.A. (202 566-8195). There are also Internet sites with lots of information, check our Website at www.rollinghomes.com for links to these sites.

Ferries

When following the tours in this book you will have the opportunity to ride the ferries of two different ferry systems.

Tour 5 of the Cascade Loop includes a short ferry ride from Mukilteo to Whidbey Island. The ferry is run by Washington State Ferries. For schedules and information call 206 464-6400. Reservations are not taken for this run.

Tour 9 of Vancouver Island takes you up the Sunshine Coast from Vancouver, then across the Strait of Georgia to Vancouver Island and, later in the tour, back to the mainland. The ferries used on this tour are all operated by the British Columbia Ferry Corporation, reservations are not available. For schedules and information from Victoria call 250 386-3431, from elsewhere in B.C. call toll-free 888 223-3779, from outside B.C. call 250 386-3431. The B.C. Ferry Corporation has a web site with lots of information, check our Website at www.rollinghomes.com for a link to the site.

There are two other ferry routes that may be of interest. There is a ferry route from Anacortes (north of Seattle) to Victoria. This can be used to connect Tours 5 and 9 in either direction. The ferry is operated by Washington State Ferries. For schedules, reservations, and information call 206-464-6400. Reservations are required for the run.

A ferry also operates across the Straight of Juan de Fuca between Victoria and Port Angeles Washington. This ferry is run by a private company, Black Ball Transport. For schedules, information, and reservations call 360 457-4491 in Port Angeles, 250 386-2202 in Victoria.

Visitor Information

We're strong believers in the usefulness of local traveler's information offices. British Columbia, Washington, and Oregon all have fine offices in virtually every town. We've given their mailing addresses at the end of each chapter so that you can send for information before you leave home. When you are on the road you will find that the offices are well-signed from most town approaches, just follow the signs to the office. They can provide you with maps, a listing of sights to see, opening times, and locations for any service you may require. Most towns also maintain a Website with useful information, you can find links to them at www.rollinghomes.com.

Internet Resources

Every day there are more and more Websites devoted to information about destinations, campgrounds, sites, parks, and transportation. New sites appear and old ones disappear or change addresses. We've found that the only way to maintain a current listing is to set up our own site. The site is **www.rollinghomes.com** and has current links to a large variety of sites that will be of interest to readers of this guide. Don't ignore this resource, it can make your trip much more rewarding.

When to Go

Camping in the Northwest is pretty much a spring, summer, and fall activity. We give dates for the period that each listed campground is open in the individual chapters. While it may be possible to visit most areas during the winter and stay at campgrounds most people would probably not find the experience enjoyable. Winter in the Northwest, at least on the west side of the Cascade Mountains, is wet and cool. Temperatures seldom fall below freezing but there are few sunny days and daytime temperatures are often in the low forty's (Fahrenheit). On the east side of the Cascades winter weather is generally much cooler, often below freezing, but the skies tend to be clearer.

The camping season generally runs from the last half of April to the end of September with the most popular period between Memorial Day (end of May) and Labor Day (beginning of September).

Chapter 2

How to Use the Tour Chapters

The portion of this book that follows contains eight tours of the Pacific Northwest. There are three major state-province sections: Oregon, Washington, and British Columbia. Each state-province section begins with a chapter devoted to the gateway city that we use as a starting point for all of the tours in that section of the book. Following the gateway city chapter each section has chapters devoted to the tours that begin there. There are three tours from Portland, three from Seattle, and two from Vancouver.

Introductory Chapter Maps

We begin each section with a map of the state or province showing the tour routes covered in the section.

Similarly, each tour chapter within the section begins with a map showing the route to be covered. The numbered circles show each night's destination.

Each of the major gateway city chapters (Portland, Seattle, Vancouver) has an overall handy city map showing the general layout of the city and the location of campgrounds.

Top Attractions

The text portion of each chapter begins with a listing of the places we think that you'll probably want to see during your travels. These are the bare minimum, there are many more sights and attractions described in the text in each chapter.

Gateway City Descriptions

The three chapters covering Portland, Seattle and Vancouver are laid out similarly. Each of these cities is important because they are the largest cities in the region and serve as the base for exploring the rest of the state or province.

For each of the cities we give a general description of the city, a brief history, an explanation of the city's layout, information about public transportation, and then some details of the things to see and do there. We also include campground information.

The Tour Chapters

These chapters are arranged in a day-by-day format. Each day has three sections: Along the Way, an area description, and campground information.

Along the Way.

Here we give a general description of the route as well as information about interesting stops along the way. We also include a map of the day's route in this section. At the beginning of the section we also give the day's driving distance, along with an estimate of the time it takes to make the drive at a relaxed pace.

Area Description

The next section is a description of the area where you will spend the night. Some of these are cities and towns, others are general recreational areas that may cover quite a bit of territory. We give you some background information about the place and also describe some of the attractions that you might want to visit. You'll also find icons describing the recreational attractions of the area, here is a key.

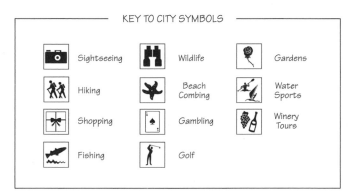

The sightseeing symbol is the most common. It indicates that there are historical, cultural, or natural sites worth a visit in the area. Usually these are described in the text.

The hiking symbol indicates that the area has hiking potential. We often do not describe the hikes but interesting possibilities should be easy to spot.

You can shop anywhere but some places are well-known for their shopping potential. We're not talking about groceries and supplies, the shopping symbol is for gifts and souvenirs.

The fishing symbol indicates that there is good fishing nearby. It might be saltwater or fresh, guided or not. Check with information centers and sporting goods stores for more information.

The wildlife symbol indicates the potential for spotting birds, whales, or other large mammals in the area. We usually include more in the text about this subject.

The beach-combing symbol usually just means there is a beach or tide pools nearby.

The gambling symbol indicates that a casino is in the area. Tourist information centers will have more information.

The golf symbol indicates that the area is a good one for golf. Almost all of our stops offer golf in the area but we only add the symbol if the golf offerings are particularly good.

The garden symbol is included if we mention a garden in the area. Gardens, like golf, are widespread, we do not include a garden symbol if the area is not known for its gardens.

The water sports symbol means that the area offers windsurfing, kayaking, river floats, or even motorized water sports. Check with information centers for more information.

The winery tours symbol is only used for destinations with well-developed wine tours since it seems that grapes are grown almost everywhere these days. Check with information centers for details.

Each destination section also includes a map to give you the lay of the land and to pinpoint campground locations. The maps are for the most part pretty easy to interpret, here is a symbol key.

MAP LEGEND

Symbol	Description	Symbol	Description
═══	Major Freeway	5	Freeway Number
━━━	Secondary and Other Roads	97	Secondary Road Number
⌁	Ferry Route	20	Other Road Number
CANADA U.S.A.	Country or State Border	🍁	Canadian National Highway
═▭═	Freeway Off-ramp	●	Start or End of Tour
Exit 19	Freeway Off-ramp Name Indicated	❶	Tour Day Number
🚐	Campground with Text Write-up	✈	Airport

Campground Information

Each gateway city and also each night's stop in the tour chapter includes a listing of campgrounds and information about them.

We begin each campground description with a series of symbols. These are designed to convey important information about the campground at a glance. Here is a key to the campground symbols.

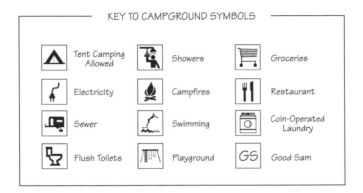

Campground prices tend to change quite a bit over time. We've classified the campgrounds in this book by price as follows:

LOW	Low	Up to $15
MED	Medium	Over $15 and up to $25
HIGH	High	Over $25

These prices are the high season charge for an RV with full hookups. If you do not require hookups or are using a tent you can expect to pay considerably less.

We've included a count of the number of sites in a campground so that you'll have some idea of the size of the campground. These are our count and may vary from the owner's count, particularly if there are tent sites at the campground since we often miss some of those.

Not all campgrounds allow tenters. We've included the tent symbol for those that do.

The electricity symbol indicates that electrical hookups are available. High-amp. hookups are not as important in the Northwest as they are in some other places since air conditioning is usually not really necessary. In the hot desert country on the eastern side of the mountains it may be, we've tried to indicate which campgrounds have 50-amp. service in the text portion of the description in those areas.

The sewer symbol means that either sewer drains or a dump station are available. Some campgrounds do not allow dumping unless you spend the night.

All of the campgrounds listed in this book have toilets, the toilet symbol in our descriptions shows which ones are flush toilets. You may also run into pit or vault (outhouse-style) toilets, particularly in provincial or federal campgrounds.

The shower symbol means that hot showers are available. There may be an additional fee for showers, usually in the form of a coin box that takes quarters or loonies (Canadian one-dollar coins).

The fire symbol means that campfires are allowed, usually at individual sites but sometimes at a central fire pit. Plan on either bringing firewood along with you or buying it at the campground, you won't be able to pick wood off the forest floor because there have been too many folks there ahead of you. Cutting standing trees is never permitted. The only exception to the bring it along or buy it rule is that most British Columbia provincial campgrounds still provide free wood.

The swimming symbol means that swimming is available either on-site or very near by. It may be a swimming pool, lake, river, or even the ocean if folks customarily swim there.

We include the playground symbol only if there is a playground for children with swings, slides and the equivalent. Even if there is no symbol the campground may offer horseshoes, a play field, or provisions for some other type of sports.

Many campgrounds have small stores. We've included this symbol if the store appears to have enough stock to be useful, or if there is an off-site store within easy walking distance.

Few campgrounds in the U.S. or Canada have restaurants, but if they do, or if there is one within easy walking distance, we include the restaurant symbol.

The laundry symbol means that the campground has self-operated washers.

Finally, many campgrounds give a discount to members of the Good Sam Club. We include the symbol if they advertise that they do.

We include both address and telephone numbers for commercial campgrounds, you'll need the information to make reservations. No address or telephone number is given for government campgrounds other than the reservation number. If there is no phone number given, the campground does not accept reservations.

In the text portion of the campground listing we try to give you some feeling for the campground as well as detailed instructions for how to find it.

Units of Measurement

The region covered by this guide uses two different sets of measurements. Canada is on the metric system while the U.S. uses miles and gallons.

We've given mileages in both kilometers and miles. In the U.S. the miles come first, in British Columbian the kilometers do. Here are some handy conversion factors: 1 km = .62 mile, 1 mile = 1.61 km, 1 liter = .26 U.S. gallon, 1 U.S. gallon = 3.79 liters, 1 kilogram = 2.21 pounds, and 1 pound = .45 kilograms.

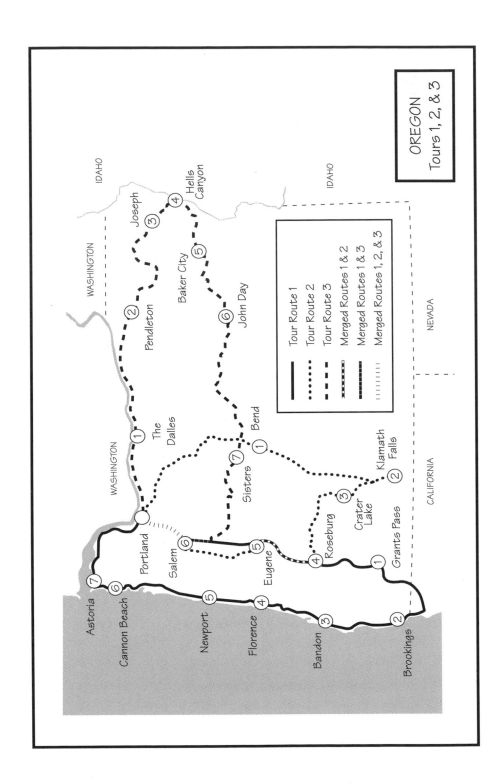

OREGON
Tours 1, 2, & 3

Tour Route 1
Tour Route 2
Tour Route 3
Merged Routes 1 & 2
Merged Routes 1 & 3
Merged Routes 1, 2, & 3

IDAHO

WASHINGTON

IDAHO

NEVADA

CALIFORNIA

Joseph ③

Hells Canyon ④

Baker City ⑤

Pendleton ②

John Day ⑥

The Dalles ①

Bend ①

Sisters ⑦

Klamath Falls ②

Crater Lake ③

Roseburg ④

Grants Pass ①

Portland

Salem ⑥

Eugene ⑤

Astoria ⑦

Cannon Beach ⑥

Newport ⑤

Florence ④

Bandon ③

Brookings ②

WASHINGTON

Chapter 3

Portland

Top Attractions

✦ Pioneer Courthouse Square and the surrounding area

✦ Tom McCall Waterfront Park

✦ Powell's Books

✦ Washington Park

✦ International Rose Test Garden

✦ Oregon Museum of Science and Industry

General

The Portland region, with a population of about 1,000,000, is by far the largest concentration of people in the state. The area population depends, of course, upon how you define the region. The population is fairly dense as far south as Salem and also crosses the Columbia to Vancouver, Washington.

For our purposes Portland at first appears to be inconveniently located at the northern border of the state. You might expect that any tour loop visiting the farther regions of Oregon would require that you spend a lot of time driving. We have found this not to be the case for two reasons. First, the most remote part of the state, the far southeast, is not where most of the interesting sights are located. We've not provided a tour to the southeast, that means we've been forced to exclude some things, but there are lots more in the places we do visit. Second, the two interstate highways that meet in Portland, north-south I-5 and east-west I-84, let you travel to the far reaches of the state quickly and fairly painlessly, particularly since you can count on little congestion other than near Portland.

History

Portland is a young city by any standards, it was founded around 1844 when the first land claim was staked in what is now downtown Portland. Although the city is older than Seattle it is only older by a few years. The location is said to have been used for years as a seasonal campsite by Indians, there was a village nearby on Sauvie Island near the mouth of the Willamette.

Actually, Europeans had been in the neighborhood for quite a few years too. Fort Vancouver, across the Columbia River, was an important Hudson's Bay Company post beginning in 1825.

Like Seattle, much of Portland's early growth came as a timber port to fuel the demand for lumber in booming San Francisco down the west coast. Gold had been discovered in the Sacramento River Valley and San Francisco was growing rapidly. Portland also served as a gateway to the Willamette River Valley which was attracting large numbers of settlers who traveled the Oregon Trail. It became much easier to reach Portland when the railroad arrived in 1883.

Lewis and Clark passed near Portland in 1805 so Portland celebrated the fact 100 years later with the Lewis and Clark Centennial Exposition, actually a world's fair. Huge numbers of tourists attended the exposition and many decided to move to Portland. The population of the city leaped ahead during the next decade.

With the development of the Columbia River Valley's farming and industry during the 1900s Portland has become even more important as a transportation hub until today, based on total tonnage, the city is the west coast's largest port.

Layout

Today's Portland and its suburbs sprawl 25 miles (40 km) from east to west and 25 miles from north to south. The northern border of the city is the Columbia River although Vancouver, Washington, on the north side of the river definitely qualifies as a suburb. The Willamette River runs right through the center of town with the downtown area on the west bank some 10 miles (16 km) from where the Willamette meets the Columbia.

Just west of the city center is a range of hills, much of them is covered by Washington Park and Forest Park, on the far side are the suburbs of Beaverton and Hillsboro. To the east rises Mt. Hood, almost on the lower slopes is the suburb of Gresham. South of Portland along the Willamette are many more suburbs, among them Milwaukie, Lake Oswego, West Linn, Oregon City, Tualatin, and Tigard.

Highway I-5 runs north and south through the center of Portland. Near downtown I-5 follows the east bank of the Willamette opposite the downtown business district. There is a short ring-road freeway, I-405, that leaves I-5 north of downtown, circles around the west side of the district, and then rejoins I-5 after less than four miles (6 km). There's a much longer ring-road freeway, I-205, around the east side of Portland. It leaves I-5 north of the Columbia River and makes a 36-mile (58-km) loop around the east side of the city before rejoining I-5 at the far southern border of the Portland suburbs. I-84 from the east also ends near the city center, it joins I-5 on the east bank of the Willamette River opposite downtown after having come in through eastern Portland.

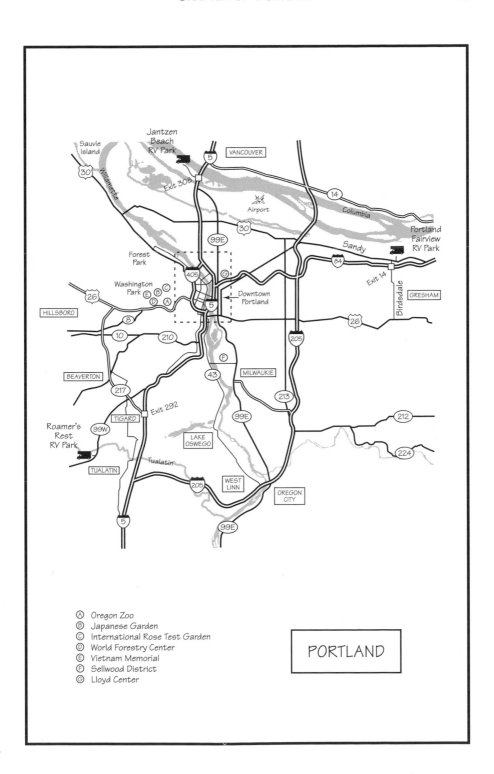

Ⓐ Oregon Zoo
Ⓑ Japanese Garden
Ⓒ International Rose Test Garden
Ⓓ World Forestry Center
Ⓔ Vietnam Memorial
Ⓕ Sellwood District
Ⓖ Lloyd Center

PORTLAND

Transportation

Portland has an award-winning public transportation system. The crown jewel is the Max light rail system with extensions running far east to Gresham and west to Hillsboro. Planned extensions will reach the airport and stretch north along I-5 to the Columbia River. Portland also has an excellent bus system.

Central Portland has a real parking problem, that means that you will probably want to visit using the public transportation system. Unfortunately the Max light rail system does not serve any of Portland's campgrounds, you'll have to use the bus at least part of the way. Once you reach downtown, however, there is free bus service in the central core and busses and the Max system provide easy access to the places you will probably want to visit.

Portland provides one bus route that is of particular interest to visitors. This is Bus 63, nicknamed Art: the Cultural Bus. It provides access to many of Portland's cultural attractions including the Memorial Coliseum, Oregon Convention Center, Oregon History Center, Oregon Museum of Science and Industry (OMSI), Pacific Northwest College of Art, Portland Art Museum, Portland Center for the Performing Arts, Tom McCall Waterfront Park, RiverPlace shops and marina, Oregon Zoo, Japanese Garden, International Rose Test Garden, World Forestry Center and the Vietnam Memorial.

Public transportation in central Portland is conveniently centered around the downtown Transit Mall. This eleven-block-long area between 5th and 6th Avenues is closed to all traffic except public transportation. The Tri-Met (transit) main office is located at Pioneer Courthouse Square.

Once you have arrived in downtown Portland you might want to start your tour by making your way to **Pioneer Courthouse Square**. It adjoins the transit mall and is bounded by Broadway, 6th Ave., Morrison, and Yamhill. Here you'll find the Tri-Met transit office and you'll also be in the center of downtown Portland's attractions. You are also in the center of Portland's upscale shopping district. Portland is a popular shopping destination with visitors because Oregon does not have a sales tax.

To find the **Greater Portland Convention and Visitor's Center** you can stroll east toward the river on Salmon St. to the three World Trade Center buildings. Across the street is **Governor Tom McCall Waterfront Park**. It stretches about a mile along the Willamette River and offers an excellent place for a promenade on a nice day. At the south end of the park is the **RiverPlace Marina** development with upscale shops and restaurants.

To really appreciate Portland you should know the names and locations of the various districts. Many are within easy walking distance of downtown, particularly since Portland's blocks are small, some downtown are only 200 feet square.

Four of the districts have their southern borders along W. Burnside Street, an east-west thoroughfare five blocks north of Pioneer Courthouse Square. The farthest west is called the **Northwest District**. Bounded on the west by NW 27th Ave. and on the east by NW 18th Ave. the district is just west of the I-405 ring road but still less than a mile from Pioneer Courthouse Square if you head northwest on Morrison. The whole district is filled with refurbished Victorian homes, many now serving as boutiques, coffee houses, book shops, theaters, pubs, and restaurants. The center of the action is known as **Nob Hill**, NW 21st through 23rd Ave.

The next district to the east and just east of the I-405 ring road is **The Pearl**, bounded on west by NW 15th Ave. and east by NW 8th Ave. It's an up-and-coming district of restored warehouses with art galleries and condominium conversions. Here you'll find one of Portland's best-known stores–**Powell's Books**. Covering a full block at 10th and Burnside this book store is the largest independent bookstore in the world.

The next district to the east is **Chinatown**. The Chinatown gates are at 4th and Burnside. Merging in from the east is **Old Town**. Many of the buildings here are from the 1880s, Portland had a fire in 1872 that razed much of this area and resulted in the building of these cast iron-fronted buildings typical of the period.

Now we've followed the districts eastward all the way to the river, there are two more just to the south. **Skidmore Historic District** and **Yamhill Historic District** adjoin the Riverfront Park from Burnside south to about Salmon St. Both are much

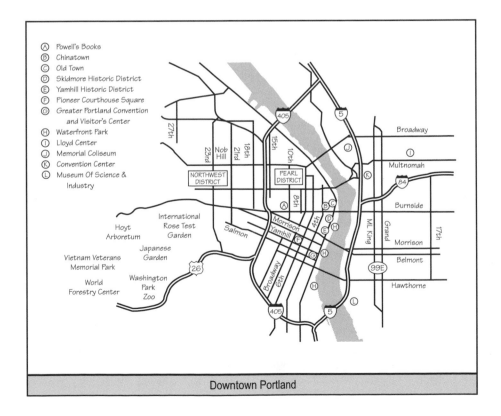

Downtown Portland

like the **Old Town** district to the north. A popular attraction in the Skidmore District is the **Saturday Market**, a street crafts market held on Saturday and Sunday all year except in the dead of winter and located just south of Burnside near the Skidmore Fountain.

There are also a couple of interesting shopping districts on the east side of the Willamette. The **Hawthorne District** is along east-west Hawthorne Boulevard from about S.E. 17th to S.E. 55th Ave. It has a kind of counter-culture (or maybe 1960s) atmosphere and offers second-hand shops, book stores, cafes and galleries.

More mainstream is the huge **Lloyd Center** shopping mall. It is located about 10 blocks east of the river near the Memorial Coliseum and the Oregon Convention Center. The easiest way to get there is via the Gresham-bound Max.

Antique hunters will want to visit the **Sellwood District**. To reach it start at the Sellwood Bridge, Portland's southernmost. Drive east on Tacoma for 7 blocks to S.E. 13th and you are there. From Tacoma St. north to about Bybe St. you'll find many antique shops and also some good restaurants.

Portland is known for its city parks, but the best must be huge **Washington Park**. It is located in the hills west of downtown Portland and is easily accessible either by taking the Hillsboro-bound Max and getting off at the Zoo Stop or from Hwy. 26 west of downtown at the Zoo Exit. In the park are a number of Portland's most popular attractions including the **Washington Park Zoo**, **International Rose Test Garden**, **Japanese Gardens**, **Hoyt Arboretum**, and the **World Forestry Center**.

Science, and technology buffs will probably enjoy the **Oregon Museum of Science and Industry** (OMSI). Located on the east bank of the Willamette, OMSI covers 18 acres and offers a variety of hands-on technology-inspired exhibits including a decommissioned submarine, an Omnimax theater, a giant walk-through heart, a shaking earthquake room, and even the bridge of the Starship Enterprise.

Portland Area Campgrounds

🚐 **Portland Fairview RV Park** `MED` 🚶 ⬛ 🔧 ⚡ 📶 🅿️   21401 NE Sandy Boulevard, Fairview, OR 97024; 503 661-1047; 407 sites, open all year - This is a huge and fairly new campground for RVs only on the east side of Portland. If you are arriving on I-84 from the east access is very convenient. The park has over 400 sites, all have full hookups, most are very large pull-throughs. Electricty is 50- or 30-amp. Parking is on paved pads with patios separated by well-tended grass. Sites are arranged on several terraces dipping shallowly to the north. Amenities include nice restrooms, swimming pool, recreation room, exercise room, playground, and laundry. A small market is nearby. To use public transportation to get to downtown Portland you take a bus and then Max light rail. To reach the campground take Exit 14 from I-84 east of Portland. Drive north one-quarter mile (.4 km) to Sandy Boulevard, turn right, and you'll see the campground on your left almost immediately.

🚐 **Jantzen Beach RV Park** `MED` 🚶 ⬛ 🔧 ⚡ 📶 🅿️   1503 N Hayden Island Drive, Portland, OR 97217; 503 289-7626 or 800 443-7248 for reservations; 169 sites, open all year - This campground is the closest to central Portland, it is the easiest campground to reach if you are approaching from the north. It is located on Hayden Island which is an island in the Columbia River that I-5 crosses approaching the city from the north. Near the campground is a large shopping center but actually the area is a comparatively quiet retreat considering how close it is to central Portland. Bus transportation is available to downtown from near the campground. Take Exit 308 which is marked Jantzen Beach, then follow the campground signs 1/2 mile (.8 km) on Hayden Island Drive to the west of the freeway on the north bank of the island.

Roamer's Rest RV Park MED 🔟 🔟 🔟 🔟 🔟 17585 SW Pacific Hwy., Tualatin, OR 97062; 503 692-6350 or 877 478-7275 for reservations; 93 sites, open all year - This small modern campground is the place to stay when approaching Portland from the south. The compact site slopes steeply to the Tualatin River. Restrooms are nice, there are individual rooms with toilet, shower and sink. Reach the campground most easily by taking Exit 292 from I-5, drive northwest on Hwy. 217 for .2 miles (.3 km), then turn left on Hwy. 99W and drive 3.8 miles (6.1 km), the entrance is on the right just after you cross the Tualatin River.

Information Resources

See our Internet site at www.rollinghomes.com for Internet site addresses.

Portland Oregon Visitor's Association, 28 SW Salmon St., Portland, OR 97204; 503 222-2223
    or 877 678-5263
Washington Park Zoo, 4001 SW Canyon Road, Portland, OR 97221; 503 226-7627
International Rose Test Garden, 400 SW Kingston Ave., Portland, OR 97201; 503 823-3636
Japanese Garden; 503 223-1321
Oregon Museum of Science and Industry, 1945 SE Water Ave., Portland, Oregon 97214-3354;
    503 797-4000 or 800 955-6674

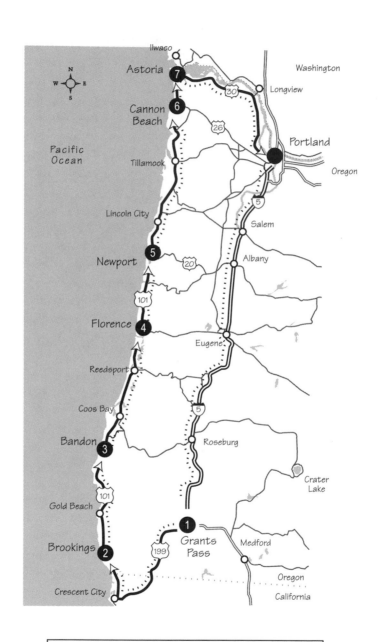

THE OREGON COAST

Chapter 4

Tour 1

The Oregon Coast

Top Attractions

- ✦ The Oregon Caves
- ✦ The Oregon coast lighthouses and jetties
- ✦ The Rogue River from a jet-powered mail boat
- ✦ The Oregon Dunes National Recreation Area
- ✦ Sea Lion Caves
- ✦ Yaquina Head near Newport
- ✦ Cannon Beach
- ✦ Seaside
- ✦ Historic Astoria and Lewis and Clark's Fort Clatsop

General Description

This tour makes a quick dash south from Portland but then makes a leisurely return north along the full length of Oregon's Pacific coast. As you drive south on Interstate Highway 5 through the Willamette Valley you may feel that you are missing lots of interesting stops, and you are. For more information about the area take a look at Tour 3 which returns north through this area after descending on the eastern side of the Cascade Mountains. But save that until later. After one day on the interstate things start to get interesting. You'll cross the coastal mountains and by the afternoon of the second day you are on the coast. There is so much to see and do that you may want to spend a month returning north to Portland. The total distance of this tour is 826 miles, driving time about 24 hours.

The Roads

During the first day you'll be traveling down Interstate Highway 5 (I-5), the major north-south highway on the west coast of the United States. On day two you'll leave the interstate at Grant's Pass and head southeast through the Siskiyou Mountains along winding Hwy. 199. For big rigs the going is slow, but there should be no problems, this is a well-traveled highway. At the coast you'll join the coastal Hwy. 101. This road is formally known as the Pacific Coast National Scenic Byway, and it lives up to it's name, it is really scenic. The standard of the road varies, but it is mostly good two-lane highway allowing vehicles of any size to easily and safely maintain the speed limit.

Hwy. 101 is well marked with mileage posts. These start in Astoria in the north and reach mile 363 at the Oregon-California border. They make a great way to locate campgrounds and interesting sights, we'll use them extensively in this chapter.

Practical Tips

You will quickly notice that our favored campgrounds on this loop are in Oregon state parks. This is generally true throughout Oregon and Washington but particularly along the coast. Any private campground owner will tell you that government campgrounds have an unfair advantage–lots of prime real estate. Many other states do not take advantage of this, but Oregon and Washington do. The state campgrounds offer full hookups (in at least one case even cable TV), beautiful settings and landscaping, lots of room, and even a reservation system.

The reservation system is key. From Memorial Day to Labor Day the coast is very popular and reservations are absolutely necessary, especially on weekends. Make them as soon as you can, particularly if you happen to have a large rig since sites for big rigs with slide-outs are at a premium in the state park campgrounds. We describe the reservation system under Campground Reservations in the first chapter of this book.

The Oregon Coast changes with the seasons. It's a great destination all year long and many campgrounds remain open during the entire year, but it's a completely different place in the winter than in the middle of the summer. This is one of the few tours in this book that is fine for winter travel although you may have to deal with snow during the drive from Grants Pass to Brookings. When snow is a problem you can use a different route to reach the coast, perhaps Hwy. 20 from south of Salem to Florence would be the best choice but there are several alternates. During wet winter weather the coastal Hwy. 101 is sometimes closed by landslides, regional news programs will have reports if this happens, the road generally opens within a day or two. In the winter you don't really need to worry about making reservations at the campgrounds.

Whale watching is a very popular pastime on the coast. Gray whales winter in Baja California and summer in the far north, therefore they pass the Oregon coast twice. During December, January, and early February they are going south, in March, April and May they are headed north. A small population also summers in Oregon waters. You can see the whales from high points on shore and also take whale-watching voyages from several ports.

Fishing is another popular activity along the coast. You can fish from charter boats from many ports, fish in salt water along the beaches, or fish the estuaries and rivers along the coast.

DAY 1 – DESTINATION GRANTS PASS
253 miles (408 km), 4.5 hours

Along the Way - From Portland we'll head south on Interstate Highway 5 (I-5). This is a major four-lane highway that actually runs the length of the westernmost states from Blaine on the Canadian border to Tijuana on the Mexican border. Along the way it seldom is within sight of the Pacific Ocean, and the section we will travel is no exception.

From Portland the highway runs straight down the length of the Willamette Valley. There are coastal mountains on the right and the Cascades on the left. After leaving the Portland metropolitan area you'll drive through farming country and pass the towns of Salem, Albany, and Eugene. After Eugene the highway begins to climb to pass across the Middle Range before dipping into the Umpqua River Valley and Roseburg and then climbing again to reach the Rogue River Valley and Grants Pass.

Twenty miles (32 km) north of Grant's Pass at Exit 76 you might enjoy a stop at **Wolf Creek Inn State Heritage Site.** Now a state park, this may be the oldest hotel in the state, it dates to the early 1880s when it was a state-coach stop. It has eight rooms, but RV travelers will be more interested in the meals served in the dining room which is decorated as it was in the early days.

Just south, at Exit 71, is the **Applegate Trail Interpretive Center**. The Applegate Trail was a southern route of the Oregon Trail, there's also a covered bridge nearby.

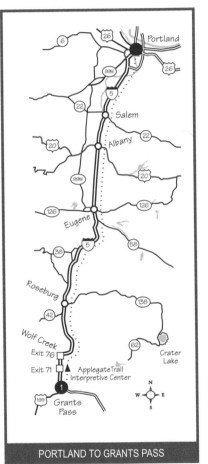

PORTLAND TO GRANTS PASS

GRANTS PASS

Grants Pass occupies the north end of a scenic stretch of I-5 along the Rogue River. Two other important towns, Medford and Ashland, are located along the highway to the southeast and are close enough that we consider them part of the same destination. Medford is 29 miles (47 km) from Grants Pass while Ashland is 41 miles (66 km).

The town of **Grants Pass** (population 17,500) is a pleasant and quiet town. It occupies the banks of the Rogue River, you may decide to take a ride on the river from this inland base, you will read about doing so from the mouth of the river at Gold Beach later in this chapter. From Grants Pass the river flows into the coastal mountains and becomes a designated Wild and Scenic River. You can ride a jet boat from downtown Grants Pass and through **Hellgate Canyon**, the jet boats are not permitted to run all the way down the river to the coast. The Rogue is popular for fishing and river raft trips, Grants Pass is a center for companies that specialize in guiding these activities. It is also possible to take a scenic drive to Hellgate Canyon. To do so take Exit 61 from I-5 about 3 miles (5 km) north of Grants Pass. Drive west through Merlin and you'll soon be in the canyon. You probably won't want to drive much past the town of Galice which serves as civilization in this part of the valley. It is actually possible to drive all the way across the Coast Range on small roads but these are not suitable for most larger RVs. Grants Pass annual events include the **Boatnik Festival** on Memorial Day, and the **Josephine County Fair** in mid-August.

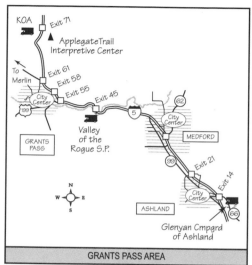

GRANTS PASS AREA

Medford (population 47,000) is the big town of the area. As the big city Medford acts as the business center for a region known for its fruit. A popular stop in Medford is **Harry and David's Country Village**. You probably know them for their mail-order gift baskets. They're located in the Southgate Mall. Take Exit 27 to visit. Medford has a **Pear Blossom Festival** in mid-April and hosts the **Jackson County Fair** on the third weekend of July.

Ashland (population 16,200) is probably best known for the **Oregon Shakespeare Festival**. It runs from late February to October in three different venues, including an outdoor theater. Performances each year include many different productions, both Shakespeare and modern. It is best to get your tickets in advance, we've included address and phone information at the end of this chapter.

Grants Pass Campgrounds

🚐 **Valley of the Rogue State Park** [MED] ⛺ 🚻 🚐 🛃 🚽 ♨ ⚟   800 452-5687 for reservations; 167 sites, open all year - This is a large state campground conveniently located right next to the freeway. The day-use portion of the park actually serves as a highway rest stop. Despite being so close to the freeway the campground is peaceful and relatively quiet, this park is an excellent base for exploration of the surrounding area. Because it is so conveniently located next to the highway this campground receives more visitors than any in the state system other than those along the coast. Camping sites are arranged off several paved circular drives. The river is nearby but not actually within sight of the camping sites. Large grassy areas surround the sites and they are well separated and quite large. There are 30-amp. full-hookup, electric only, and no-hookup sites. The restrooms offer hot showers and flush toilets. To reach the campground take Exit 45 and follow the signs to the park on the south-west side of the highway.

🚐 **Glenyan Campground of Ashland** [MED] [icons] 5310 Hwy. 66, Ashland, OR 97520; 541 488-1785; www.glenyancampground.com/; 68 sites, open March 1 through October 31 - Located just a few miles from Ashland this campground makes a good base for attending the Shakespeare Festival. Take Exit 14 from I-5 and follow the signs about 4 miles (6 km) to the southeast on Hwy. 66.

🚐 **Grants Pass-Sunny Valley KOA** [MED] [icons] [GS] 140 Old Stage Rd., Wolf Creek, OR 97497; 541 479-0209 or 800 KOA-7557 for reservations; 70 sites, open all year - A large full-service campground near the freeway about 14 miles (23 km) north of Grants Pass. Take Exit 71 from I-5 and follow the signs. Nearby attractions include the Applegate Trail Museum and a covered bridge.

DAY 2 – DESTINATION BROOKINGS
100 miles (161 km), 3.5 hours

A long the Way - Take Exit 55 from Highway 5 just east of Grant's Pass. This is the most convenient exit for Highway 199 and is clearly marked. Highway 199 is a mostly two-lane road but it's OK for larger rigs. Portions are winding and somewhat narrow, just take it easy on those sections and you'll have no problems.

About twenty-eight miles (45 km) from Grants Pass you'll reach Cave Junction, from here a small paved road leads east 20 miles (32 km) to the **Oregon Caves**. This side trip is well worth your while, the caves are unique in the Northwest, they have marble formations from mineral-laden water flows. Unfortunately the road is not recommended for large RVs. If you have a smaller vehicle available (tow vehicle or towed car) you can leave your larger rig or trailer in the parking lot at Illinois Valley Visitor Center in Cave Junction and make the side trip in it. There are also a few campgrounds near the junction if you choose to stay overnight in the area.

FROM GRANTS PASS TO BROOKINGS

Some 15 miles (24 km) beyond Cave Junction you reach the California border. You'll be stopped and asked if you have any fruits on board, then you're on your way. You're in California, but not for long. After 35 miles (56 km), much of it along road bordered by tall **redwoods** (this portion of the road is named the Redwood Highway), you'll see the sign for US 101 north to the Oregon Border and, six miles (10 km) beyond, Brookings.

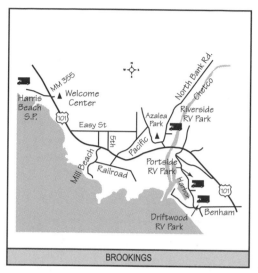

BROOKINGS

Brookings (population 6,300) is the first town you come to as you head in to Oregon from California along the coast. The town is increasingly popular and growing, largely because it has better weather than most towns along the Oregon coast. Warm air descending from the Rogue Valley mixes with marine air to produce comfortable temperatures year-round. Unfortunately, as is common along the entire coast, there is still lots of rain, particularly in the winter. Almost all of the Easter lilies produced in the U.S. come from near Brookings.

Brookings has a split personality with a downtown area on high ground north of the Chetco River and smaller unincorporated Harbor along the south shore of the Chetco River outlet. There are also many stores and other businesses strung out along the highway south of town.

There is a State Welcome Center, (open May through October 8 a.m. to 6 p.m. on Monday-Saturday and 9 a.m. to 5 p.m. on Sunday) which is located at a rest area near Mile 355.6. This is just across the highway from the Harris Beach State Park and about a mile north of Brookings. It has pamphlets covering the whole state and is designed to provide information for folks driving north from California. There's lots of parking for RVs.

While you are in Brookings you may want to visit **Brookings Harbor** for a meal at one of the seafood restaurants and perhaps even book a fishing charter. Brookings Harbor is said to be the safest port on the Oregon coast, coastal ports have dangerous entrances due to waves coming across the sand bars at river and estuary entrances. There's river fishing here too, the Chetco for steelhead and salmon and the Winchuck River a little to the south for rainbows and cutthroat.

The town is proud of **Azalea Park**, a small park just north of the river with many Azaleas, they bloom from April to June. It's a pleasant place for a picnic. **Harris State Park** is located just north of town. It's our favorite place to camp but also has a day-use area with picnic tables overlooking huge rocks and a beach that is large enough to allow you to indulge in your first beach combing of the trip. Inland from Brookings along the Chetco River near Loeb State Park is the **Redwood Nature Trail** which runs through some of the world's northernmost redwoods, drive eight miles (13 km) east on North Bank Road to reach the trail.

Brookings has a **Beachcomber's Festival** each March, an **Azalea Festival** on Memorial Day weekend, and **Easter in July** on July 1 to celebrate the blooming of the Easter lilies.

Brookings Campgrounds

Harris Beach State Park 800 452-5687 for reservations; 149 sites, open all year - This is our pick for a base during a visit to Brookings/ Gold Beach. It is conveniently located within hiking distance of downtown Brookings. In addition to the large campground located in a protected area well above the beach there is a picnic area near the shore. Huge rocks divide the beach into several stretches of sand. Harris Beach also has a hiker/biker camp area and some rental yurts. Electricity is 30-amp., some sites even have cable TV hookups. Many of the sites are large enough for the largest rigs although none are pull-through sites. To find the campground just drive right through town on Hwy. 101, the campground is on the left about a mile north.

Driftwood RV Park 16011 Lower Harbor Road, Brookings, OR 97415; 541 469-9089; 100 sites, open all year - Located near the harbor this campground has large sites, some pull-throughs, 50-amp. power, and some instant phone sites for Internet access. It is located in the harbor area.

Portside RV Park, Inc. 16219 Lower Harbor Road, P.O. Box 2187, Brookings, OR 97415; 541 469-6616; 115 sites, open all year - Another conveniently located park near the harbor. The campground has long pull-throughs, 50-amp. power, and advertises that it has a computerized golf simulator. It too is located near the harbor.

Riverside RV Park 97666 N Bank Chetco River Rd., Brookings, OR 97415; 541 469-4799 or 888 201-9506 for reservations; 25 sites, open all year - Located in a nice setting along the north side of the Chetco River just .4 miles from the highway.

Gold Beach Side Trip

Gold Beach is 27 miles (44 km) north of Brookings. From there you can ride a **jet mail boat** up the Rogue River. This is one of the most popular day trips along the entire Oregon Coast, most people thoroughly enjoy it. Until a road was built to reach the small town of Agnes, some 32 miles (52 km) up the Rogue, mail was delivered by mail boat. Today you can drive to Agnes, but the boats are more fun! Two outfits in Gold Beach offer rides, they are Jerry's Rogue River Jet Boats and Rogue River Mail Boat Trips. A variety of trips are offered.

Fishing is also good in the area. The Rogue is a famous fishing river, and offshore fishing is also popular.

DAY 3 – DESTINATION BANDON
84 miles (135 km), 3 hours

Along **The Way** -The 29-mile (47 km) section of coastline from Brookings north to Gold Beach is very scenic. The road closely follows the coastline which is alternately rocky cliffs and sandy beaches. From Mile 343 to Mile 353 you are in the **Samuel H. Boardman State Scenic Corridor**. There are many pull-offs giving you the opportunity to make short walks and take some photos from scenic viewpoints.

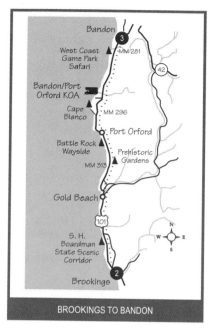

BROOKINGS TO BANDON

The town of **Gold Beach** is located at Mile 328. It sits at the mouth of the Rogue River. Jet boat trips from here are described as a side trip in the Brookings section above.

You might find a visit to the **Prehistoric Gardens** at Mile 313.1 interesting, particularly if you have some youngsters along. There are full-sized dinosaur replicas in a rain forest setting.

Port Orford is the western-most incorporated city in the contiguous U.S. You'll pass through this small town at Mile 301. Take the time to stop at **Battle Rock Wayside** at the south end of town for views and steep access to the beach. Those with small easy to maneuver rigs can turn left at the sign in town and drive out to the **Port Orford Heads Wayside**. There's a trail to a headland which can be an excellent whale-watching spot but turn-around room is limited.

Cape Blanco is the westernmost point in the contiguous U.S. You reach it by taking a five-mile (8 km) paved road from Mile 296.6 of US 101. The lighthouse on the cape is the oldest on the Oregon coast, there's also a small state park campground with electrical hookups. There's plenty of room to turn big rigs just before the end of the road.

HIGHWAY 101 ALONG THE OREGON COAST

About six miles (10 km) south of Bandon you'll pass the **West Coast Game Park Safari** at Mile 281.5. This is a large private zoo with a reported 75 different species. Some of the animals are free-roaming while others are in exhibit areas.

Finally, at Mile 270 you'll reach your destination for the day, the town of Bandon.

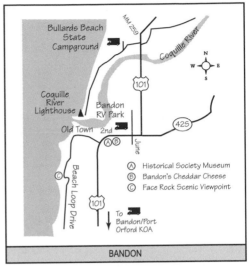

For such a small town Bandon (population 2,800) has lots to offer. Today's tourists know the town as an artists colony and laid-back tourist town with interesting tourist attractions including a cheese factory, cranberries, and the cute little Old Town sitting just south of the harbor. Bandon is located near the mouth of the Coquille River and has its own jetties and lighthouse. It has been a port attracting visitors since the 1800s.

Once you have set yourself up in a campground take a stroll around the **Old Town**. The **Chamber of Commerce** is located along the highway at the entrance to the area. You'll find shops and good restaurants. Don't miss the stores selling cranberry sweets and products. There's even a museum - **The Bandon Historical Society Museum**, located in the old Coast Guard Station.

On the main highway just a block or so from the Old Town is what must be the town's most popular attraction. Seems like everyone passing on the highway stops to sample the cheeses at **Bandon's Cheddar Cheese**. Try the fresh curds if they happen to be available the day you visit.

As you approached the town of Bandon you may have noticed fields that are surrounded by dikes and flooded with water. Those aren't rice paddies, they're growing **cranberries**. Check with the Chamber of Commerce visitor center for the location of these fields, they may be able to set you up with a visit or tour during the fall harvest activities.

Bandon has good beaches and also a good selection of sea stacks - big rocks offshore. You can best see them from **Beach Loop Drive** which follows the coast on the south side of the Coquille River. The **Bandon State Natural Area** and **Face Rock Scenic Viewpoint** provide several beach access points, necessary since this stretch of coast is fairly built-up with private residences and motels.

Bandon is another fishing town. Charter boats are available at the boat basin next to the old town, the Coquille River offers salmon, and in the lower section it is possible to catch crabs. Surf fishing is popular from the beach north and south of the river mouth.

Bandon's lighthouse, the **Coquille River Lighthouse**, is located on the north bank of the river near the mouth. It makes a good photograph from town but to reach it you must follow Highway 101 north to Bullards Beach State Park. The same road provides access to the campground, the lighthouse, and long sandy Bullards Beach. This lighthouse is not operational but serves as an interpretive center. The state park also offers hiking trails and the river mouth area of the park is popular with windsurfers.

On Memorial day Bandon hosts the **Wine and Seafood Festival** and **Sandcastle-Building Contest** but the big event of the year is the **Cranberry Festival** in October.

Bandon Campgrounds

Bullards Beach State Campground [MED] [△] [♿] [⛽] [♨] [🔥] [♨]   800 452-5687 for reservations; 185 sites, open all year - This is a large attractive campground set in evergreens about a mile from the beach. Sites are arranged off 2 big loops and are attractively landscaped, many are screened by vegetation from their neighbors. All sites are back-in, many are large enough for long rigs with pop-outs. Most sites have either electricity and water or full hookups. There is a dump station, restrooms with flush toilets and hot showers, yurt rentals, and a hiker/biker tent camping area. Nearby, in the park, are a horse camping area, boat ramp, picnic area, lighthouse, and beach access. Trails through the sand and also a bike trail lead to the beach from the campground. Like all of the state park campgrounds this one is easy to find because it is well signed. It is located some 3 miles (5 km) north of Bandon just across the Coquille River bridge. If you've been watching the mileposts you will note that you lose eight miles (13 km) just north of Bandon, this is due to a change in the routing of the road since the posts were placed. Watch for the turn toward the ocean at Mile 259.2. The campground is on the right about a quarter-mile down this road, the road continues to the lighthouse at the mouth of the river.

Bandon/Port Orford KOA [MED] [△] [♿] [⛽] [♨] [🔥] [♨] [▣] [🛒] [▣]   46612 Hwy. 101, Langlois, OR 97450; 541 348-2358 or 800 KOA-3298 for reservations; 72 sites, open all year - A full service campground located off Hwy. 101 about 16 miles (26 km) south of Bandon.

Bandon RV Park [MED] [♿] [⛽] [♨] [🔥] [▣]   935 2nd St. SE Hwy. 101, Bandon, OR 97411; 541 347-4122; 46 sites, open all year - This small RV park is short on amenities but has full hookups and an excellent location, you can easily stroll in to Bandon's Old Town. The campground is located right in Bandon a short distance east of the harbor and right on Highway 101.

Day 4 – Destination Oregon Dunes and Florence
76 miles (123 km), 2.5 hours (to Florence)

Along The Way - Not far north of Bandon is Coos Bay, center of commercial life on the southern Oregon coast. Rather than concentrating on Coos Bay we'll leave the main highway south of Coos Bay, visit some interesting coastal destinations, and then rejoin Hwy. 101 in the northern suburbs of Coos Bay, thereby bypassing much of the city.

To do this drive north from Bandon and take the left turn at Mile 256.9 marked Charleston. The Seven Devils Road winds through the forest and passes **South Slough National Estuarine Reservation**. You'll find a visitor's center and paths down to and around the estuary. Continuing on you'll enter Charleston and see signs pointing left for **Sunset Bay State Park**, **Shore Acres State Park**, and **Cape Arago State Park**.

These three small state parks along the shore offer a variety of options. **Shore Acres State Park** is the former estate of a timber magnate: Louis J. Simpson. There are formal gardens with roses, azaleas, and rhododendrons, and also a Japanese garden. There's a bluff-top lookout with views along the rocky coast. **Cape Arago State Park**, at the end of the road, also offers a coastal lookout, often with views of sea lions and seals, not to mention whales on occasion. The park also has excellent tide pools. **Sunset Bay State Park,** the first park you come to has a small bay where the water gets warm enough for the hardy to swim.

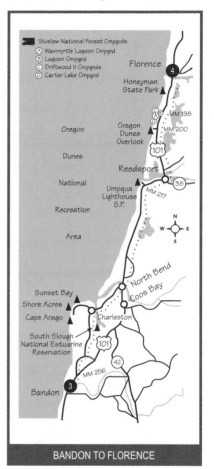

BANDON TO FLORENCE

As you drive back inland stop for a while in **Charleston**, the most attractive of the Coos Bay-area towns. It is a fishing village, with more convenient access to the ocean for fishing boats than Coos Bay and North Bend which are located farther from the estuary mouth. In Charleston you'll find a fishing pier, fishing charter companies, restaurants, and shops.

Follow the highway across the bridge and northeast through suburbs of Coos Bay, you'll eventually hit Hwy. 101 again. Turn north and you'll soon be entering Oregon's dune country. For about 40 miles (66 km) between Coos Bay and Florence the highway passes inland of a large area of shifting sand dunes. Much of the area is incorporated into the **Oregon Dunes National Recreation Area**. Many visitors come here to roar across the dunes on sand buggies, it can be a lot of fun. Others enjoy hiking through sections closed to motorized vehicles or visit the beaches. If you didn't bring your own sand buggy they can easily be rented in the area. The Recreation Area charges a $3 daily fee, you must display a pass when parked at trailheads.

Watch for the road west to **Umpqua Lighthouse State Park** near Mile 217 just south of Winchester Bay. The lighthouse is on the south shore of the mouth of the Umpqua River, nearby is the **Umpqua River Whale Watching Station**, whales are often sighted in the estuary.

The official center of the dunes area is **Reedsport** at Mile 211.5 of US 101, a town of about 5,000 near the mouth of the Umpqua River, the largest river between the Columbia and the Sacramento. Reedsport is the location of the **Oregon Dunes National Recreation Area Visitor Center**. Hwy. 38 joins Hwy. 101 here, if you drive 3 miles (5 km) east you'll reach the **Dean Creek Elk Viewing Area**, a refuge where you can usually see and photograph elk.

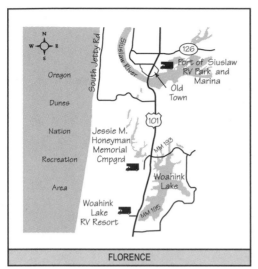

FLORENCE

About 10 miles (16 km) north of Reedsport is the **Oregon Dunes Overlook** at Mile 200.8. There's a special deal on the recreation area daily fee here, only $1. Boardwalks and ramps make it easy to see and understand the dunes. As you continue north on US 101 you'll pass Jessie M. Honeyman State Park (see camping below), and arrive at Florence at Mile 191.

Florence (population 6,700), originally a lumber mill town, is located near the mouth of the Siuslaw River. It has become an attractive tourist destination, particularly in the **Old Town** area along the waterfront. Like the old towns in several other cities along the coast it has interesting shops and restaurants, this one is not as flashy as some. There's also a marina and an RV park run by the port.

Just south of the river the **South Jetty Dune and Beach Access Road** leads out to the coast and then north to the Siuslaw River south jetty. This is the best beach access in the area and also provides access to the off-road vehicle portion of the dunes.

The Siuslaw River is navigable for 20 miles (32 km) upstream and fishing for a variety of species is popular.

Golfers will probably appreciate the Sand Pines Golf Course and the Ocean Dunes Golf Links, both take advantage of the rolling dunes in the area.

Florence has a **Rhododendron Festival** during the third week of May.

Florence Campgrounds

Jessie M. Honeyman Memorial Campground MED 800 452-5687 for reservations; 371 sites, open all year - Another great Oregon state campground, this one is really huge. In addition to the camping area there is a large day-use area with picnicking and swimming in Cleawax Lake. Trails lead to the dunes, you can walk through them to the coast some 2 miles distant. There's another day-use area on much larger Woahink Lake which is located across the highway, also with a swimming area. All sites are back-ins, some large enough for long rigs with pop-outs. There are good restrooms with flush toilets and hot showers, fire rings at all sites, a dump station, rental yurts, and a hiker/biker tent camping area. The campground is just off US 101 at Mile 193.4, about 3 miles (5 km) south of Florence.

Port of Siuslaw RV Park and Marina MED 1st and Harbor, Florence, OR 97439; 541 997-3040; 84 sites, open all year - Within walking distance of Florence's old town. Heading north watch for 1st St. on the right after crossing the bridge into Florence, turn right and follow 1st to the end.

Woahink Lake RV Resort MED GS 83570 Hwy. 101 South,

Florence, OR 97439; 541 997-6454, or 800 659-6454 for reservations; 78 sites, open all year - This is a modern commercial campground with some pull-through sites and 50-amp. power. The campground has access at the back to the dunes so it is a good place to stay if you have your own buggy. It also has it's own dock on Woahink Lake across the highway from the campground.

There are many Siuslaw National Forest Service Campgrounds in the Oregon Dunes National Recreation Area. Here is small selection:

Waxmyrtle, Lagoon, and Driftwood II Campgrounds LOW
800 280-2267 for reservations; 166 sites, open all year - All of these campgrounds are located near each other off the Siltcoos Beach Access Road which leaves Hwy. 101

OREGON COAST LIGHTHOUSE

and heads west some seven miles (11 km) south of Florence. Driftwood II is primarily for off-road vehicle users and has access to the portion of the dunes where they operate, the other two campgrounds do not and are quieter. Driftwood II has the largest sites. There is swimming in the Siltcoos River. Reservations are available only for Driftwood II at 800 280-2267, there is a reservation fee.

Carter Lake Campground [icons] 800 280-2267 for reservations; 24 sites, open May 1 through September 30 - This campground is on Carter Lake which is used for swimming and fishing. The dunes are overgrown in the immediate area but trails lead into nearby dunes not open to off-road vehicles. To reach the campground drive 8.5 miles (13.7 km) south from Florence, and then west a short distance on Forest Road 1084.

Day 5 – Destination Newport
50 miles (81 km), 2 hours

Along The Way - Today's drive is short, but it passes some very scenic coast and interesting stops.

The twenty miles (32 km) or so between Mile 186 and Yachats at Mile 165 are very scenic. They're in the Siuslaw National Forest.

Sea Lion Caves, at Mile 179.3, have long been a do-not-miss stop for travelers along the coast. There is a good parking area for big RVs. This is a commercial operation. An elevator drops through the cliff to a lookout window which lets visitors watch a colony of undisturbed Stellar sea lions in a large natural sea cave. In the distance you can also see the Heceta Head Lighthouse to the north. Just north of the caves is a pull-off where you can sometimes see sea lions on the rocks and in the water below. This is also an excellent spot to get a photo of the lighthouse and to watch for whales.

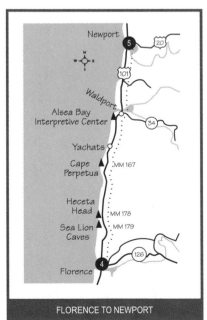

FLORENCE TO NEWPORT

Heceta Head Lighthouse is one of the most scenic of the eight along the Oregon coast. You can walk to the lighthouse using a trail that leads from **Heceta Head Lighthouse State Scenic Viewpoint** at Mile 178.3. There is also a bed and breakfast here in the former assistant lighthouse keeper's house, **Heceta House**.

You may want to stop at the **Cape Perpetua Interpretive Center** at Mile 167.3. The center, run by the Forest Service, has exhibits covering the forest and coastline in this area. Nature trails and tide pools are accessible from the center. This is also another popular whale-watching site. There is adequate parking for larger rigs.

At Mile 165 you'll pass through little **Yachats**, and then at Mile 156 reach **Waldport**. The highway crosses the new Alsea Bay Bridge here, and at the south end of the bridge is the **Alsea Bay Interpre-**

tive Center with displays covering transportation along the coast. The flat coastline is less scenic along this section, at Mile 143 you'll find that you are approaching Newport.

NEWPORT

Newport (population 8,800) is one of the two most popular tourist destination towns along the coast, the other is Seaside to the north. One reason is that the town is only two highway hours from Portland.

South of the big bridge over the outlet of Yaquina Bay are two ocean-oriented attractions. These are the **Oregon Coast**

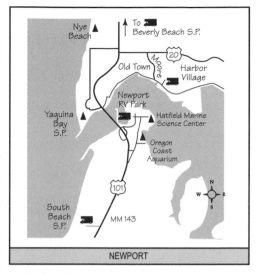

Aquarium and the **Hatfield Marine Science Center**. The very impressive aquarium is probably best known as the former home of Keiko the killer whale but don't let Keiko's absence stop you from visiting. The aquarium is modern and well thought out with great displays of the region's marine life including tide pools, a seabird aviary, seals, sea lions, and sea otters. The science center next door is a branch of Oregon State University and has a public wing with marine displays.

On the north side of the bridge the main attraction is probably the **Old Town** situated along the north shore of Yaquina Bay. Here you'll find a variety of tourist-trap-type attractions including restaurants, shops, and, believe it or not, a Ripley's Believe It or Not! The Old Town can be a lot of fun, and the presence of an actual working fish-processing plant or two is a nice touch. Large murals grace the walls of some buildings.

Seaward from the Old Town, west of the bridge, is **Yaquina Bay State Park**. There you'll find **Yaquina Bay Lighthouse**, views of the harbor entrance, and trails to the beach. A little farther north is **Nye Beach**, an old and established beachside neighborhood where most resort hotels are located.

Newport has a big charter fishing fleet. Also offered are whale-watching tours and boat tours of local oyster beds and the harbor.

Newport's big event is in February, the **Newport Seafood and Wine Festival**, there's also **Loyalty Days and Sea Fair** in May.

Newport Campgrounds

South Beach State Park [MED] ⬛ ⬛ ⬛ ⬛ ⬛ ⬛ ⬛ ⬛ 800 452-5687 for reservations; 244 sites, open all year - This large campground has sites with electricty and water situated off several paved loops near a sandy beach that stretches for miles. There's lots of room for big rigs. The campground is just two miles south of Newport off Hwy. 101.

Newport RV Park at South Beach [MED] ⬛ ⬛ ⬛ ⬛ ⬛ ⬛ ⬛ [GS] 2301 SE Marine

Science Dr, Newport, OR 97365; 541 876-3321; 116 sites, open all year - This is a good big-rig campground with 50-amp. power. It is within walking distance of the Oregon Coast Aquarium across the river from Florence. Follow signs from the south end of the Newport bridge.

Harbor Village RV Park and Mobile Homes `LOW` 923 SE Bay Blvd., Newport, OR 97365; 541 265-5088; 140 sites, open all year - Small with limited facilities and many permanent residents, this RV park has location going for it. You can easily walk along the edge of the harbor to Newport's old town. From the junction of Hwy. 101 with Hwy. 20 in town go .5 miles east on Hwy. 20, turn south on S.E. Moore Dr. and drive down to the waterfront, turn left and you'll see the campground entrance in about a block on the left.

Beverly Beach State Park `MED` 800 452-5687 for reservations; 258 sites, open all year - This large state campground has access under the highway to a long scenic beach between Yaquina Head and Cape Foulweather. The campground stretches inland for quite some distance from the beach so you have a choice between crowded but convenient (to the beach) and uncrowded but less convenient. This state campground has some big pull-through sites. There's also a hiker/biker camp, and yurts. The campground is 7 miles (11 km) north of Newport.

SEA LIONS ON THE DOCK IN NEWPORT

DAY 6 – DESTINATION CANNON BEACH
113 miles (182 km), 4 hours

A long The Way - Just outside Newport to the north, at Mile 137.6, a road leads to **Yaquina Head**. This area is run by the Bureau of Land Management and has seen improvements over the last few years that now make it one of the most interesting stops along the coast. The head is occupied by Yaquina Head lighthouse. Below the cliffs and easily accessible is an excellent area of tide pools. New is another tide pool area, created out of an old rock quarry and fully wheelchair accessible. In 1999 this area had not yet accumulated much in the way of tide pool life, but each year there will be more. Offshore is Colony Rock, a sea-bird rookery where you can sometimes see puffins although they nest on a rock face that is difficult to see. Yaquina Head has a new and very nice visitors center with excellent exhibits about the tide pools and nearby lighthouse.

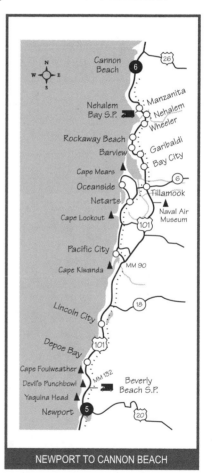

NEWPORT TO CANNON BEACH

A few miles north, just past the entrance to the Beverly Beach State Park Campground, a road leads west to the small town of Otter Crest and a parking area and viewpoint for the **Devil's Punchbowl**. The Punchbowl is a bowl that has been worn in the rocks by the wave action. If waves and tide are right the vertical spray can be impressive. Watch for the turn at Mile 132.5. Turn-around room for big rigs is limited. It's also a good place for an impressive coastal picture to the south.

When Captain Cook explored this coast he must not have been enjoying the weather when he passed the cape he named **Cape Foulweather**. There is an excellent viewpoint and a small shop just down from the highway on a short access road from Mile 131.2.

At Mile 128.0 you'll find yourself in tiny **Depoe Bay**. As you cross the bridge look inland to see one of the smallest and snuggest harbors along the entire coast. Then stop and take a look at the very narrow entrance to the harbor. Depoe Bay was the site of the charter-fishing sequence in the movie *One Flew Over the Cuckoo's Nest*. You can catch a whale-watching cruise from the harbor or check out the many shops and restaurants.

Lincoln City appears at Mile 120. It continues for about 7 miles (11 km). With a population of over 7,000 people this is one of the largest cities on the coast and it draws many tourists. The attraction is the beach, you won't see it from the road. You will find access at **Siletz Bay** at Mile 118, the **D River Wayside** at Mile 115, and at **Roads End State Recreation Site** at Mile 112.8.

As you continue north you may want to avoid the pleasant but relatively uninteresting inland section of Highway 101 leading into Tillamook by following the **Three Capes Loop**. The south junction is at Mile 90.4. The 28-mile (45 km) loop will lead you past **Pacific City**, **Cape Kiwanda**, **Cape Lookout**, and **Netarts**. A side trip from near Netarts will take you to Oceanside and **Cape Mears**. The loop road rejoins Highway 101 in Tillamook at the west end of Third Street.

Most people probably know **Tillamook** for its cheese, and cheese factories are a big part of the draw here. The **Tillamook Cheese Visitors Center** is north of town along Highway 101 at Mile 63.9. There is another factory nearby, the **Blue Heron French Cheese Company**, at Mile 65. Our favorite attraction in Tillamook is the **Tillamook Naval Air Station Museum**. It is located south of town near Mile 68.1. The museum is housed in a huge blimp hanger, you really can't miss it. Inside is the beginning of what will hopefully become an excellent collection of World War II fighters and bombers along with other interesting aircraft.

From Tillamook Highway 101 winds its way north through a series of towns along Tillamook Bay, Nehalem Bay, and the coast. These are **Bay City** (Mile 60.8), **Garibaldi** (Mile 55.6), **Barview** (Mile 53.7), **Rockaway Beach** (Mile 50.8), **Wheeler** (Mile 47.0), **Nehalem** (Mile 44.7), **Manzanita** (Mile 43.0), and finally, Cannon Beach. We'll spend the night in Cannon Beach, but there are many other excellent stops for RVers along this coast.

CANNON BEACH

Cannon Beach (population 1,300) is cute and upscale. That's a pretty good description for this little town. There's an excellent beach, big rocks called sea stacks just offshore, and lots of little restaurants, shops and galleries. Art activities are big here in the summer. In addition to the many studios and galleries the Portland State University Haystack Program in the Arts and Sciences puts on classes, there's a **Sunday Concerts in the Park** series from the Fourth of July to Labor Day, and even an annual **Sandcastle Contest**, usually in late May. One of Cannon Beach's big advantages in the way of ambiance is that the highway bypasses the town.

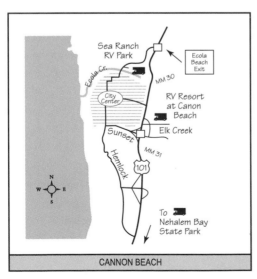

CANNON BEACH

Adjoining Cannon Beach to the north is **Ecola State Park**. It encompasses **Tillamook Head**, there is a hiking trail through the park from Cannon Beach to Seaside. Captain William Clark of the Lewis and Clark expedition is thought to have viewed the Cannon Beach area from a vantage point in the park, it was probably the farthest point south along the coast reached by the expedition.

Cannon Beach Campgrounds

RV Resort at Cannon Beach [MED] 345 Elk Creek Road, P.O. Box 219, Cannon Beach, OR 97110; 503 436-2231 or 800 847-2231 for reservations; 100 sites, open all year - This RV campground offers a hard to beat combination: a convenient location and excellent facilities. It is located on the east side of the highway near the second (from the north) Cannon Beach exit and is within a mile or so of what is called the Midtown area of Cannon Beach. The campground has 100 sites, all large paved sites wide enough for big rigs with pop-outs and with full hookups including cable TV. There are top quality restrooms, an indoor pool and spa, laundry, grocery, and even a shuttle in to town for those not wanting to make the 15-minute walk. You can easily find the campground by taking the Cannon Beach Exit at Mile 30.8 and heading east. You'll immediately see the entrance.

Sea Ranch RV Park [MED] 415 North Hemlock, P.O. Box 214, Cannon Beach, OR 97110; 503 436-2815; 71 sites, open all year - Even more convenient to Cannon Beach than the campground above, but the facilities aren't as upscale. Traveling north take the Ecola Beach Exit, you'll soon see the campground on the left, it's on the main access road into town from the north.

Nehalem Bay State Park [MED] 800 452-5687 for reservations; 281 sites, open all year - A large state park campground with electrical sites, yurts, and even an air strip. The campground sites right next to a long, sandy beach and with walking distance of the village of Manzanita. To find the campground follow the signs from Hwy. 101 just north of Nehalem.

DAY 7 – DESTINATION ASTORIA
65 miles (105 km), 2.5 hours

A long The Way - Today's drive is a short one, but en route you'll pass through Seaside, one of the most-visited cities on the coast, and end the day near Astoria which is one of the coast's most historical sites. There's lots to see so don't spend too much time eating a leisurely breakfast in Cannon Beach.

Just 3 miles (5 km) north of Cannon Beach at Mile 25 you'll begin to pass through the road-side outskirts of Seaside, the center of town is between the highway and the ocean. Take the time to pull off the road, park, and wander around Seaside. The town is about 100 years old, and the main business here has always been tourism. The main drag leading from Highway 101 to the beach is Broadway, there's a turnaround at the end of it. With a large rig a better bet is the public parking lot at Columbia Avenue and First Street which is just north of Broadway and near the beach. Seaside has a variety of attractions. There's the two-mile paved **Promenade** along the beach, shopping and restaurants along **Broadway**, and the **Seaside Aquarium**. If you are interested in the town's history visit the **Seaside Museum**. There almost always seems to be something going on in Seaside, particularly in the summer, check at the Seaside Chamber of Commerce for information.

Continuing north you will spot the southern access road to Fort Stevens and Warrenton at Mile 7.5. Both of our campgrounds listed below are on this road. There's

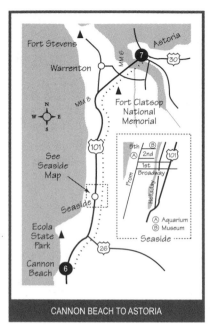

CANNON BEACH TO ASTORIA

another access road at Mile 6.5, either one will work. Astoria is northeast across the long bridge across the mouth of the Youngs River.

Between the two Fort Stevens access roads, at Mile 7.0, old Highway 101 leads three miles (5 km) east to **Fort Clatsop National Memorial**. This is where the Louis and Clark Expedition spent the winter of 1805-1806. There is a reconstruction of their fort here and an excellent visitor center.

Astoria

Some folks claim Astoria (population 10,100) is the oldest town in this part of the country, but that can be disputed since it has not been continually occupied since the early days of Fort Astoria. Only since the 1840s was the town site permanently occupied, and by that time Oregon City on the outskirts of today's Portland had begun to grow.

The Columbia River is the town's reason for existence. Even today the river pilots that guide the huge ships across the bar are based here. There's an excellent museum, the **Columbia River Maritime Museum**, that gives the whole fascinating story on Columbia River shipping.

Another river-oriented site here is the huge Astoria-Megler Bridge. You can't miss it because it towers over the little town and stretches 4.1 miles (6.6 km) north

across the Columbia to Washington State. There's a toll, but on a nice day the drive across is worth the money for the views. Once across you might look around. The **Lewis and Clark Campsite Heritage Area** just 2.4 miles (3.9 km) to the west occupies the spot where Lewis and Clark first saw the Pacific Ocean. At 3.0 miles (4.8 km) is **Fort Columbia State Park**. This was a second fort (of three) guarding the entrance to the Columbia, Fort Stevens was on the south bank and Fort Canby was farther west on the north shore.

Back in Astoria there are at least two more must-see attractions. The **Astoria Column**, erected by the Northern Pacific Railroad in 1926, offers great views after a 164-step climb up the interior spiral stair-

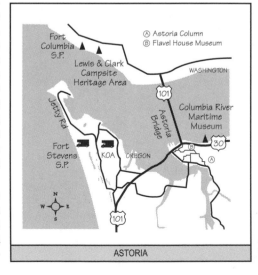

ASTORIA

way. The **Flavel House Museum** is a Victorian-style mansion built by Oregon's first steamship captain, it has the original furnishings and was built in 1883.

Finally, our campground, Fort Stevens State Park, has a great deal of historical interest. Fort Stevens was built during the Civil War. It was also shelled by a Japanese submarine during World War II. You can find out more at the **Museum** in the park. At the far north end of the park is a huge **jetty** jutting out into the Pacific. It was designed to help protect the entrance to the Columbia and to help control the sand bars that want to close the shipping channels. It is not entirely successful, extensive dredging is still required and the entrance to the Columbia is one of the world's more dangerous shipping routes, particularly during winter storms.

The area near the mouth of the Columbia River is well-known for its fishing, and also as a fairly treacherous piece of water. Fishing charters from Astoria and Warrenton/ Hammond are available.

Astoria celebrates the **Great Astoria Crab Feed and Seafood Festival** on the last weekend in April, the **Astoria Scandinavian Festival** during the last half of June, and the **Astoria Art Festival** in September.

Astoria Campgrounds

▄ **Fort Stevens State Park** ⎅MED⎅ △ ⎙ ⎚ ⎚ ⎚ ⎚ ⎚ ⎚ 800 452-5687 for reservations; 605 sites, open all year - This is the largest of the Oregon state campgrounds. It has 209 full hookup sites, 126 sites with electricity and water, and many tent sites. Sites have large paved parking areas, many suitable for the largest rigs. Restrooms are good with flush toilets and hot showers. There are also yurt rentals, a hiker/biker area, 14 miles (23 km) of bicycle and hiking trails, and a very long beach. You can drive to the campground by heading northwest from either Mile 6.5 or Mile 7.5 of US 101. Signs will guide you along back roads to the campground.

▄ **Astoria/Warrenton/Seaside KOA** ⎅HIGH⎅ △ ⎙ ⎚ ⎚ ⎚ ⎚ ⎚ ⎚ ⎚ ⎚ 1100 Ridge Road, Hammond, OR 97121; 503 861-2606 or 800 KOA-8506 for reservations; 259 sites, open all year - This large KOA is located right across from the entrance to Fort Stevens State Park and offers a commercial alternative with virtually the same location. It has 50-amp. power, an indoor swimming pool, and lots of pull-throughs. Follow the directions given for the state park above to reach the campground.

DAY 8 - DESTINATION PORTLAND
85 miles (137 km), 2 hours

From Astoria it is an easy drive back to Portland along US 30. This highway generally follows the south bank of the Columbia but is seldom within view of the river. For most of the distance it is a decent two-lane road. It is possible to cross the river at a bridge from Rainier in Oregon to Longview in Washington. There you can pick up the I-5 interstate, the same road we followed south from Portland on this trip. I-5 follows the north bank of the Columbia to Portland and is quicker than U.S. 30. It also offers easier access to Portland campgrounds.

Information Resources

See our Internet site at www.rollinghomes.com for Internet site addresses.

Destination Grants Pass

Applegate Trail Interpretive Center, 500 Sunny Valley Loop, Sunny Valley, OR 97497; 888 411-1846 or 541 472-8545

Grants Pass Visitors and Convention Bureau, 1995 NW Vine St., P.O. Box 1787, Grants Pass, OR 97526; 541 476-7717 or 800 547-5927

Hellgate Jetboat Excursions, 953 SE 7th Street, Grants Pass, OR 97526; 800 648-4874

Medford Visitors and Convention Bureau, 101 E 8th St., Medford, OR 97501; 541 779-4847 or 800 469-6307

Harry and David's Country Village, 1315 Center Drive, Medford, OR 97501; 541 776-2277

Ashland Chamber of Commerce, 110 E Main St., P.O. Box 1360, Ashland, OR 97520; 541 482-3486

Oregon Shakespeare Festival Box Office, 15 S Pioneer St., Box 158, Ashland, OR 97520; 541 482-4331

Destination Brookings

Oregon Caves, 20,000 Caves Hwy., Cave Junction, OR 97523; 541 592-3400

Brookings-Harbor Chamber of Commerce, P.O. Box 940, Brookings, OR 97415; 800 535-9469 or 503 409-3181

State of Oregon Welcome Center, Hwy. 101 Mile 355.6, Brookings, OR 97415; 503 469-4117

Gold Beach Visitor Center and Chamber of Commerce, 29279 Ellensburg #3, Gold Beach, OR 97444; 800 525-2334 or 541 247-7526

Jerry's Rogue River Jet Boats, P.O. Box 1011, Gold Beach, OR 97444; 541 247-4571 or 800 451-3645

Rogue River Mail Boat Trips, P.O. Box 1165G, Gold Beach, OR 97444; 541 247-7033 or 800 458-3511

The Prehistoric Gardens, 36848 Hwy. 101 S, Port Orford, OR 97465; 541 332-4463

Port Orford Visitor Center at Battle Rock, P.O. Box 637, Port Orford, OR 97465; 541 332-8055

Destination Bandon

West Coast Game Park, Rt. 1, Box 1330, Bandon, OR 97411; 541 347-3106

Bandon Chamber of Commerce, 300 2nd Street, P.O. Box 1515, Bandon, OR 97411; 541 347-9616

Bandon Cheddar Cheese, Hwy. 101, Bandon, OR 97411; 800 548-8961 or 541 347-2456

Destination Florence

Reedsport-Winchester Bay Chamber of Commerce, 855 Highway Ave., P.O. Box 11, Reedsport, OR 97467; 541 271-3495 or 800 247-2155

Oregon Dunes National Recreation Area Visitor Center, 855 Hwy. 101, Reedsport, OR 97467; 541 271-3611

Florence Chamber of Commerce, 270 Highway 101, P.O. Box 26000, Florence, OR 97439; 541 997-3128

Destination Newport

Newport Chamber of Commerce, 555 SW US 101, Newport, OR 97365; 541 265-8801 or 800 262-7844

Destination Cannon Beach

Depoe Bay Chamber of Commerce, 630 SE Hwy 101, Depoe Bay, OR 97341; 541 765-2889

Lincoln City Visitor and Convention Bureau, 801 SW US 101, Lincoln City, OR 97367; 800 452-2151 or 541 994-8228

OREGON COAST

Cannon Beach Chamber of Commerce, P.O. Box 64, 201 E. 2nd, Cannon Beach, OR 97110; 503 436-2623

Astoria Segment

Seaside Chamber of Commerce, 7 N Roosevelt Street, Seaside, OR 97138; 503 738-6391

Seaside Aquarium, 200 North Promenade, Seaside, OR 97138; 503 738-6211

Seaside Historical Museum, 570 Necanicum Drive, Seaside, OR 97138; 503 738-7065

Fort Clapsop National Memorial, Route 3 Box 604FC, Astoria, OR 97103; 503 861-2471

Astoria Chamber of Commerce, P.O. Box 176, 111 W Marine Dr., Astoria, OR 97103; 503 325-6311

Columbia River Maritime Museum, 1792 Marine Dr., Astoria, OR 97103; 503 325-2323

Flavel House, 441 8th St., Astoria, OR 97103; 503 325-2203

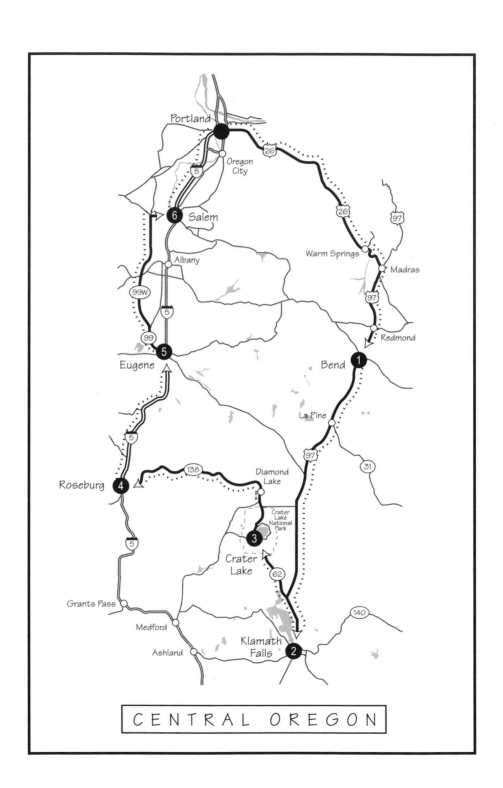

CENTRAL OREGON

Chapter 5

Tour 2

Central Oregon

Top Attractions

- ✦ Mt. Hood
- ✦ Mt. Bachelor
- ✦ Cascade Lakes Highway
- ✦ Newberry National Volcanic Monument
- ✦ High Desert Museum
- ✦ Klamath Basin National Wildlife Refuges
- ✦ Lava Beds National Monument
- ✦ Crater Lake National Park
- ✦ Umpqua River Valley
- ✦ McKenzie River Valley
- ✦ Robert Aufderheide Memorial Drive
- ✦ Willamette Valley

General Description

On this tour you will have a chance to explore Oregon's section of the Cascade Mountains. First you'll cross the mountains from Portland and drive south along the eastern slopes. You'll visit Bend and Klamath Falls. Then you'll drive northwest to spend some time at Crater Lake National Park before descending to the western slopes. There, in Oregon's historical heartland, you'll visit the towns of Roseburg, Eugene, and Salem. Each has its own access to the wild Cascades to the east, as well as covered bridges, wineries, and historical sites in the fertile farming country nearby. Total driving distance is 638 miles (1,029 km), time on the road about 17 hours.

The Roads

Oregon's Cascades are much more accessible than Washington's. While Washington has only six east-west highways Oregon has 10 of them. Rather than zigzag our way back and forth across the mountain range we'll only cross twice, once in the north and again toward the south. Both of the routes you will follow are very suitable for big rigs of all kinds with easily handled two-lane highways and medium grades.

On the east side of the mountains and headed south the tour follows Hwy. 97 which is mostly two lanes and fairly flat. There is quite a lot of traffic on Hwy. 97 but it moves right along.

On the west side of the mountains headed north you'll travel on either the I-5 interstate or good rural roads.

Even though the tour only crosses the Cascades twice it still gives you the opportunity to drive in the mountains. We suggest possible mountain driving tours from Bend and Eugene. If you are driving an unwieldy larger rig you can leave it parked in the campground and do the exploring in your tow car.

Practical Tips

This would generally be considered a summer tour. Some of the destinations, however, do offer possibilities in the winter. On the east side of the Cascades the weather is usually decent, and you'll see that the campgrounds at lower elevations around Bend are open all year. This is a very popular winter sports area with Mt. Bachelor's skiing nearby. The Klamath Falls area also has its winter attractions, during the months of December through February the area attracts the Lower 48's largest concentration of bald eagles.

A problem with a winter visit is the higher elevations, of course. Crater Lake National Park is snowed in until June most years so you'll probably be better off to cross westward to I-5 using Hwy. 97 to Weed. Once you make it north to Roseburg you'll again find the valley campgrounds to be open, although winter days are short and the weather generally wet.

DAY 1 - DESTINATION BEND
149 miles (240 km), 4 hours

Along the Way - From the ring road around the east side of Portland (I-205) take Exit 19 and follow the signs for Hwy. 26. Once you leave the populated areas around Gresham the highway will take you up across the south slopes of Mt. Hood and down the far side into the dry country on the eastern slopes of the Cascade Mountains. As you start to descend you'll be amazed at how fast the evergreens disappear and the temperatures rise.

Ninety-five miles (153 km) after leaving Hwy. 205 you will reach the town of Warm Springs in the 600,000-acre **Warm Springs Indian Reservation**. You may want to take a break and tour **The Museum at Warm Springs**. It documents the heritage of the tribes that make up the Confederated Tribes of Warm Springs: the

Wasco, Paiute and Warm Springs (Walla Walla) Tribes. If you decide to stay longer you can drive north on Hwy. 3 to **Kah-Nee-Ta Vacation Resort** which boasts an RV park and a golf course as well as the **Indian Head Gaming Center** (Casino).

In another 14 miles (23 km) along Hwy. 26 you will reach Madras and Hwy. 97, the east-of-the-Cascades north-south highway. As you drive south you'll pass through Redmond and in just a few more miles reach the northern outskirts of Bend.

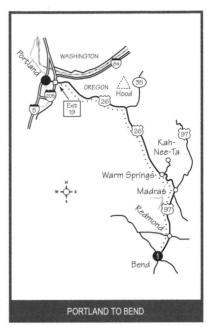

PORTLAND TO BEND

BEND, OREGON

The Bend area (population about 50,000) offers a wealth of outdoor recreational opportunities. The town is large enough to offer pretty much anything you would need, it makes a great base.

The **Deschutes National Forest** is to the west and south. It has miles of trails and back roads. There are dozens of Forest Service campgrounds in the forest, at least 25 are convenient to the Bend area. The Deschutes River is very popular for white-water rafting.

An interesting drive is known as the **Cascade Lakes Highway**. This scenic two-lane paved road heads west from Bend to **Mt. Bachelor**, a very popular winter ski area. In the summer you can ride the lift up the mountain for the view. The highway passes around the north side of the mountain and then south along a chain of lakes. After passing the mountain you will find that a maze of Forest Service roads - some paved, some not - offer the opportunity to do lots of exploring, fishing, and camping.

South of Bend is the **Newberry National Volcanic Monument**. There are many good stops in the monument, we like the road up to Paulina and East lakes in the volcano's caldera, there are several excellent Forest Service campgrounds up there as well as an interesting flow of lava composed of obsidian.

Just south of Bend (about 3 miles) you'll find the **High Desert Museum**. With live animals, western art, and historical dioramas this is a nationally-acclaimed do-not-miss attraction.

Bend has at least 24 **golf courses** nearby, it would be hard to find a better place to get out on the fairways.

The events that Bend celebrates include the **Cascade Festival of Music** in late summer and the **Bend Summer Fest** on the second weekend in July.

Bend Area Campgrounds

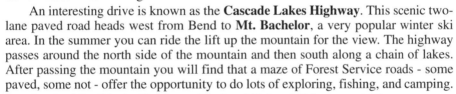 **Bend Kampground** 63615 N Hwy. 97, Bend, OR 97701; 541 382-7738 or 800 713-5333 for reservations; 77 sites, open all year - This is a conveniently located campground suitable for all types of rigs, includ-

ing tents. 50-amp. power is available. Amenities include a swimming pool, a fishing pond, playground, store, gas station, and dump station. You'll have no problem finding this place, it is on the right as you approach the northern edge of Bend on Hwy. 97. It is almost exactly 1 mile north of the intersection of Hwy. 97 and Hwy. 20.

Crown Villa RV Park 60801 Brosterhous Road, Bend, OR 97702; 541 388-1131; 131 sites, open all year - A campground seemingly aimed at big rigs and older campers, it is a little out of the way but offers quiet and huge, widely-spaced sites with 50-amp. power. From Hwy. 97 near the south end of town turn east on Murphy Road just opposite the Albertsons. Drive 1.1 miles east on Murphy until it intersects Brosterhous Rd, turn right and you'll see the campground entrance on the right.

LaPine State Park 800 452-5687 for reservations; 137 sites, open all year - A large state park campground with full hookups and big sites located along the Deschutes River. Drive south from Bend for 22 miles (35 km) to the entrance road, then west 5 miles (8 km) to the campground.

National Forest Campgrounds - There are many federal campgrounds located within striking distance of Bend. Here are a few.

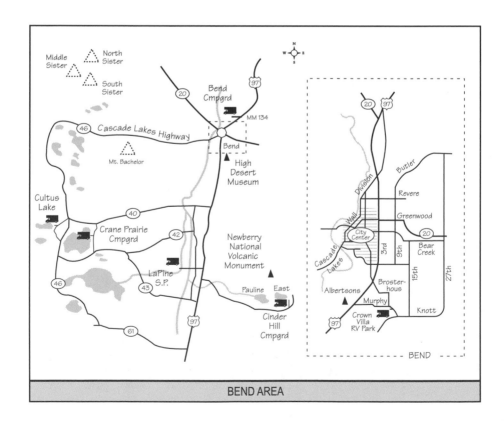

BEND AREA

Crane Prairie Campground [LOW] [△] [⚲]   146 sites, open April through October - A reservoir-side campground with good fishing. For the easiest access drive 27 miles (44 km) south on Hwy. 97 from Bend to Wickiup Junction, turn west on Road 43 for 11 miles (18 km), then 5.4 miles (8.7 km) west on Forest Service Road 42, and then 4.2 miles (6.7 km) north on Forest Service Road 4270.

Cultus Lake [LOW] [△] [⚲] [⟋]   55 sites, open May through September - A campground off Cascade Lakes Highway on Cultus Lake. Popular for windsurfing and small boats. Drive west on the Cascade Lakes Highway from Bend for 46 miles (74 km), turn right on Forest Service Road 4635. The campground is two miles (3 km) from the turn on this paved road.

CAMP SITE IN NEWBERRY NATIONAL VOLCANIC MONUMENT

🚐 Cinder Hill Campground `LOW` `△` `🚐` `🔥` `L`   110 sites, open May through October - A lakeside campground on East Lake in the Newberry Volcanic Monument. There are several more campgrounds nearby, all arranged around two lakes in the volcano's caldera. An excellent base for hiking, mountain bikes, and canoeing. To reach the campground drive south from Bend for 23.5 miles (38 km) on Hwy. 97, turn into the Newberry Volcanic Monument access road (Rd. 21) and drive 18 miles (29 km) to the campground. This campground is at 6,400 feet, a surprisingly long climb from Hwy. 97 at about 4,300 feet.

Day 2 - Destination Klamath Falls
133 miles (215 km), 3 hours

A long the Way - The drive from Bend to Klamath Falls couldn't be simpler. You just follow Hwy. 97 south. The road is mostly two-lane although there are many places where it has been widened to three or four lanes for passing, there is quite a bit of traffic along this highway since it is the main north-south corridor on the east side of Oregon's Cascades.

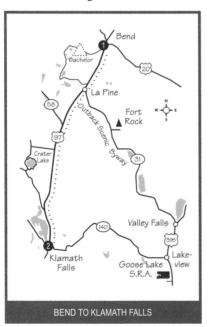

BEND TO KLAMATH FALLS

There is another highway route from Bend to Klamath Falls. This is **The Outback Scenic Byway** which follows Hwy. 31 south from La Pine (29 miles (47 km) south of Bend on Hwy. 97) to Valley Falls, then Hwy. 395 south to Lakeview, and then Hwy. 140 west to Klamath Falls. The drive is probably named as it is because the country it traverses resembles the remote Australian outback. Along the way you can visit **Fort Rock**, a formation that stands in for Australia's Ayers rock to make the comparison even more realistic. If you take this route plan on a long day, the distance via this route to Klamath Falls is 270 miles (435 km). You could make it a two-day trip by spending the night at the **Goose Lake State Recreation Area** campground south of Lakeview and right on the California border.

Klamath Falls

Founded in 1876 and originally called Linkville, the town of Klamath Falls (population 19,000) occupies the Klamath Basin. It is surrounded by national wildlife refuges set aside for migrating birds. The refuges extend south across the California border. At one time there were even more wetlands in the area, many were drained to create farm land early in the century.

Many visitors to the town come for the bird watching. There's something to see all year long. A good place to start is with a visit to the **Refuge Headquarters and**

Visitors Center about 5 miles (8 km) west of Tulelake which is across the border in California, about 14 miles (23 km) south of Klamath Falls. There are actually six different refuges in the area. They offer auto tour routes, canoe trails, trails, and photography blinds.

In Klamath Falls you will probably enjoy a visit to the **Favell Museum of Western Art and Indian Artifacts**. This is an outstanding museum with exhibits including a huge arrowhead collection, Indian artifacts from all the western states, a miniature firearm collection, and western art created by over 300 artists including Charles Russell.

The **Kla-Mo-Ya Casino** is located in the small town of Chiloquin about 22 miles (35 km) north of Klamath Falls on Hwy. 97.

Lava Beds National Monument is in California, but not far from Klamath Falls. The monument actually adjoins the wildlife refuges to the south. The monument is a large area covered by shield volcano lava beds, hundreds of lava tube caves make this a popular and easy place to explore underground. It's as dry as the wildlife refuges are wet. There is a visitors center and also a campground in the monument.

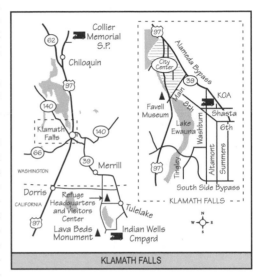

KLAMATH FALLS

The visitor center sells inexpensive protective helmets, highly recommended if you plan to do any spelunking. The area was the scene of the Modoc Indian War, several sites in the monument are related to that 1872 conflict. To get there drive south on Hwy. 39 to Tulelake, about 4 miles (6 km) beyond Tulelake you'll see the entrance to the monument. From there a paved road circles around the south end of Tule Lake Wildlife Refuge and then south through the monument to the visitor center and campground.

Klamath Falls Campgrounds

Klamath Falls KOA [MED] [icons] 3435 Shasta Way, Klamath Falls, OR 97603; 541 884-4644 or 800 KOA-9036 for reservations; 84 sites, open all year - This well-run KOA is the best place to stay if you want to actually spend the night in Klamath Falls. There is a paved bike path running along an adjoining canal. You can find the campground most easily if you are approaching town from the north by taking the Alameda Bypass which leaves Hwy. 97 just north of the downtown area. It is signed as Hwy. 39. Shasta Way crosses Alameda some 4.1 miles (6.6 km) from the intersection, turn right at the light and you'll see the campground on your right. This route has good signage for the campground from Hwy. 97.

Collier Memorial State Park [MED] [icons] 68 sites, open mid-April through October 31 - A large campground with full hookups and big sites along the Williamson River. Nearby is a state-run outdoor logging museum and pioneer village.

The campground is located about 30 miles (48 km) north of Klamath Falls on Hwy. 97.

🚐 Indian Well Campground in Lava Beds National Monument
40 sites, open all year - A desert campground with widely-spaced sites, some large enough for fairly large rigs. To reach the campground drive south on Hwy. 39 to Tulelake. About 4 miles (6 km) beyond the entrance road to the monument goes right. The campground is near the southern border of the monument, a distance of about 25 miles (40 km).

DAY 3 - DESTINATION CRATER LAKE NATIONAL PARK
57 miles (92 km), 2 hours (to Crater Lake Lodge)

A long the Way - From Klamath Falls drive north on Hwy. 97 toward Bend. The intersection with Hwy. 62 is 20 miles (32 km) north, turn on to Hwy. 62 and follow it 30 miles (48 km) through Fort Klamath to the south entrance of the park.

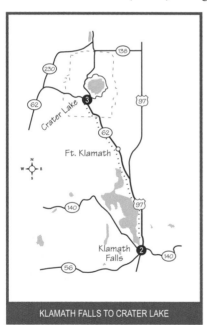

KLAMATH FALLS TO CRATER LAKE

If you plan to camp in the park you have arrived. However, camping in the park is limited (see below). If you plan to go on to Diamond Lake you should have plenty of time to drive the road around the crater, stop and take in some of the sights, and then drive on out the north park entrance to those campgrounds. See the directions in the following section for the drive on to Diamond Lake.

CRATER LAKE NATIONAL PARK

Crater Lake was designated a National Park in 1902. The primary attraction here is the deep blue lake in the volcanic caldera of Mount Mazama. The caldera and lake are a fairly recent geologic occurrence, the mountain blew its top off about 7,500 years ago, well within the time that this region was populated by Native Americans. The explosion is calculated to have been 42 times as powerful as the recent eruption of Mt. St. Helens. The lake in the caldera is definitely one of the scenic wonders of the world. It is the deepest lake in the U.S. at 1,932 feet.

A 37-mile (60 km) road circles the rim of the caldera offering many viewpoints. While some folks follow the rim drive in their RV's it is best to use a smaller rig if you have one available. The road is narrow in many places and parking at viewpoints is sometimes tight, particularly on weekends and during August.

Facilities in the park are limited. There are two visitor centers. **Steele Visitor Center** is open all year, the **Rim Visitor Center** is only open during the summer when melting snow allows the opening of the rim drive. This varies from year to year, usually the road is open from early July to about the end of October.

One popular activity in the park is the narrated **boat tour** of the lake. It takes about an hour and forty-five minutes and circles the lake with a stop at Wizard Island. To take the tour you must walk the 1-mile **Cleetwood Cove Trail** down to the lake, not too difficult on the way down but another story climbing the 700 vertical feet back out. Remember, you are at an altitude of 6,176 feet at the lake's surface, Don't try this unless you are in reasonably good shape. At the peak of the season there are 9 trips each day, tickets are sold at the parking lot.

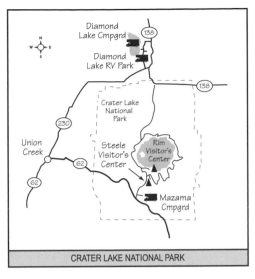

CRATER LAKE NATIONAL PARK

Crater Lake Campgrounds

There is only one campground in the park suitable for RVs. Diamond Lake, north of the park, has both Forest Service campgrounds and a commercial campground.

CRATER LAKE

Mazama National Park Campground `MED` `⛺` `♨` `⚟` `🔥` `🏪` 199 sites, open mid-June through September, varies - This large campground is the only one inside the park suitable for vehicle camping. There are many large sites suitable for the largest rigs, some are pull-throughs. No hookups are available, but there is a dump station and water fill point. Amenities include an amphitheater where rangers give nightly presentations and also a small nearby store and gas station. This campground accepts no reservations but often does not fill up. Plan to arrive early to insure a spot, particularly in August.

Diamond Lake Campground `LOW` `⛺` `♨` `⚟` `🔥` `🏖` 877 444-6777 for reservations; www.reserveuse.com/; 238 sites, open May 15 to September 30 - This is an Umpqua National Forest campground that runs for about 3 miles (5 km) along the shore of Diamond Lake. Sites are suitable for rigs up to about 30 feet, there are no hookups. The lake has excellent fishing and there is an 11-mile (18 km) paved bike trail that circles it. To reach the campground from the junction of Hwy. 138 (to Roseburg) and Hwy. 230 (to Medford) follow Hwy. 230 toward Medford for .2 mile, turn right onto the Diamond Lake recreation area road. You'll have to drive several miles along the lake before you see the entrance road and greeting station on the left.

Diamond Lake RV Park `MED` `🚿` `♨` `⚟` `🔥` `📷` `GS` Diamond Lake, OR 97731; 541 793-3318; www.chatlink.com /~dlrvp/index.html; 130 sites, open mid-May through October 1 - A nice commercial campground in a location offering nearby hiking, boating and fishing. The campground is not on the lake shore but it is near. To reach the campground from the junction of Hwy. 138 (to Roseburg) and Hwy. 230 (to Medford) follow Hwy. 230 toward Medford for .2 mile, turn right onto the Diamond Lake recreation area road, you'll soon see the campground entrance on your right.

Day 4 - Destination Roseburg
101 miles (163 km), 3.5 hours

Along The Way - When you are ready to depart Crater Lake make your way out the north entrance. Soon after you pass the entrance station the road intersects Hwy. 138. Head westward toward Roseburg. Four miles (6 km) after that intersection you'll come to another, this one with Hwy. 230 toward Medford and Grants Pass. At this point you are very near Diamond Lake, with some of the best base campgrounds for the Crater Lake Area. See **Crater Lake Campgrounds** above.

From Crater Lake Hwy. 138 leads down the canyons of the Clearwater and North Fork of the Umpqua River to Roseburg. This is a very scenic route with many places to pull off and enjoy views of the river and surrounding

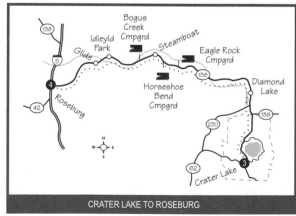

CRATER LAKE TO ROSEBURG

mountains.

The North Fork of the Umpqua is a well-known fishing river. If you have a fly rod you may find the clear water flowing through gravel-bottom pools formed by basalt formations too attractive to pass by.

The route along the Umpqua is well supplied with small Umpqua National Forest campgrounds, by our count there are at least 9 of them along the highway and several others up side roads.

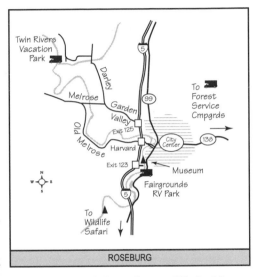

ROSEBURG

Little Roseburg (population 20, 200) is the main town of the Umpqua Valley. The Umpqua River, like the Rogue farther south, actually flows from the Cascades and then through the Coastal Mountains to the Pacific. At Roseburg the valley widens and becomes good farm land. Roseburg is an old town for Oregon, it was established by the Hudson Bay Company in 1836 as a fur-trading post.

Probably the best known of Roseburg's sights is the **Wildlife Safari**. It is located just northwest of Winston which is about 7 miles (11 km) south of Roseburg. At Wildlife Safari you drive your vehicle through fenced areas filled with wildlife from Africa, Asia, and North America on a 3-mile loop.

The Umpqua Valley is also a **wine-growing region**. Pick up a tour map at the visitor center that will lead you on a circuit to 7 of the valley's wineries and tasting rooms. You'll need the map to find these small wineries hidden on back roads.

Roseburg also has an excellent museum - The **Douglas County Museum of History and Natural History**. It is located right next to the RV park at the Douglas County Fairgrounds. Take Exit 123 from I-5 and follow the signs.

Roseburg hosts the **Douglas County Fair** the second week of August.

Roseburg Area Campgrounds

🚐 **Douglas County Fairgrounds RV Park** [LOW] 50 sites, open all year - This campground is handy to the freeway and the closest campground to central Roseburg. It has large sites, some are pull-throughs. All have 30-amp. electricity and water, there is also a dump station. These are well-spaced sites with some shade. Restrooms with showers are available across the access road inside the fairground fence. Next door is the Douglas County Museum, very convenient. To find the campground get on I-5. Take Exit 123 which is just south of Roseburg. From the exit follow the signs a short distance to the fairgrounds and campground on the east side of the freeway.

Twin Rivers Vacation Park `MED` `⚡` `◻` `♨` `◻` `▤` `◻` `GS` 433 River Forks Park Rd., Roseburg, OR 97470; 541 673-3811; 85 sites, open all year - A much nicer park than the one at the fairgrounds, but not quiet as handy because it is some distance from town. The campground is located right next to a large day-use area on the Umpqua River. From Exit 125 of I-5 go west 2.2 miles (3.5 km) on Garden Valley Road to a Y. Take the right fork on Darley Road and drive 2.5 miles (4 km). Turn left just after the bridge and drive 1.6 miles (2.6 km) on Old Garden Valley Road, turn left on River Forks Road and you'll soon see the campground on the left.

Forest Service campgrounds up the Umpqua River.

Bogus Creek Campground `LOW` `△` `♨` `♨` 16 sites, open May 20 to October 15 - This is the closest of the North Umpqua Forest Service campgrounds to Roseburg. Some of the sites will accommodate large rigs. It is a popular launching point for white water boating on the river. The campground is 35 miles (56 km) east of Roseburg on Highway 138.

Horseshoe Bend Campground `LOW` `△` `♨` `♨` 24 sites, open May 20 to September 30 - The campground sits some distance from the highway so that road noise isn't a problem. Some sites here will accommodate large rigs and this also is a popular white water launching point. It's also a good spot for fishing and hiking. The campground is 46 miles (74 km) east of Roseburg on Highway 138.

Eagle Rock Campground `LOW` `△` `♨` 25 sites, open May 20 to September 15 - The campground is located in an area of impressive rock formations. It too is handy for fishing, white water, and hiking. The campground is 51 miles (82 km) east of Roseburg on Highway 138.

Day 5 - Destination Eugene
68 miles (110 km), 1.25 hours

Along The Way - The route from Roseburg to Eugene is an easy one, just follow the I-5 freeway north.

EUGENE

Eugene (population 134,000), home to the University of Oregon, has a lot to offer. Actually, this is a twin city, Springfield (population 52,000) is just to the east. Often considered one of the most livable middle-sized towns in the U.S., Eugene has the cultural attractions of a university town and the outdoor attractions of the nearby McKenzie River Valley climbing east into the Cascades.

Eugene is laced with **bike paths**, particularly along the Willamette River. If you are a bike rider, jogger, or walker you should take advantage of them.

The **University of Oregon** campus covers 250 acres near downtown Eugene. It is very attractive and a good place for a stroll. It has two good museums: the **Museum of Art** and the **Museum of Natural History**.

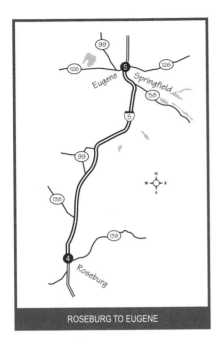

ROSEBURG TO EUGENE

Eugene occupies the south end of the fertile Willamette Valley. There are several small **wineries** in the area that deserve a visit.

Hwy. 126 leads east toward Bend up the **McKenzie River Valley**. While Sisters is 90 miles (145 km) away, you can find a lot to enjoy by just making a side trip as far as McKenzie Bridge, 50 miles (81 km) up the valley. Watch for the **Goodpasture** covered bridge at about Mile 22 just west of Vida. You can make an excellent loop trip out of the drive by following the paved **Robert Aufderheide Memorial Drive** (a National Forest Service Byway), from a point five miles (8 km) short of McKenzie bridge, south 57 miles (92 km) to meet Hwy. 58 and then return 41 miles (66 km) to Eugene on that highway. As you near Eugene on Hwy. 58 you'll have a chance to visit 5 more covered bridges. You'll also find a wealth of Forest Service campgrounds along the route since the eastern portion is within the Willamette National Forest.

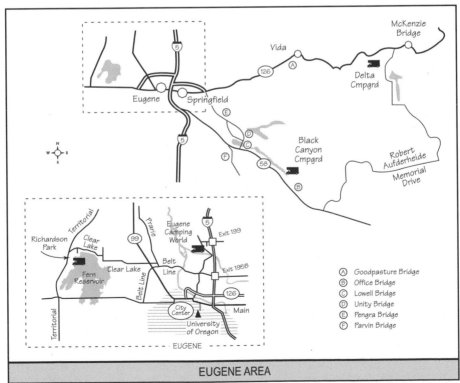

Ⓐ Goodpasture Bridge
Ⓑ Office Bridge
Ⓒ Lowell Bridge
Ⓓ Unity Bridge
Ⓔ Pengra Bridge
Ⓕ Parvin Bridge

EUGENE AREA

Eugene Area Campgrounds

Richardson Park Campground [LOW] [△] [icons] 541 682-6940 or 541 935-2005 for reservations; 96 sites, open April 15 to October 15 - This Lane County campground is located east of town near the Fern Reservoir. Sites are large, well-spaced, most have plenty of shade, and 50-amp. power is available. Driveways and parking pads are paved, restrooms offer showers. Nearby you'll find a swimming beach and boat launch. To reach the campground take Exit 195 and follow Beltline west to the Hwy. 99 (No. 6) Exit. Go north .6 miles (1 km) to Clear Lake Road. Turn left and drive west 8.1 miles (13 km) to the entrance which is on your left.

Eugene Kamping World [MED] [△] [icons] 90932 S Stuart Way, Coburg, OR 97408; 541 343-4832 or 800 343-3008 for reservations; 152 sites, open all year - This is a large modern campground. It has big sites, many are pull-throughs, 50-amp. power is available. Expect to find the place filled with luxurious bus-style rigs, several manufacturers and big dealers are nearby. Conveniently located just west of I-5 at Exit 199 about 7 miles (11 km) north of Eugene.

Willamette Forest Campgrounds

Delta Forest Service Campground [LOW] [△] [🔥] 38 sites, open May 14 to September 13 - This is a very scenic campground with large sites on the McKenzie River among old growth Douglas fir and cedar. From Eugene drive 88 miles (142 km) east on Hwy. 126 and turn south on Robert Aufderheide Memorial Drive, you'll soon see the sign for the campground directing you to the right on Road #400.

Black Canyon Forest Service Campground [LOW] [△] [🔥] [icons] 72 sites, open April 21 to September 30 - A campground with large sites located at the upper end of Lookout Point Reservoir and offering reservoir and river recreational activities like swimming, fishing, and boating. The campground is located about 30 miles (48 km) east of Eugene on Hwy. 58.

DAY 6 - DESTINATION SALEM
80 miles (129 km), 2.5 hours

Along The Way - While it is possible to drive right up I-5 from Eugene to Salem, a distance of 59 miles (95 km), there is a better alternate route. This is the old US 99.

Follow US 99 out of Eugene toward Junction City. At first the highway is lined with commercial activities of various kinds with quite a few stop lights, but soon you'll be driving through flat quiet farming country.

At Junction City the highway splits into 99 West and 99 East. Much of the old 99 East is parallel to or covered by the I-5 Interstate but 99 West remains a quiet rural route.

Forty-three miles (69 km) north of Junction City is **Corvallis**. It is a pleasant city with a population of about 50,000. It is home to Oregon State University.

From Corvallis continue north on US 99. You'll pass through little Monmouth and then catch Hwy. 22, the Willamena-Salem Highway, east to Salem.

SALEM

Salem (population 127,000), Oregon's state capital, is an excellent base for exploring the upper Willamette Valley. This region was the goal of most of the trekkers of the Oregon Trail. Oregon City some 35 miles (56 km) north of Salem is considered the end of the Oregon Trail.

Since Salem is one of the older towns in the Willamette Valley you would expect the central area to have some sights of interest and you wouldn't be mistaken. Start at **Mission Mill Village** which is easy to find since it houses an information center for the town as well as being a woolen museum set in the buildings of the old Thomas Kay Woolen Mill. Just follow the information signs posted near the entrances to town.

From the Mission Mill Village you can visit

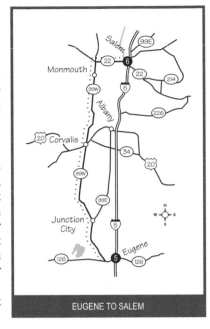

EUGENE TO SALEM

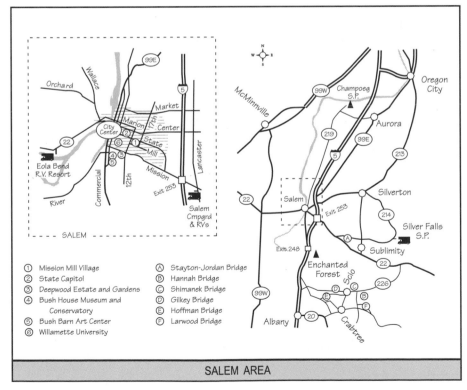

① Mission Mill Village
② State Capitol
③ Deepwood Estate and Gardens
④ Bush House Museum and
    Conservatory
⑤ Bush Barn Art Center
⑥ Willamette University

Ⓐ Stayton-Jordan Bridge
Ⓑ Hannah Bridge
Ⓒ Shimanek Bridge
Ⓓ Gilkey Bridge
Ⓔ Hoffman Bridge
Ⓕ Larwood Bridge

SALEM AREA

the other sites of downtown Salem including **Willamette University**, the **state capitol and grounds** and surrounding **historic area, Deepwood Estate and Gardens, Bush House Museum and Conservatory,** and the **Bush Barn Art Center**.

The Salem area is home to a large collection of **covered bridges** dating from the early 20th century. You can follow a loop visiting six of these bridges from Exit 253 off I-5 in Salem. The loop goes east on Hwy. 22, then loops south to Albany on Hwy. 226 from Mehama. You'll need a guide pamphlet available from most area visitor's centers to find all of the bridges since they are tucked away on side roads.

Near Salem is the premier Oregon **wine growing area**. It is centered around McMinnville in Yamhill County to the west of Salem. The county has some 30 wineries, many offer tours. Pick up a guide to the wineries at the McMinnville tourist information center or other area information centers.

The area between Salem and Portland is full of interesting historical sites, particularly **Oregon City, Aurora,** and **Champoeg**. A driving tour from Salem north on I-5 to Oregon City, then south on 99E, west on country roads to Champoeg State Park, and then returning to Salem can make a good day trip. Once again, check with local information centers for more details.

If you have kids along they will probably be ready for something less historical after visiting all of the above. The answer is **Enchanted Forest**, a theme park located right along the I-5 freeway at Exit 248.

Salem Area Campgrounds

Salem Campground & RVs [MED] ▲ ♿ 🖥 🚻 🔧 ☂ 🛒 🍽 GS   3700 Hagers Grove Rd. SE, Salem, Oregon 97301; 503 581-3736 or 800 826-9605 for reservations; 185 sites, open all year - This is a large campground convenient to I-5. There are a variety of shaded sites including large pull-throughs and tent sites. Full hookups are the most common with 30-amp. power. The campground has a small store and supermarkets are located nearby. A trail under the freeway leads to a small park with playground and swimming area. To reach the campground take Exit 253 from I-5. Follow the campground signs about a quarter-mile east to Lancaster Drive. Turn right on Lancaster and then almost immediately turn right onto Hagers Grove Road which is also the entrance road to the campground.

Eola Bend R.V. Resort [HIGH] ♿ 🖥 🚻 🔧 ☂ 🍽 GS   4700 Salem-Dallas Hwy. 22, Salem, OR 97304; 503 364-7714; 180 sites, open all year - This is a nice newer campground located just east of Salem in a rural setting on the far side of the Willamette River. As you approach Salem from the west on Hwy. 22 you'll see the campground below you near the river on the right side of the highway. It is 5 miles (8 km) east of the junction of Hwy. 99W and Hwy. 22. From the other direction it is 4.4 miles (7 km) from the bridge over the Willamette into downtown Salem.

Silver Falls State Park [MED] ▲ ♿ 🖥 🚻 🔧 🔥   800 452-5687 for reservations; 105 sites, open all year - Oregon's largest state park is located 22 miles (35 km) east of Salem. It has ten waterfalls, nice hiking trails, and a large campground. To reach the campground drive east on Hwy. 22 about 6 miles (10 km) to the junction with Hwy. 214, then follow Hwy. 214 some 13 miles (21 km) to the park.

DAY 7 - DESTINATION PORTLAND
50 miles (81 km), 1 hour

The drive north to Portland goes by pretty quickly. You're barely on the road before you start to arrive in the suburbs.

Information Resources

See our Internet site at www.rollinghomes.com for Internet site addresses.

Destination Bend

The Museum at Warm Springs, 2189 Hwy. 26, Warm Springs, OR 97761; 541-553-3331

Bend Chamber/Visitor Bureau, 63085 N Hwy. 97, Bend, OR 97701; 541-382-3221 or 800 905-2363

High Desert Museum, 59800 S Hwy. 97, Bend, OR 97702; 541 382-4754

Destination Klamath Falls

Klamath Falls Information Center, 1451 Main, Klamath Falls, OR 97601; 800 445-6728 or 541 884-0666

Kla-Mo-Ya Casino, 34333 Hwy. 97 North, P.O. Box 490, Chiloquin, OR 97624; 541 783-7529

Favell Museum, 125 West Main St., Klamath Falls, OR 97601; 541 882-9996

Klamath Basin National Wildlife Refuges, Route 1, Box 74, Tulelake, CA 96143; 530 667-2231

Lava Beds National Monument, P.O. Box 867, Tulelake, CA 96134; 530 667-2282

Destination Crater Lake

Crater Lake National Park, P.O. Box 7, Crater Lake, OR 97604; 541 594-2211 ext 402

Umpqua National Forest, P.O. Box 1008, 2900 NW Stewart Parkway, Roseburg, OR 97470; 541 672-6601

Destination Roseburg

North Umpqua Ranger District, Umpqua National Forest, 18782 North Umpqua Highway, Glide, OR 97443; 541 496-3532

Roseburg Visitors & Convention Bureau, 410 SE Spruce, P.O. Box 1262, Roseburg, OR 97470; 541 672-9731 or 800-444-9584

Douglas County Museum of History and Natural History, P.O. Box 1550, Roseburg, OR 97470; 541 957-7007

Wildlife Safari, P.O. Box 1600, Winston, OR 97496; 800 355-4848 or 541 679-6761

Destination Eugene

Eugene Chamber of Commerce, 1401 Willamette St., Eugene, OR 97401; 541 484-1314

Convention & Visitors Association of Lane County Oregon, 115 West 8th, Suite 190, P.O. Box 10286, Eugene, OR 97440; 800 547-5445 or 541 484-5307

Destination Salem

Corvallis Convention & Visitors Bureau, 420 NW Second St., Corvallis, OR 97330; 541 757-1544 and 800 334-8118

Salem Convention & Visitors Association, 1313 Mill St. SE, Salem 97301; 503 581-4325 or 800 874-7012

Visitor Services, Oregon State Capitol, Salem, OR 97310; 503 986-1388

Enchanted Forest, 8462 Enchanted Way SE, Turner, OR 97392; 503 363-3060 or 503 371-4242

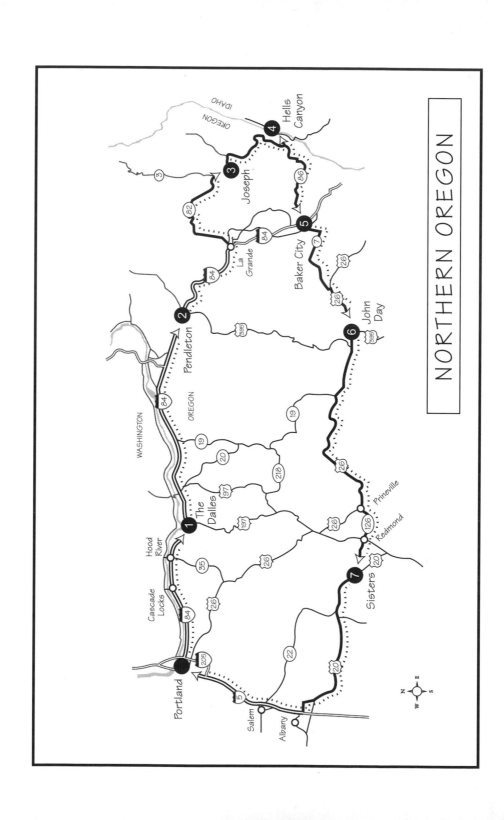

NORTHERN OREGON

Chapter 6

Tour 3

Northern Oregon

Top Attractions

✦ Columbia River Scenic Highway

✦ Bonneville and The Dalles Dams

✦ Wallowa Lake

✦ Hells Canyon

✦ Oregon Trail

✦ John Day Fossil Beds

✦ Metolius River

✦ McKenzie Pass

General Description

The tour laid out in this chapter crosses Northern Oregon to the Idaho border, then returns along a more southerly route. Along the way it stops for the night at a variety of interesting places. Most nights are spent in or near popular outdoor destinations although, surprisingly, the route does not pass through or near any national parks. It, however, does visit a national scenic area, a national recreation area and a national monument. The total driving distance of this tour is 858 miles (1,383 km), driving time will be about 24.5 hours.

The first day is spent near Portland as you tour the southern shore of the Columbia Gorge. The following day the route travels east to Pendleton where you can spend the night at an Indian-owned resort offering a golf course and a casino. Day 3 heads into the wild northeast corner of the state for a night at beautiful Wallowa Lake. The next day's route follows small (but paved) roads through the Wallowa National Forest to the spectacular Hells Canyon. Heading westward finally you can visit the Oregon Trail in Baker City. Day 6 offers a visit to the John Day Fossil Beds National Monument and then you'll spend the final evening in scenic Sisters near the famous Metolius River.

The Roads

You'll find lots of variety in this chapter. The first day you'll visit one of the most famous roads in the country - the Columbia River Scenic Highway. This is a very scenic but narrow road so larger rigs may want to drive directly to Cascade Locks, park the rig in a campground, and then explore the highway in a smaller tow car or truck.

The following two days will find you on I-84, a major east-west freeway route, for most of the time. When you do leave I-84, however, you'll be on paved two-lane highways for most of the remainder of the trip. Only on the last day will you again drive on a freeway when you join I-5 south of Albany to drive north to Portland.

All of the two-lane roads in this section are entirely suitable for any size rig except one. This is the Hells Canyon National Scenic Byway through the Wallowa National Forest from Joseph to Hells Canyon. It is a paved national forest road but is not built to normal highway standards. It did not appear overly challenging to us. When we drove the route we saw several 35-foot motorhomes pulling tow cars and the road was engineered for rigs at least as big as logging trucks. And it is paved. You'll have to make your own decision on this one, we've given the address and phone number for the information center at Enterprise which you can check for advice and road condition information.

Practical Tips

For RVers this is a summer or fall trip. The road between Joseph and Hells Canyon is not open in the winter and many campgrounds throughout the route are also not open in the winter.

For the most part this route is not as heavily traveled as the Oregon Coast route but reservations are still a good idea, particularly in the state park campgrounds.

You can easily combine this tour with the Central Oregon Tour to make a two or three week trip. The last night on this tour is spent at Sisters which is just a few miles from Bend, the first night's stop on that tour.

The theme of this tour could easily be the Oregon Trail. Locations with Oregon trail exhibits along the way are the **Columbia Gorge Discovery Center and Waasco County Historical Museum** in The Dalles, the **Tamástslikt Cultural Institute** just outside Pendleton, **Oregon Trail Interpretive Park** near the Blue Mountains summit east of Pendleton, and the **Oregon Trail Interpretive Center** near Baker, Oregon.

Day 1 - Destination The Columbia Gorge
93 miles (150 km), 3 hours (to The Dalles)

Along the Way - The section of the gorge covered on this day's itinerary is actually fairly compact. It stretches from the eastern suburbs of Portland to The Dalles. The first section, as far as Cascade Locks, is the most impressive with most of the interesting stops. While this Along the Way section will take you all the way to The Dalles you might want to stop for the night in or near Cascade Locks and continue on to Pendleton the next day with stops in Hood River and The Dalles. Cascade Locks makes a good base for RVers because it is handy to the western portion of the Scenic Highway, US 30. This highway is a prime attraction of the Gorge, but it is fairly narrow and most of the stops along the way lack adequate parking for larger rigs. If you have a large rig and a smaller tow car consider driving directly from Portland to Cascade Locks on Highway 5, a distance of 35 miles (56 km), and parking your rig. Use your smaller vehicle to tour the western section of the Scenic Highway. Rigs of all sizes find US 30 adequate if they take it easy, but parking can be challenging.

Regardless of the above, we'll assume that you are going to drive the route from west to east without backtracking. From Portland take I-84 east. To begin the Colum-

MULTNOMAH FALLS

bia River Scenic Highway tour leave the freeway at Exit 18 just past the Sandy River bridge.

The **Historic Columbia River Scenic Highway** was completed in 1915. It was considered an engineering triumph and was built as much as a scenic attraction as a transportation route. I-84 obliterated much of the highway but two good sections remain. The first is about 23 miles (37 km) long and runs between Exit 18 of I-84 to Exit 35. This section of road has famous scenic viewpoints and many waterfalls. The second section leaves I-84 at Exit 69 and climbs the bluffs to Rowena Crest Viewpoint before descending to meet I-84 at Exit 76, just west of The Dalles.

The Columbia Gorge, Cascade Locks, Hood River, and The Dalles

After leaving I-84 at Exit 18 you will follow the quiet Sandy River for several miles before starting to climb. Make a stop at the **Portland Women's Forum State Scenic Viewpoint** for an excellent view of the **Crown Point Vista House** ahead and

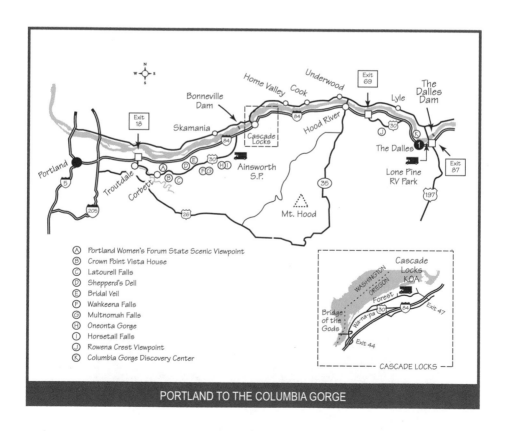

(A) Portland Women's Forum State Scenic Viewpoint
(B) Crown Point Vista House
(C) Latourell Falls
(D) Shepperd's Dell
(E) Bridal Veil
(F) Wahkeena Falls
(G) Multnomah Falls
(H) Oneonta Gorge
(I) Horsetail Falls
(J) Rowena Crest Viewpoint
(K) Columbia Gorge Discovery Center

PORTLAND TO THE COLUMBIA GORGE

slightly lower against the backdrop of the Gorge. This is a very popular photographic viewpoint. In just over a mile you will arrive at the Vista House, the views here of the gorge are outstanding and there's also a gift shop and some exhibits about the highway and local wildflowers.

After the Vista House the highway descends and the waterfalls start. They're all different and all worth a stop. In order they are **Latourell Falls**, **Shepperds Dell**, **Bridal Veil**, **Wahkeena Falls**, **Multnomah Falls**, **Oneonta Gorge**, and **Horsetail Falls**. Multnomah Falls is the best known and has the best facilities. There is a lodge with restaurant and information office as well as good paved trails up to a scenic walking bridge just below the falls. The falls themselves have a drop of 620 feet and are clearly viewable from the lodge below.

You'll reach I-84 at Exit 35 after passing Ainsworth State Park Campground. In just 5 miles (8 km) you'll reach the **Bonneville Dam** exit. This dam offers one of the best of the many dam touring opportunities on the Columbia, if you want to see a dam up close this is a good one. There is plenty of room for parking big rigs here. Take a look at the visitor's center which has exhibits and a fish-viewing room. Just a short walk from the center you can view the generator room. This dam also has huge locks, you may be lucky enough to watch a tug with barges passing through. Finally, the dam has a fish hatchery with a unique sturgeon-viewing pond.

The Cascade Locks Exit (for traffic from the west) is four miles (6 km) beyond Bonneville Dam. **Cascade Locks** (population 1,100) is a small town and a good base for a visit to the western end of the gorge. Before the Bonneville Dam was built there was a set of locks here to let boats on the river bypass the **Cascades of the Columbia**, a treacherous series of rapids. Bonneville Dam flooded the locks, but there is a pleasant waterfront park, and the top of the drowned locks are still above lake level. You can take a cruise on the **Columbia Gorge sternwheeler** which is based here during the summer. There is a bridge across the river at Cascade Locks, it is called the **Bridge of the Gods**. The name comes from an Indian legend, probably based upon the fact that a huge landslide once stopped up the Columbia at this point. The Cascades Crest Hiking Trail crosses the Columbia on the bridge.

Eastward from Cascade Locks you continue to follow I-84. You'll want to make a stop at **Hood River** (population 5,200). This little town has become the windsurfing capital of the U.S. Drive down the hill and across the railroad and park next to the river, if there's wind there will be lots of **windsurfers**. Watching them can be very entertaining.

East of Hood River is another chance to leave I-84 and follow the original US 30. Take Exit 69. The road climbs onto the cliffs above the river. There is an excellent overlook with lots of parking room some 12 miles (19 km) along, it's called **Rowena Crest Viewpoint** and offers great views up and down the river. From there the road once again descends and rejoins I-84 at Exit 76.

Next stop is The Dalles (population 11,800). There's a new attraction here, the **Columbia Gorge Discovery Center and Waasco County Historical Museum**. It is a very well-done facility, particularly the Waasco County section. Take Exit 82 and follow the signs. They have lots of parking for big rigs.

Just past The Dalles is the second dam on the river. Take Exit 88 for **The Dalles Dam**. It is much the same as Bonneville Dam, but is unique in that you make a short train trip to reach the visitor facilities.

Campgrounds

⌦ **Cascade Locks KOA** [MED] [△] [♿] [⛟] [🚻] [🚰] [🔥] [🖊] [📯] [🛒] [⊙] [GS] 81 NW Forest Lane, Cascade Locks, OR 97014; 541 374-8668 or 800 KOA-8698 for reservations; 115 sites, open March 15 to October 15 - This KOA makes a good base for exploration of the western end of the Gorge. Leave your big rig here and tour the falls in your tow car. The campground has about 120 sites with a variety of hookup options. Many are pull-throughs with room for big rigs. Evergreens provide lots of shade without blocking all the light. To reach the campground from the west take Exit 44 from I-84. Follow the main road through town, Wa-na-pa Street, and then turn left on Forest Lane Road. This turn is 1.2 miles (1.9 km) from the freeway exit. You'll see the campground on the left 1 mile (1.6 km) from the turn.

⌦ **Ainsworth State Park Campground** [MED] [♿] [⛟] [🚻] [🚰] [🔥] 45 sites, open mid-March through October 31 - This is the only campground actually located on the scenic highway. If you can get in it offers the best access to the sights and trails nearby. The campground is located near the eastern end of the western section, about 1.2 miles (1.9 km) west of where the scenic highway meets I-84 at Exit 35.

⌦ **Lone Pine RV Park** [MED] [♿] [⛟] [🚻] [🚰] [🍴] [⊙] 335 Lone Pine Dr., The Dalles, OR 97058; 541 298-2800; 40 sites, open May through October (varies) - A convenient and simple commercial campground near Exit 87 in The Dalles. It offers a view of The Dalles Dam.

DAY 2 - DESTINATION PENDLETON
119 miles (192 km), 2 hours

Along the Way - The route from the Columbia Gorge to Pendleton follows I-84. The distance from Cascade Locks to Pendleton is 162 miles (261 km), from The Dalles to Pendleton the distance is 119 miles (192 km).

From The Dalles eastward the highway continues to follow the Columbia River.

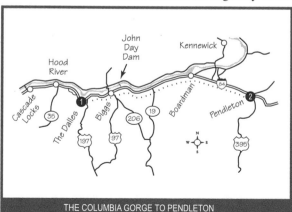

THE COLUMBIA GORGE TO PENDLETON

You will have the opportunity to visit another dam along this section if you desire. At first you will be following the shore of Celilo Lake behind The Dalles Dam but soon you will spot **John Day Dam**. Take Exit 109 for a visit to the dam, you can take a self-guided tour to see the fish ladder, fish viewing windows, and generator room.

After John Day Dam you will be driving along above Lake Umatilla. About 50 miles (84 km) east of John Day Dam you will reach Boardman and the highway leaves the river and cuts inland for 54 miles (87 km) to Pendleton through a rolling landscape filled with irrigation circles.

PENDLETON

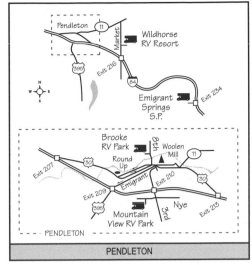

PENDLETON

Pendleton (population 17,000) bills itself as "The real west". The little town does indeed have a western flavor. It is very well known for its **Pendleton Round-Up**, a 4-day rodeo held during mid-September. Make sure you have reservations if you visit during the round-up, you'll have lots of company. You should also buy your tickets to the rodeo early to avoid being disappointed.

The name Pendleton may make you think of wool blankets. This is the home of the **Pendleton Woolen Mills**. The company began operations in 1909 when it started making woolen Indian blankets, today they have 14 mills scattered around the country. The one in Pendleton has a store and gives tours of the factory.

Four miles (6 km) east of Pendleton is the **Wildhorse Resort**. This entertainment complex, run by the Confederated Tribes of the Umatilla Indian Reservation, has a casino, an 18-hole golf course, an RV park, and a museum. The museum is known as the **Tamástslikt Cultural Institute** and describes the Cayuse, Umatilla and Walla Walla tribes and cultures and their interaction with the travelers on the Oregon Trail. The easiest way to enjoy the resort is to stay at the convenient RV park.

Pendleton Area Campgrounds

Wildhorse RV Resort MED 72781 Hwy. 331, Pendleton, OR 97801; 541 966-1646 or 800 654-9453 for reservations; www.wildhorseresort.com; 100 sites, open all year - Just a short drive east of Pendleton is the entertainment complex of the Confederated Tribes of Umatilla. You'll find a good RV park and also, within walking distance, a casino, a golf course, and a museum. Sites are all large with full hookups, 50-amp. power is available. They are surrounded by clipped grass and have good separation but no shade. There is a swimming pool with spa and restrooms with hot showers. You can walk about a quarter-mile to the casino which has a restaurant, there is also a free shuttle bus for transportation to the casino, museum, or golf course. To reach the campground take Exit 216 from I-84 about 4 miles (6 km) east of Pendleton. Follow signs .3 mile north to the access road for the complex. The RV park entrance is .3 mile up the entrance boulevard, on the right.

Brooke RV Park LOW 5 NE 8th Street, Pendleton, OR 97801: 541 276-5353; 43 sites, open all year - A small RV park located along the Umatilla River near central Pendleton. 50-amp. power is available. In downtown Pendleton find 8th Street, follow it north across the river, the campground is the first left on the far side.

Mountain View R.V. Park MED GS 1375 SE 3rd, Pendleton, OR

97801; 541 276-1041;) 70 sites, open all year - A large modern campground convenient to the I-84 freeway but some distance from the central business district. This is
a good big-rig campground with large sites and 50-amp. power. Take Exit 210 but go
south away from town, go one block and turn right on SE Nye Ave (before the
Doubletree Inn), the campground entrance will be on your left down SE 3rd Street.

Emigrant Springs State Park [MED] ▲ ⌇ 🖫 🐟 ♨ 51 sites, open mid-April
through October 31 - 18 full hookup sites and 33 with no hookups, located high in the
Blue Mountains near the interstate at Exit 234, 26 miles (42 km) east of Pendleton.

Day 3 - Destination Joseph and Lake Wallowa
121 miles (195 km), 3 hours (to Joseph)

Along The Way - Wallowa Lake and the adjoining town of Joseph lie about 50
miles (81 km) northeast, as the crow flies, of Baker Oregon. The drive from
Pendleton is very scenic, first on I-84 through the Blue Mountains and then from La
Grande on back roads through farming country and through wooded canyons.

From Pendleton take I-84 eastward. Almost immediately you'll reach the long
grade up into the Blue Mountains. The scenery changes quickly from dry grasslands
to pine forests. Emigrant Springs State Park, an alternate campground for Pendleton,
is just off the freeway at Exit 234.

PENDLETON TO JOSEPH AND LAKE WALLOWA

You'll pass the Blue Mountains Summit (elevation 4,194
feet) and reach an interesting
stop, the **Oregon Trail Interpretive Park at Blue Mountain
Crossing**. To reach it take Exit
248 and follow a winding road
for 3 miles (5 km) to the park.
You'll find a short trail that leads
up the hill to a section of the Oregon Trail, ruts are visible and an
interpretive trail and volunteers
help you make sense of what you
see.

Back on the freeway you'll
soon descend into the Grand Ronde Valley. There are several exits for the town of La
Grande, take Exit 261 which is marked for Elgin. You will want to go left toward the
northeast, but you might want to make a brief detour to the right to take a look at La
Grande.

Head out of La Grande on Highway 82, this highway takes a few unexpected
turns but you will have no problem following it if you just watch for signs for Elgin
and then Enterprise. If you zero your odometer when you leave the freeway you'll
reach Elgin at 19 miles (31 km), Enterprise at 63 miles (102 km) , and Joseph at 70
miles (113 km).

You may want to make two stops in Enterprise before going on to Joseph. Just
before you arrive in town you'll pass the **Wallowa Wilderness Mountains Visitor**

Center. A stop here will bring you up to speed on the area's attractions. Then, in Enterprise you'll find the last large supermarket in this neck of the woods, you might stop and pick up groceries for the next few nights.

JOSEPH AND WALLOWA LAKE

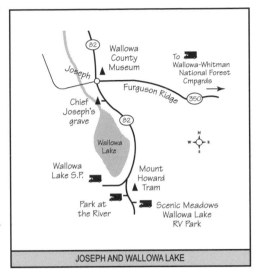

JOSEPH AND WALLOWA LAKE

The small town of Joseph and nearby Wallowa Lake make a very attractive destination. Almost anyone can find something of interest in this area.

Joseph itself is a small town with a population of some 1,300 people. It has become a bit of an art colony in the last few years. The town is known for its bronze foundries that produce bronze statues of all sizes, most with western themes. There are showrooms and you can tour a couple of the foundries, just ask at the showrooms.

The Wallowa Lake area was the traditional summer home of the Nez Percé Indians. You can visit the **Wallowa County Museum** in Joseph to learn more about them. South of town and overlooking the lake you'll find **Chief Joseph's grave**. This is the grave of old Chief Joseph, father of the Chief Joseph who led his people on the "Trail of Tears" toward Canada in 1877.

Wallowa Lake is a 4-mile-long jewel extending from near Joseph back into high mountains. At the south end of the lake is a tourist area with the state park, a couple of private RV campgrounds, miscellaneous attractions for the tourist hordes, and some trail heads for hikes into the Wallowa Mountains. The lake is very popular for water sports of all kinds including water skiing and fishing. The top tourist attraction here must be the **Mount Howard Tram** which lifts visitors to 8,200 feet for several miles of hiking trails and great views in all directions.

Joseph celebrates **Chief Joseph Days** in late July and **Alpenfest** on the third weekend after Labor Day.

Joseph Area Campgrounds

🚐 **Wallowa Lake State Park** [MED] 🔺 ⛏ 🔥 🚻 🛁 ⚡ 🏊 🖼 🏪 800 452-5687 for reservations; 210 sites, open all year - This state park is actually world famous, National Geographic once chose it as one of the six best state parks in the west. The reason is that there is lots to do here and the setting is magnificent. There is a boat launch and swimming area along the lake shore. Within walking distance you'll find restaurants, mini-golf, the tram to the top of Mount Howard, horse rides, and go-karts. To reach the campground just follow Highway 82 south 6 miles (10 km) from Joseph. The road reaches the lake at 2 miles, then follows the eastern lake shore for 4 miles (6 km) to the south end. At a Y there go right to the park entrance. This is a very popular park, even during the week you should have reservations or arrive very early in the day.

🚐 **Scenic Meadows Wallowa Lake RV Park** [MED] [⛺] [👤] [🔌] [🐴] [🐿] [🔥] [🍳] 59781 Wallowa Lake Hwy., P.O. Box 912, Joseph, OR 97846; 541 432-9285; 19 sites, open May 1 through October 1 - A nice little well-run RV park with amenities some will like and others hate including a go-kart track, mini-golf, and horses. Kids love it. 50-amp. power is available. Located in the south Wallowa Lake tourist area. From the Y at the south end of Wallowa Lake go left, the campground is on the left in .4 mile.

🚐 **Park at the River** [MED] [👤] [🔌] [🐴] [🐿] 59888 Wallowa Lake Highway, Joseph, OR 97846; 541 432-8800; 48 sites, open all year - This medium-sized RV park is quieter than Scenic Meadows and almost across the street. All sites are full hookup, 50-amp. power is available. From the Y at the south end of Wallowa Lake go left, the campground is on the right in .3 mile.

🚐 **Wallowa-Whitman National Forest Campgrounds** - The area surrounding Joseph is full of small national forest campgrounds. They have no hookups and their small sites are not suitable for big rigs. Here is a selection of campgrounds between Joseph and Hell's Canyon along tomorrow's route:

    🚐 **Lick Creek Campground**, 5 sites, 24 miles (39 km) from Joseph

    🚐 **Blackhorse Campground**, 16 sites, 38 miles (61 km) from Joseph

    🚐 **Ollokot Campground**, 12 sites, 38 miles (61 km) from Joseph

---

DAY 4 - DESTINATION HELLS CANYON
68 miles (110 km), 3 hours (to Copperfield)

Along The Way - The drive from Wallowa Lake to Hells Canyon runs through the Wallowa-Whitman National Forest. This is an extremely pleasant drive on sometimes narrow forest service roads. It has been designated a Scenic Route by the state of Oregon. The entire distance is now paved.

RVers with extremely large rigs may not want to follow the route, the alternative would be to backtrack to La Grande, follow I-84 to Baker City, and then drive in to the canyon on Highway 86. It is a good idea to check with the visitor center in Enterprise for information about the condition of the road, it is not cleared in winter.

From near the center of Joseph follow Highway 350 east toward Imnaha and Furguson Ridge. After 8.1 miles (13.1 km) take the right turn marked Highway 39 and Wallowa Mountain Road. Signs will tell you it is now 64 miles (103 km) to Halfway and 37 Miles (60 km) to the **Hells Canyon Scenic Overlook**.

You soon enter the Wallowa-Whitman National Forest. The road climbs to Salt Creek Summit which is 8 miles (13 km) from the junction. Five miles (8 km) after the summit the road enters Hells Canyon Recreation Area.

Twenty-four miles (39 km) from the summit you'll see a sign directing you left to **Hells Canyon Overlook**. This three-mile (5 km) spur road is paved, follow it to a nice overlook area with great views of Hells Canyon. You can't actually see the river from here, but it will give you a much different view of the canyon than the one you see from the bottom.

Back at the main road continue south. The road descends in 19 miles (31 km) to meet Highway 86.

Turn left and follow Highway 86 down to the river, a distance of 8 miles (13 km). Two miles (3 km) before reaching the river you'll pass through Pine Creek which has gasoline and a small grocery store.

HELLS CANYON

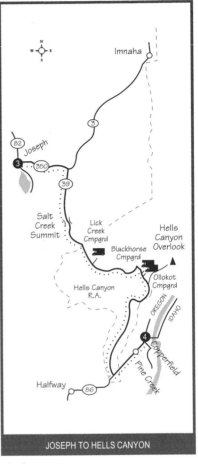

JOSEPH TO HELLS CANYON

Hells Canyon stretches along the Oregon-Idaho border for 110 miles (177 km) from Oxbow Dam to the Oregon-Washington border in the north. The canyon is sometimes called the deepest in the U.S. with a depth of about 8,888 feet. This is measured from the top of nearby He Devil Mountain so purists might be right is saying that the Grand Canyon is actually a deeper canyon. Irregardless, Hells Canyon is impressive, particularly from the bottom. The bordering ridges average 5,500 feet above the river.

The portion of the canyon that we are concerned with here is the top part, a 30-mile (48 km) stretch actually beginning above the canyon with road access along the entire length. There are three dams in this area operated by the Idaho Power Company: Brownlee, Oxbow, and Hells Canyon. These dams are very controversial in ecological circles since they do not have fish ladders and act as a barrier to the migration of salmon up the Snake River. Some people would like to see the dams removed entirely.

As with most of this type of controversy there are arguments for keeping the dams. In addition to economic and flood control arguments there is the one about the recreational potential of the lakes behind the dams. In this case the recreational opportunities are outstanding. The three lakes offer flat-water water sports action, vehicle-accessible camping along the shores, sightseeing, and excellent fishing.

Highway 86 reaches the river at Copperfield, a few miles below Oxbow Dam. The river here is actually a narrow lake, Hells Canyon Reservoir. You can cross the lake into Idaho and follow an excellent paved road to the left (down river) for 23 miles (37 km) to a point just beyond Hells Canyon Dam. The scenery along this section of road is spectacular with barren cliffs rising thousands of feet from the river. The drive has been designated a Scenic Drive by the state of Idaho. When you reach **Hells Canyon Dam** you can drive across it and then descend a steep road to a National Forest information center. This center is at a put-in point for popular float trips of the lower river which is designated as a wild river for 31.5 miles (50.8 km) and then as a scenic river for another 36 miles (58 km). Large rigs (over about 26 feet or towing a

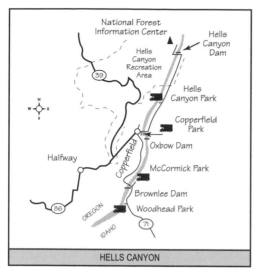

HELLS CANYON

trailer) will not want to make this final crossing of the dam and descent to the information center because there is a sharp switchback and limited maneuvering room at the information center. Drivers of large rigs should watch carefully for the appearance of the dam ahead, about the time they see it they will reach a large flat turn-around area, the last place to do so before the dam. Unfortunately there are no warning signs so you are on your own.

From Copperfield the road also extends upriver on the Oregon side of the river. It soon passes **Oxbow Dam**, which is barely visible off to the left and not accessible by vehicle, and runs along the shore of Oxbow Reservoir. This section of road is not as impressive as the section downstream but it's still outstanding. After 11 miles (18 km) the road crosses the river just below hulking **Brownlee Dam** and then climbs the cliff face to reach huge Brownlee Reservoir. After following the shore of the reservoir for a few miles the road heads east into Idaho and away from the river toward Cambridge.

Hells Canyon Area Campgrounds

🚐 **Copperfield Park** ⌞ᴸᴼᵂ⌝ △ ⌂ ⌸ ⌦ ⌧ ♨ ⌲ 62 sites, open all year - The first thing you'll see when you arrive at the river is this beautiful RV park. It's an Idaho Power facility, as are the three campgrounds mentioned below. It is on the Oregon side of Hells Canyon Reservoir. The sites are paved and set off a paved drive on terraces sloping toward the river. All have 30-amp. electricity and water hookups, none have sewer. Sites range from short to long including a few pull-throughs. Even the largest rigs should find a site that fits here. The restrooms are spotless and have flush toilets and showers in separate rooms. There is a dump station. A favorite evening activity here is fishing from the bridge across the reservoir. You can't miss this campground since it sits right where Highway 86 reaches the river.

🚐 **Hells Canyon Park** ⌞ᴸᴼᵂ⌝ △ ⌂ ⌸ ⌦ ⌧ 24 sites, open all year - Also on Hells Canyon Reservoir, on the Idaho side, this pleasant smaller campground also has sites with electricity and water but with parallel parking.

🚐 **McCormick Park** ⌞ᴸᴼᵂ⌝ △ ⌂ ⌸ ⌦ ⌧ 34 sites, open all year - The oldest of the Idaho Power campgrounds in the canyon this one has sites arranged as back-in slots around a gravel area.

🚐 **Woodhead Park** ⌞ᴸᴼᵂ⌝ △ ⌂ ⌸ ⌦ ⌧ ♨ 124 sites, open all year - A huge and beautiful campground facility on the Idaho side of Brownlee Reservoir. Sites here are on terraces above the lake, water level of the lake varies considerably.

HELLS CANYON

DAY 5 - DESTINATION BAKER CITY
70 miles (113 km), 2 hours

Along the Way - From Hells Canyon Hwy. 86 leads west to Baker City. For the most part the road runs through open range and irrigated farmland with one decent summit with a good climb just past the town of Halfway, the top is at 3,653 feet.

As you approach Baker City you will spot the **Oregon Trail Interpretive Center** on top of Flagstaff Hill to your right. This must-see attraction is described below.

Baker City

Although the **Oregon Trail** passes near Baker City (population 10,100) the town really dates from a gold-mining period in the 1860s. Located on I-84, Baker City is more than a spot to stop for gas and a quick bite, the town has a surprising number of interesting nearby tourist attractions.

First on the list must be the

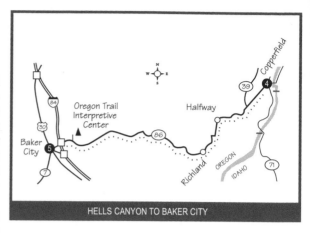

HELLS CANYON TO BAKER CITY

new **Oregon Trail Interpretive Center**. Completed in 1992 this modern museum presents a fascinating look at the Oregon Trail. The trail itself passes below, you can see the ruts from the center but there are trails leading down for a closer look. In the center itself you pass along a winding path past dioramas, slide shows, and exhibits –plan on at least an hour to take it all in. RVers should especially appreci-

BAKER CITY

ate this monument to some of the first of our kind.

In Baker City itself there are a number of worthwhile sites. The **Central Oregon Regional Museum** is a huge building with a large variety of exhibits. The **Geiser Grand Hotel**, dating from 1889, has recently been restored and is designated a National Historic Landmark.

Baker's annual celebration is the **Miner's Jubilee**, held during the third week of July.

East of town on Hwy. 7 is the **Sumpter** gold field area. Attractions include the **Sumpter Railroad**, **Sumpter Gold Dredge**, and also Sumpter itself. They are described in the next Along the Way section below.

Baker City Area Campgrounds

Union Creek Campground 58 sites, open April through October - This is a large, modern national forest campground offering utility hookups and sites large enough for big rigs, an unusual combination that makes this a great place to stay when you are in the Baker City area. The campground is next to Phillips Reservoir, a five-mile-long lake which offers fishing and boating possibilities. Head east from Baker City on Highway 7, the campground is 17 miles (27 km) out of town.

Mountain View Holiday Trav-L-Park 2845 Hughes Lane, Baker City, OR 97814; 541 523-4824; 83 sites, open all year - This is a good base if you wish to stay in Baker City. The campground has long pull-throughs with 50-amp. power. From Exit 302 of I-84 head west, take a left and drive past the Oregon Trails West RV park, take a right on Hughes Road, you will see the campground on the left in 1 mile (1.6 km).

Oregon Trails West RV Park 42534 N Cedar, Baker City, OR 97814; 541 523-3236; 61 sites, open all year - This campground has full-hookups with 50-amp. power and pull-through sites. Definitely the easiest to find of the Baker City campgrounds, this one is right at Exit 302 of I-84 on the west side of the freeway.

DAY 6 - DESTINATION JOHN DAY
79 miles (127 km), 2.5 hours (to John Day)

Along the Way - From Baker follow Hwy. 7 eastward out of town. The road follows the Powder River toward the old dredge tailing piles near Sumpter. Seventeen miles (27 km) after leaving town you'll pass the entrance road for Union Creek Campground. 4.8 miles (7.7 km) farther along take a left to visit **Railroad Park**. From here, on weekends, you can ride to the dredge at Sumpter behind a historic steam locomotive. Driving on, in just 2.3 miles (3.7 km), you'll reach a junction, take

SUMPTER GOLD DREDGE

a right and visit the historic gold mining town of Sumpter.

Sumpter offers a number of attractions. The main street is lined with several restaurants, small stores, and other tourist-oriented establishments. The most interesting attraction, however, is the **Sumpter Gold Dredge**. This is part of a state park that also includes the Sumpter Valley Railroad. Neglected for many years the dredge had sunk in it's pond, but has been raised and is being restored. You can wander through it now, it is already a well-done exhibit that will only get better.

Back on Hwy. 7 you'll climb over 5,124 foot Tipton Summit and then link up with Hwy. 26 and travel westward. The highway soon crosses another summit, this one the 5,279-foot Dixie Mountain Pass, and finally reaches the town of John Day.

JOHN DAY REGION

John Day is a town of 2,075 souls. Today it is the largest town in Grant County, although Canyon City (population 725), two miles south, is the county seat. In the 1860s these towns served the nearby **Strawberry Mountain gold fields**. You can visit the fields near Canyon City, the **Grant County Historical Museum** has exhibits describing this period.

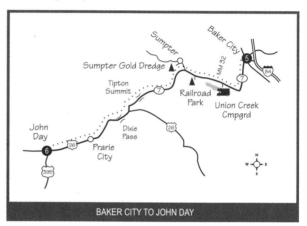

BAKER CITY TO JOHN DAY

During the 1800s large numbers of Chinese came to the west from southern China. They worked the railroads and fish canneries, and they also worked the mines. John Day had one of the largest Chinese populations in the western mining areas, and the tiny **Kim Wah Chung and Co. Museum** in John Day offers a fascinating look back at this period. It occupies the rickety building that served as home, store, opium den, card room, and Chines herbal pharmacy for a pair of Chinese entrepreneurs. The building was locked up and remained undisturbed for years following the owner's deaths, when reopened it was a treasure house of interesting things including Chinese herbs and groceries from the early part of the century.

The **Grant County Fair** is held in John Day during the second week of August.

To the west of John Day are the three units of the **John Day Fossil Beds National Monument**. The main visitor's center is now located in the Cant family ranch house which is located on Hwy. 19 some 2 miles (3 km) north of its intersection with Hwy. 7 and 40 miles (65 km) from John Day.

The visitor center is located in the **Sheep Rock section** of the monument. Other interesting attractions in this section are **Picture Gorge** (which you pass through just before reaching the visitor center), **Sheep Rock** to the east of the visitor center and viewable from an overlook just to the south, **Blue Basin** with hiking trails 3 miles (5 km) north of the visitor center, and the **Forsee Area**, also with hiking trails, about 7 miles (11 km) north of the visitor center.

There are two other sections of this monument. Far to the north, off Hwy. 218 near the town of Fossil, is the **Clarno Unit**. The prime attraction here is the **Palisades**, a rugged cliff rising from the flatlands. There are several trails here offering you a look at plant fossils.

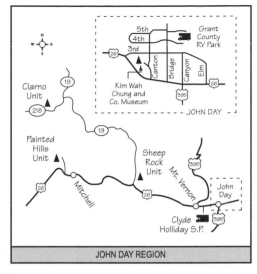

The other section of the monument is known as the **Painted Hills**. They are more conveniently located for us since this tour's route passes right by them en route to Sisters. Just west of Mitchell, 66 miles (106 km) west of John Day along Hwy. 26, a small paved road leads north into the section. You'll find an overlook offering you the opportunity to take photos of smoothly rounded hills with bands of colored minerals. The area also offers hiking trails and a small area with picnic tables and restrooms.

John Day Area Campgrounds

Camping facilities are not plentiful in this region. We like the state park as a primary destination with the county campground in John Day as a backup if the state campground happens to be full.

🚐 **Clyde Holliday State Park** LOW 🏕 🍴 🖥 🚻 🚿 🔥 30 sites, open March through December 1 - This medium-sized state park campground is set on a fairly small plot of land next to the John Day River. There are only 30 hookup sites, they have 50-amp. electricity and water, there is a dump station instead of sewer hookups. Shade is plentiful, sites are paved and off a paved drive, some are very long so a big rig isn't a problem if you happen to be able to get one of them. The restroom buildings are older but offer hot showers and flush toilets. This campground also offers a hiker/biker camp and two rental Indian teepees. The campground is hard to miss if you are traveling on US 26. Watch for it on the left about 8 miles (13 km) after leaving John Day, when you get to Mt. Vernon you've gone too far.

🚐 **Grant County RV Park** LOW 🍴 🖥 🚻 🚿 ✒ 541 575-0110; 25 sites, open all year - There are 25 large RV spaces with full hookups and showers at the fairgrounds in John Day. The fairgrounds are well signed from Hwy. 26 as it passes through town.

DAY 7 - DESTINATION SISTERS
160 miles (258 km), 5 hours

Along **The Way** - The drive from John Day to Sisters follows Hwy. 26 eastward to Prineville, then branches south on Hwy. 126 to pass through Redmond and on to Sisters. Until the highway reaches the Prineville area this is a very sparsely populated part of Oregon, and also extremely scenic with miles and miles of open pine forest.

Along the way you'll have the opportunity to visit two of the sections of the **John Day Fossil Beds National Monument**. They are described in the previous section and include the **Sheep Rock** section near Mile 38 of this day's drive and the **Painted Hills** section near Mile 66 of the drive.

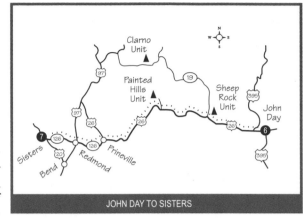

JOHN DAY TO SISTERS

Sisters (population 900) is one of those theme towns, it may remind you of Leavenworth or Winthrop in Washington. It's a cute little place with a number of restaurants, shops, and art galleries. Plan to spend an hour or two wandering around.

Sisters also serves as a good base for exploring some beautiful countryside. The town of Bend, covered in Tour 3, is only 21 highway miles (34 km) to the southwest so you might consider some of the sights covered in the Bend section. Sisters, however, has its own set of sights.

Probably your first trip should be to the **Metolius Meadows**. The Metolius River starts at a spring, it is thought to pass underground from the nearby mountains, and then flows through a beautiful area of Ponderosa Pine and grasslands. The river is a famous fishing spot (fly fishing only), the area is extremely scenic with many hiking trails. The commercial center of the area is called Camp Sherman, it amounts to little more than a store and post office, there are quite a few homes, condos, and resorts set in seclusion among the pines in the surrounding area. To get there just follow Hwy. 20 some 9 miles (15 km) toward Salem and then take the Camp Sherman road (Rd. 14) to the right. After 2.7 miles (4.4 km) there is a fork, take the right (Rd. 14) to visit the source of the Metolius River and the National Forest Service Campgrounds downstream. A left at the fork puts you on Rd. 1419 and a drive through an area of lodges and other facilities. You can take a right after another 2.2 miles (3.5 km) to reach the Camp Sherman Store which has groceries, gas, a deli, and a post office.

A popular drive from Sisters is the **McKenzie-Santiam Pass Loop**. This 82-mile (132 km) loop is a designated National Forest Scenic Byway. The loop follows Hwy. 242 westward from Sisters and across **McKenzie Pass**. There you'll find the **Dee Wright Observatory,** built of lava and offering an easy wheelchair-accessible trail through a lava flow. After the pass the road descends to the intersection with Hwy. 126. Turn north and follow this highway up the McKenzie River Valley. There are a number of small National Forest Service campgrounds along this section of the road as well as the McKenzie River National Recreation Trail which offers access to the river and several waterfalls. Watch for signs for **Koosah and Sahalie Falls**, both are easily accessible. You'll come to another intersection, this time with Hwy. 20, and turn east. This highway will take you over **Santiam Pass** and past the Metolius River Recreation Area back to Sisters. The first portion of the route, Hwy. 242, is narrow and steep and not suitable for large rigs, that's why it is listed here only as a day trip. Also, snow closes this portion of the loop from November until late June.

Sisters holds the **Sisters Rodeo** during the second week of June.

Sisters Area Campgrounds

Mountain Shadow RV Park 540 Hwy. 20 West, P.O. Box 938, Sisters, OR 97759; 541 549-7275; 104 sites, open all year - This is the most conveniently located campground to the central area of Sisters since it is located only a mile from the downtown area. Many sites are large pull-throughs with 50-amp. electrical service. The campground is modern and very spiffy, sites are paved and have patios with picnic tables and stands for barbecues. There are large, clean restrooms and also an indoor swimming pool with spa. From Sisters proceed west on Hwy. 20. At the fork on the outskirts of town where Hwy. 20 and Hwy. 126 split go right on Hwy. 20. The campground is on the left just past the Comfort Inn exactly .4 miles from the fork.

Sisters KOA 67667 Hwy. 20 West, Bend, Oregon 97701; 541 549-3021or 800 KOA-0363 for reservations; 75 sites, open March 1 through December 31 - This fine KOA is located only 4 miles (6 km) southeast of Sisters on Highway 20 in the direction of Bend. Amenities include available 50-amp.

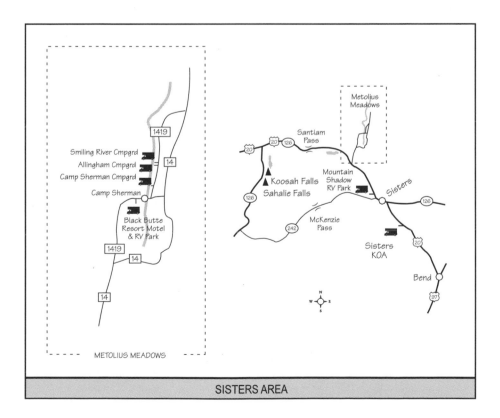

SISTERS AREA

power, mini golf, and a fishing pond.

⛟ Black Butte Resort Motel & RV Park [MED] [🛁] [🚐] [🍴] [⚙] 25635 SW Forest Service Rd. 1419, Camp Sherman, OR 97730; 541 595-6514 or 877 595-6514 for reservations; http://www.centormall.com/ black_butte_resort/; 29 sites, open all year - For hookups only a few hundred yards from the Metolius River try this place. To reach the campground take the Camp Sherman exit from Highway 20, take the left fork at 2.7 miles (4.3 km) and then drive 2.2 miles (3.5 km) to a stop sign, turn right and you will see the campground entrance after another .3 miles (.5 km).

⛟ Metolius Area National Forest Campgrounds http://www.fs.fed.us/r6/ deschutes/desnf /recreate/facility/recfacil.html - There are a number of these along the banks of the Metolius River north of the Camp Sherman Store. All have vault toilets, they're your typical forest service campground, few amenities but a great location.

⛟ Camp Sherman Campground [LOW] [⛰] [🔥] 15 sites, open April through October - From the Camp Sherman cutoff on Hwy. 20 drive 6.1 miles (9.8 km) on Rd. 14, then a half mile (.8km) north on Road 1419.

⛟ Allingham Campground [LOW] [⛰] [🚐] [🔥] 10 sites, open May through Sepember - From the Camp Sherman cutoff on Hwy. 20 drive 6.1 miles (9.8 km) on Rd. 14 then a mile (1.6 km) north on Road 1419.

⛟ Smiling River Campground [LOW] [⛰] [🚐] [🔥] 38 sites, open May through October - From the Camp Sherman cutoff on Hwy. 20 drive 6.1 miles (9.8 km) on Rd. 14 then a mile (1.6 km) north on Road 1419.

DAY 8 - DESTINATION PORTLAND
148 miles (239 km), 4 hours

From Sisters the easiest route back to Portland for big rigs is Highway 20 across Santiam Pass (4,817 feet) and Tombstone Summit (4,236 feet) to Highway I-5 just south of Albany.

Cascadia State Park, 59 miles (95 km) from Sisters, makes a good place to take a break. The park is located along the South Santiam River at the site of a spring long famous for it's healthful soda water. There's a historic covered bridge nearby. Once you reach I-5 it's about 55 freeway miles (89 km) north to Portland.

Information Resources

See our Internet site at www.rollinghomes.com for Internet site addresses.

Destination Columbia Gorge

Cascades Locks Visitor Information Center, P.O. Box 307, Cascade Locks, OR 97014; 541 374-8619

Columbia River Gorge National Scenic Area, USDA Forest Service, 902 Wasco, Suite 200, Hood River, OR 97031; 541 386-2333

The Dalles Chamber of Commerce, 404 West 2nd Street, The Dalles, OR 97058; 800 255-3385 or 541 296-2231

Hood River Chamber of Commerce, 405 Port Way, Hood River, OR 97031; 541 386-2000 or 800 366-3530

Columbia Gorge Discovery Center, 5000 Discovery Drive, The Dalles, OR 97058; 541 296-8600

Destination Pendleton

Pendleton Chamber of Commerce, 501 S Main Street, Pendleton, OR 97801; 541 276-7411 or 800 547-8911

Pendleton Round-Up, 1205 SW Court, P.O. Box 609, Pendleton, OR 97801; 800 457-6336 or 541 276-2553

Pendleton Woolen Mills, 1307 SE Court Place, Pendleton, OR 97801; 541 276-6911

Wildhorse Casino and Resort, 72777 Hwy. 331, Pendleton, OR 97801; 541 278-2274

Destination Joseph and Wallowa Lake

Hells Canyon National Recreation Area/Wallowa Mountains Visitor Center, 88401 Highway 82, Enterprise, OR 97828; 541 426-5546

Wallowa County Chamber of Commerce, 107 SW 1st St., P.O. Box 427, Enterprise, OR 97828; 541 426-4622 or 800 585-4121.

Destination Hells Canyon National Recreation Area

Snake River Campground Information, Idaho Power Company, P.O. Box 169, Oxbow, Oregon 97840; 541 785-3323

Hells Canyon Chamber of Commerce Visitors Information Center, P.O. Box 841, Halfway, OR 97834; 541 742-4222

Destination Baker City

Bureau of Land Management, National Historic Oregon Trail Interpretive Center, P.O. Box 987, Baker City, OR 97814; 541 523-1843 or 800 523-1235

Baker County Visitors & Convention Bureau, 490 Campbell Street, Baker City, OR 97814; 541 523-3356 or 800 523-1235

Greater Sumpter Chamber of Commerce, P.O. Box 250, Sumpter, OR 97877; 541 894-2290

Destination John Day

Grant County Chamber of Commerce, 281 W Main, John Day, OR 97845; 541 575-0547

John Day Fossil Beds National Monument, HCR 82, Box 126, Kimberly, OR 97848; 541 987-2333

Destination Sisters

Sisters Chamber of Commerce, 164 N Elm St., P.O. Box 476, Sisters, OR 97759; 541 549-0251

Metolius Recreation Association, PO Box 64, Camp Sherman, OR 97730; 541-595- 6117

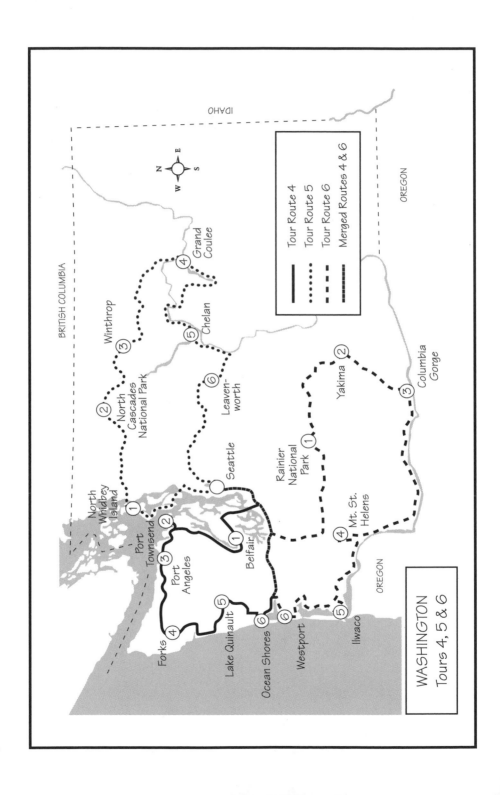

WASHINGTON
Tours 4, 5 & 6

Chapter 7

Seattle

Top Attractions

✦ Pike Place Market

✦ Seattle Waterfront

✦ Pioneer Square

✦ International District

✦ Space Needle

✦ Puget Sound Ferries

General

The Seattle Metropolitan Area is the Northwest's giant with an area population (including Everett, Tacoma, and the Eastside) of almost 1,500,000 people. It is ideally located to serve as the base for the three Washington state tours in this book. We'll concentrate in this section mostly on the city of Seattle itself.

Access to Seattle is easy. Seattle-Tacoma International Airport (locally called Sea-Tac) provides connections to national and international flights. If you happen to be arriving in your own RV the city is conveniently located at the intersection of the West Coast's I-5 and east-west I-90 which connects this part of the Northwest with points east.

Seattle makes an extremely interesting tourist destination. It is very popular with visitors from both the U.S. and other countries.

History

The city of Seattle was founded in 1851 by a band of settlers who established themselves on Alki Point just across Elliott Bay from the present downtown. At that time the Puget Sound area was becoming a magnet for settlers, they wanted to farm and cut timber. Some of the Alki settlers soon moved to the present location of downtown Seattle, that's where the big trees were. With the construction of Yesler's Mill Seattle became a mill town. From that beginning it is easy to trace the growth of the city through a series of events: arrival of the telegraph in 1864, a wagon road opened over Snoqualmie Pass in 1867, the Great Fire burnt down downtown Seattle in 1889, the Great Northern Railroad reached Seattle in 1893, the Klondike gold rush began in 1897, in 1898 the Denny Regrade project began and the hills to the north of downtown were leveled and the dirt dumped in Elliott Bay. In 1900 Weyerhaeuser was formed when a huge amount of timberland was purchased from James A. Hill, the railroad baron. Boeing's first airplane flew in 1916, the building of airplanes during World War II gave Seattle a big spurt of growth, and the 707 passenger jetliner first flew in 1954. The city hosted the World's Fair in 1964 and Microsoft moved to Bellevue from Albuquerque in 1979.

Layout

The location and landscape of Seattle seem to conspire to make getting around the city difficult. There are Puget Sound to the west, Lake Washington to the east, and a number of steep hills including Queen Anne, Capitol and Beacon rising in inconvenient locations.

Downtown Seattle is surrounded by virtually self-sufficient neighborhoods and suburbs. Directly across Elliott Bay is West Seattle, but the Duwamish River makes access a challenge. On the hill to the east of downtown are the First Hill and Capitol Hill neighborhoods. On the hill to the north of Seattle is the Queen Anne neighborhood. North of Queen Anne an east-west canal connects Puget Sound to Lake Washington through Lake Union, this canal is another barrier to transportation and is crossed by four drawbridges that must open for canal traffic as well as by two soaring freeway bridges. Along the canal's north shore, from west to east, are the neighborhoods of Ballard, Freemont, Wallingford, and the University District. Farther afield, on the east side of Lake Washington, are Renton, Mercer Island, Bellevue, Kirkland, Redmond, and Issaquah. Large cities, not really suburbs at all, lie farther to the north and south: Everett in the north and Tacoma in the south. Finally, across Puget Sound but home to ferry commuters are Vashon Island, Bremerton, and Bainbridge Island.

Transportation

Driving in Seattle can be confusing and the roads congested. Roads must detour around lakes and hills. A major highway, I-5, runs north and south right through the middle of the city, sometimes it is as much of a barrier as the hills, lakes, and canals. A ring-road freeway, I-405, circles east of Lake Washington, others were planned but never built. Two major freeways connect I-5 and I-405 across Lake Washington on floating bridges. One of those sank several years ago, but it has been replaced. Even with all this concrete there is not nearly enough highway for the number of cars, so be sure to avoid the extended rush hours.

The city has no light rail or subway system, but it does have a pretty good bus system. Most of the campgrounds listed below have decent bus transportation available that can get you to downtown Seattle. Unfortunately it is more difficult to use the busses from the campgrounds to reach the outlying neighborhoods and suburbs since

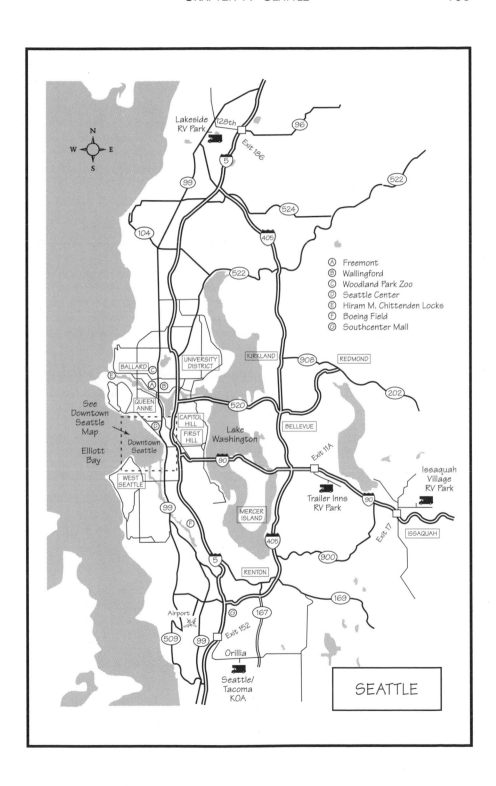

Lakeside RV Park
128th
Exit 186
96
5
99
522
524
104
405
522

(A) Freemont
(B) Wallingford
(C) Woodland Park Zoo
(D) Seattle Center
(E) Hiram M. Chittenden Locks
(F) Boeing Field
(G) Southcenter Mall

KIRKLAND
REDMOND
BALLARD
UNIVERSITY DISTRICT
908
202
(E) (C)
(A) (B)
QUEEN ANNE
520
See Downtown Seattle Map
(D)
CAPITOL HILL
BELLEVUE
FIRST HILL
Lake Washington
Elliott Bay
Downtown Seattle
90
Exit 11A
Issaquah Village RV Park
WEST SEATTLE
Trailer Inns RV Park
90
99
MERCER ISLAND
Exit 17
ISSAQUAH
(F)
405
900
5
RENTON
169
Airport
(G)
167
509
99
Exit 152
Orillia
Seattle/ Tacoma KOA

SEATTLE

the lines tend to radiate from the center rather than circle it. That means that you will probably want to use the bus to go downtown because both traffic and parking are difficult there. When bound for destinations away from the city center you will probably want to use your tow car or smaller RV.

Seattle has two other transportation options, both are tourist destinations in their own right. The state's ferry fleet serves the far shore of Puget Sound from a terminal in downtown Seattle. No visit to Seattle would be complete without a ferry outing. Also, Seattle still has its monorail, originally built for the 1964 World's Fair. The monorail's usefulness is limited but it does provide a good way to visit the Space Needle and Seattle Center from downtown.

THE CITY

Seattle's **central downtown area** is fairly compact, about 9 blocks deep from the water up to the I-5 freeway and 13 wide from Jefferson to Olive. The streets in this section don't run north and south like they do in most of the rest of Seattle, they are cocked at a 45-degree angle to parallel the waterfront. The area is compact, but walking it can be tiring because the streets climb steeply uphill from the water. It is good to know that bus service in the central area is free, just climb on and ride.

When you arrive in town you will probably alight near the uptown shopping district centered around **Westlake Center** at 4th and Pine at the north end of the downtown area. There are a cluster of large stores here including the flagship Nordstrom department store. Westlake is also the terminal for the monorail, more on that later.

Directly toward the water from Westlake is one of Seattle's most famous attractions. **Pike Place Market**, at 1st and Pike, is an actual operating farmer's market, but much more. In addition to produce you'll find fish, exotic foods of all kinds, arts and crafts, and even restaurants. It's set in several funky buildings dating from 1907, although there are lots of upscale additions in the vicinity.

Just down 1st Avenue from the market is the new **Seattle Art Museum**. It offers permanent displays of Asian and Northwest Indian art as well as temporary traveling exhibits. You can find the museum by watching for the **Hammer Man** sculpture out front, you really can't miss it.

From the market or museum you can descend to the waterfront using either stairs or a handy elevator. The **downtown Seattle waterfront** stretches for over a mile from Pier 70 next to Myrtle Edwards Park in the northwest to the Colman Dock ferry terminal (Pier 52) in the southeast. The piers between the two offer restaurants, stores, a marina, and even public parks. The area draws crowds on any sunny day. Don't miss the **Seattle Aquarium** on Pier 59. You can easily travel the length of the waterfront on a streetcar running on the far side of the road, the streetcar line turns inland at the south end of the waterfront and runs east through Pioneer Square to the International District.

At the south end of the waterfront is Colman Dock, the terminal for the **Washington State Ferry System**. Walk onto a ferry for an inexpensive two-hour round trip ride to the far side of the sound. You'll find commercial tour-boat operators along the waterfront, they'll take you on a **sightseeing tour** of Elliott Bay or through the ship canal. You can also travel to **Tillicum Island** for a traditional-style salmon bake.

To the south of the central downtown area is the **Pioneer Square Historical District**. This is the original Seattle. The whole swampy mess burned down in 1893 and handsome brick buildings were built as replacements. Later, fill from projects to flatten Seattle's hills (called the Regrade) was used to raise the street levels and fill the tidelands to the south. Today you'll see two huge sports arenas built on the fill, one for baseball and one for football. The center of the action in this part of town is tiny **Pioneer Square** which is located at the foot of Yesler, the original "**Skid Road**" and near the location of Seattle's first large employer, the steam-powered Yesler's Mill. The mill is long gone but the square and surrounding streets do offer lots of shops and restaurants, and you can take a tour of Seattle's "**underground**". The underground is actually the first floors of the nearby buildings. When the streets were raised during the Regrade the first floors of these buildings were abandoned, entrances were moved up to the second floors.

East of the Pioneer Square area is Seattle's **International District**. One easy way to reach it is to ride the trolley from the waterfront or Pioneer Square area. Covering

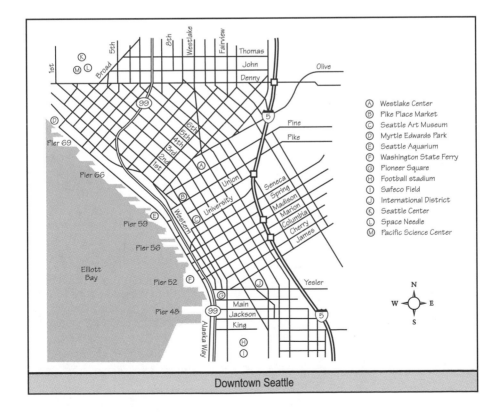

Downtown Seattle

about 30 blocks the district is filled with Chinese, Japanese, Korean, Filipino, and Southeast Asian shops and restaurants. Worth a walk-through is the large Uwajimaya Asian supermarket.

Back at the central shopping district you have one more thing to do. Hop on the monorail and ride to the **Seattle Center**. This was the site of the 1964 World's Fair and continues to offer a number of attractions including the **Space Needle**, Seattle's professional basketball arena, the **Pacific Science Center**, and even an amusement park. You can ride the elevator to the top of the Space Needle for the view or tour the child-friendly exhibits of the Science Center.

North of the downtown Seattle area and probably most easily reached using your own set of wheels is another of Seattle's popular attractions. The **Hiram M. Chittenden Locks** mark the beginning of the canal that connects the salt water Puget Sound with Lake Washington. You can watch work boats and yachts as they float up and down and also take a peek through **viewing windows** at the fish ladder that lets salmon and steelhead bypass the locks.

If you drive eastward near the north shore of the canal you'll pass through Ballard, Freemont, and Wallingford and find yourself in the **University District**. Most of the stores and restaurants here are along the north-south 45th Avenue, usually just called the "Ave". The campus lies just a block east of the Ave and is huge, 35,000 students attend class here. The University grounds are very attractive, you'll enjoy a walk on the campus.

Seattle has a very nice zoo, **Woodland Park Zoo**. If you follow 50th Street eastward from the University District you'll see the entrance on the right just after you pass under Hwy. 99 (the only underpass on this street). The zoo collection includes over 300 species and is known for its realistic habitat landscaping.

Because Seattle is home to Boeing it is known for aviation. There are two interesting aviation-oriented destinations in the region. The first is the **Museum of Flight**, which is located south of downtown along the west side of Boeing Field. The museum has a collection of more than 40 aircraft including Air Force 1 (a Boeing 707), a B-17, a B-29, and a Blackbird supersonic spy plane. North of Seattle at Paine Field near Everett is the **Boeing 747, 767, 777 Production Facility**. The tour of this huge hanger is very popular, call first to inquire about the best time to arrive. You reach it by driving west from Exit 189 off I-5 on Hwy. 526 near Everett. Drive 3.5 miles (5.6 km) from the freeway and then follow signs.

Seattle Area Campgrounds

🚐 **Seattle/Tacoma KOA** [icons] 5801 So. 212th St., Kent, WA 98032; 253 872-8652 or 800 KOA-1892 for reservations; 152 sites, open all year - Located south of the Southcenter shopping area near the Green River this campground is your best choice if you are approaching Seattle from the south. It has all the expected KOA amenities and bus service is available nearby to reach downtown Seattle. There is a handy bike path nearby too. From Highway I-5 south of Seattle take Exit 152 and follow Orillia Road South to the southeast for 2 miles. You'll see the campground on the right.

🚐 **Lakeside RV Park** [icons] 12321 Hwy. 99 South, Everett, WA 98204; 425 347-2970 or 800 468-7275 for reservations; 157 sites, open all year - From the north this is your best bet. The rigs are really packed onto this paved site.

The crowding is somewhat offset by the small adjoining lake and walking trail. Facilities are modern and there is bus service available nearby to both Seattle and Everett. This campground is north of Seattle off Hwy. I-5, take Exit 186, drive west on 128 St. SW for 1.5 miles (2.4 kilometers), turn left on Hwy. 99 and you'll see the campground on the left in .2 miles (.3 km).

🚐 **Trailer Inns RV Park** [HIGH] [⛺] [🏕] [🚻] [🏕] [♿] [📶] [📷] 15531 SE 37ᵗʰ St., Bellevue, WA 98006; 425 747-9181 or 800 659-4684 for reservations; 100 sites, open all year - The closest campground to downtown Seattle, this one is located near the Eastgate interchange right next to I-90 on the east side of Lake Washington. The campground is a large paved lot with the RVs parked very close together, spaces are large enough for big rigs, however. There is a good indoor swimming pool. The entrance roads are somewhat confusing because Eastgate has lots of freeway on- and off-ramps. From the east take Exit 11 and follow signs for 150ᵗʰ. Drive south across the freeway, then take the first left. Follow the frontage road for .2 miles (.3 km). Bear right at the Y, the campground is just beyond on the right. From the west on I-90 take Exit 11A (which is east of the intersection of Hwy. I-405 and I-90), following signs for SE 37ᵗʰ. You'll come to a stop sign at the top of the ramp, proceed directly ahead onto the frontage road. Take the right fork in .2 miles (.3 km) and the campground is just beyond on the right.

🚐 **Issaquah Village RV Park** [HIGH] [⛺] [🏕] [🚻] [🏕] [📶] [📷] 650 1ˢᵗ Ave NE, Issaquah, WA 98027; 425 392-9233 or 800 258-9233 for reservations; 115 sites, open all year - This campground is also on the east side of town and located near I-90 but it is farther out than the Trailer Inns RV Park. Sites are much farther apart, however, and there is also grass between them. There is bus service to Seattle from Issaquah. Take Exit 17 from I-90 and drive one block north to 229ᵗʰ Ave. SE, turn right and follow 66ᵗʰ Ave SE for a block, then turn right on 1ˢᵗ Street and follow it to the campground which is on the left.

Information Resources

See our Internet site at www.rollinghomes.com for Internet site addresses.

Seattle-King County Tourism Bureau, 800 Convention Place, Seattle, WA 98101; 206 461-5840

Argosy Cruises, Pier 55, Suite 201, Seattle, WA 98101; 206 623-1445

Seattle Metropolitan Transit System; 206 553-3000

Seattle Aquarium, 1483 Alaskan Way, Seattle, WA; 206 386-4300

Underground Tours, 610 1ˢᵗ, Seattle, WA 98104; 206 682-4646

Pacific Science Center, 200 2ⁿᵈ Ave. N, Seattle, WA 98109; 206 443-2001

Woodland Park Zoo, 5500 Phinney Ave. N, Seattle, WA 98103; 206 684-4800

Museum of Flight, 9404 E Marginal Way S, Seattle, WA 98109; 206 764-5720

Boeing 747, 767, 777 Production Facility, Everette, WA; 206 544-1264 or 800 464-1476

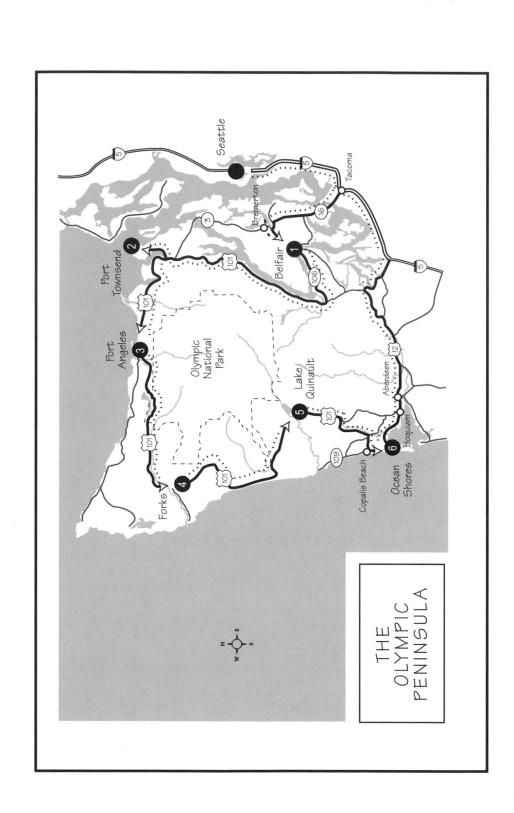

THE
OLYMPIC
PENINSULA

The Olympic Peninsula

Top Attractions

✦ Hood Canal

✦ Kitsap Peninsula

✦ Port Townsend

✦ Olympic National Park

✦ Dungeness Spit

✦ Sol Duc Hot Springs

✦ Rialto Beach

✦ Hoh Valley Rain Forest

✦ The North Beaches

General Description

This is the shortest of the Seattle tours. Northwest residents often drive the Olympic loop over a weekend. That's pretty fast, it doesn't give you time to enjoy an area that is filled with natural wonders. Total distance driven on this tour is 509 miles (821 km), driving time should be about 13.5 hours.

The tour follows Highway 5 south from Seattle to Tacoma. In Tacoma you leave Highway 5 and cross the Tacoma Narrows to the Kitsap Peninsula. The campgrounds along Hood Canal make a good place to stop for the night and also a good base for exploring Bremerton and the rest of the Kitsap Peninsula.

During the following days the tour leads you north to Port Townsend and then Port Angeles along the Strait of Juan de Fuca and then circles on around the Olympic Peninsula. This is a sparsely populated region famed for natural attractions and dominated by Olympic National Park.

Finally, on the last day of the tour you reach the ocean-side resort of Ocean Shores. You'll find a lot to do here and in the small towns scattered along the beaches to the north as well as in Hoquiam and Aberdeen to the east.

The Roads

The greater part of this tour follows Highway 101 in a loop around the Olympic Peninsula. You will be driving this two-lane paved highway from a point near Hoodsport on Hood Canal until you reach Aberdeen, a distance of 252 miles (406 km). This is a uniformly good road, no problem at all for RVs.

Practical Tips

Like the Oregon Coast Tour from Portland this is a tour that can be fun at any time of the year. During the winter you must expect a lot of rain, but temperatures rarely descend below about 40 degrees Fahrenheit. Coastal storms actually attract visitors during the winter.

You could easily combine this tour with our Southern Washington tour in either of two ways. From Aberdeen you could head south to Westport and then do the entire Southern Washington tour in a counter-clockwise direction. Alternately, instead of returning to Seattle you could drive to Packwood and start the tour in a clockwise direction.

It is also easy to connect with the Vancouver Island tour by taking a ferry north from Port Angeles to Victoria.

DAY 1 - DESTINATION THE HOOD CANAL AND KITSAP PENINSULA
67 miles (108 km), 2 hours (to Belfair)

A long the Way - Rather than deal with the crowded and somewhat expensive (especially for RVs) ferries that ply the waters of Puget Sound we'll do an end run and drive around the south end of the sound.

From Seattle head south on I-5. You'll pass through Tacoma and take Exit 132 (marked for Gig Harbor) and Highway 16 to drive across the Tacoma Narrows Suspension Bridge. Don't give it a thought, but this is the bridge that replaced the infamous "Galloping Gertie", that bridge collapsed in 1940.

Almost immediately you will find yourself in another world, you pass from the crowded Seattle-Tacoma metropolis to the green countryside of rural western Puget Sound and the Kitsap Peninsula. You might want to stop and take a look at **Gig Harbor**, sometimes called the northwest's Sausalito. The little waterfront town is filled

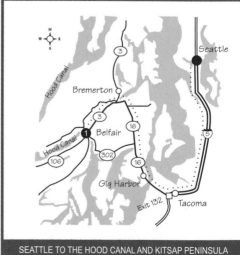

SEATTLE TO THE HOOD CANAL AND KITSAP PENINSULA

with small shops and has a nice nautical flavor. Parking for big rigs, however, is scarce.

Stay on Highway 16 as it leads north to Bremerton. Just short of that city the highway will meet Highway 3, turn left there toward Belfair and in just 8 miles (13 km) you'll find yourself entering the town of Belfair, located right at the end of Hood Canal.

BELFAIR, HOOD CANAL, AND THE KITSAP PENINSULA

Belfair is located at the very end of the long warm-water Hood Canal, and also at the base of the Kitsap Peninsula. It is a popular destination for water-oriented weekenders, and with its good state park campground and also a private alternative this little town is also an excellent base for exploring Bremerton and the lower Kitsap Peninsula.

The word canal is really not an accurate description of **Hood Canal**. Actually, Hood Canal is a 70-mile-long inlet. On a map the canal appears to be a giant hook

BELFAIR AND THE KITSAP PENINSULA

which forms the western boundary of the Kitsap Peninsula. Because the canal is so long and shallow its waters are fairly warm. It is quite popular with water sports enthusiasts. Oysters grow here, you will probably see them if you walk the beaches. Many folks from the more populous regions of Puget Sound have summer cabins along the shore of the canal.

A popular attraction near Belfair is the **Theler Wetlands** just south of Belfair where the Union River enters Hood Canal. This is a salt-water marsh with excellent paths and boardwalks offering access.

If you decide to head north and explore the Kitsap Peninsula you might want to make your first stop **Port Orchard**. This little harbor town is a good place to shop for antiques, arts, and just plain knickknacks.

Port Orchard is directly across Sinclair Inlet from much larger **Bremerton**, known as the home of the Puget Sound Naval Shipyard. You'll have to drive around the west end of Sinclair Inlet to get there if you want to take your car. The alternative is a passenger-only ferry running across the inlet. The waterfront in Bremerton is the center of interest. There you'll find a boardwalk and shipyard-related sights including the destroyer **Turner Joy** which is open to self-guided tours, and the **Bremerton Naval Museum**. There are a number of moth-balled ships in Bremerton, you can take a commercial harbor tour to see them but you are not allowed on board the ships.

If you find that you enjoy the Bremerton Naval Museum you may want to drive a few miles north on Highway 3 through Silverdale and then turn east on Highway 308 to Keyport. There you'll find the **Naval Underwater Museum**. The Kitsap Peninsula plays an important part in supporting the U.S. submarine fleet; along the west coast of the peninsula on Hood Canal is the **Bangor Trident Nuclear Submarine Base** and Keyport is home to the **Naval Undersea Warfare Center**, neither is open for tours, however.

Since you've come so far north already you might as well visit **Poulsbo**, it's only about three miles (5 km) farther north. Poulsbo is another cute harbor town offering antiques and shops, the difference here is that Poulsbo is proud of its Norwegian heritage and shows it off with Scandinavian-theme architecture and products.

Belfair Area Campgrounds

Belfair State Park   MED 🔺 ⚡ 🏕 🚻 🐟 🔥 ⚓ 📷   800 452-5687 for reservations; 184 sites, open all year - This state park is located on the north shore of Hood Canal. Here near the end of the canal water temperatures get warm enough for swimming, reason enough for the popularity of this park, swimming is in a swimming lagoon where the water is even warmer than in the canal. The park is located three miles (5 km) west of Belfair on State Route 300.

Snooze Junction RV Park   MED 🔺 ⚡ 🏕 🚻 🐟 ⚓   621 NE Gladwin Beach Rd, Belfair, WA 98528; 360 275-2381; 36 sites, open all year - Just a short distance from Belfair State Park is the commercial alternative. This small quiet campground is located on the shore of the canal. To get there follow State Route 300 west from Belfair for 2 miles (3 km) and turn left on Gladwin Beach Road. You'll soon see the campground.

Twanoh State Park   MED 🔺 ⚡ 🏕 🚻 🐟 🔥 ⚓ 📷   47 sites, open April 1 to October 31 - Much smaller than Belfair State Park, this campground has camping south of the highway and a day-use area north of the highway on the beach. It is located about 8 miles (13 km) west of Belfair on the south shore of the Hood Canal along Hwy. 106.

DAY 2 - DESTINATION PORT TOWNSEND
86 miles (139 km), 3 hours

Along the Way - From Belfair we'll follow the scenic route along the south and west side of Hood Canal and then north to Port Townsend. Don't be surprised if you find yourself tempted to stop a day or two at one of the attractive campgrounds you'll see along the way.

The first section of the route, on Highway 106, follows along the south shore of the canal. It's a leisurely drive along a shoreline lined with beautiful homes. Take it easy, there's no hurry, and much of the traffic here is local. You'll pass Twanoh State Park, which we have listed as an alternative to Belfair State Park in this area.

Eventually Highway 106 meets Highway 101. For much of the remainder of this trip we will be following 101 as it circles around the peninsula. Our route now passes up the west side of the Hood Canal. There aren't nearly as many residences along here, the views are great. Near Hoodsport you'll pass Potlatch State Park, which makes a good place to spend the night if you find this area attractive. There are also a number of other campground in the immediate area. You'll see several commercial ones and, if you follow the road that leads from Hoodsport up to Lake Cushman, several small Forest Service campgrounds.

Eventually the highway leaves the shore of the canal and approaches the north shore of the Olympic Peninsula. Just before you get there you will see a sign for Port Townsend (Highway 20). Take the right turn and in 13 miles (21 km) you will find yourself entering one of the most interesting towns on the peninsula.

PORT TOWNSEND

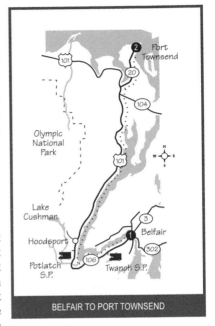

BELFAIR TO PORT TOWNSEND

Today Port Townsend (population 7,000) is not particularly large or economically important, but at one time this was the major metropolis on Puget Sound. The city was established in 1851. It had an extremely handy location at the entrance to Puget Sound so it was the logical place for a port to serve the area. The town is filled with historic Victorian buildings dating from this era when Port Townsend ruled the sound. Unfortunately for Port Townsend, railroads eventually reached the Northwest, and they led to Tacoma and Seattle, not Port Townsend.

The resulting economic bust in Port Townsend was very fortunate for today's tourist trade. The movers and shakers eventually moved out but left the town pretty much as it was at the end of the nineteenth century. Over 70 commercial buildings and homes in the town date from the era and have been preserved.

Port Townsend actually has two old business areas and one new one. As you come into town from the south you will be in the newest one. Behind the Safeway on the left is a parking lot where you can leave your rig and ride a shuttle in to town, parking for big rigs is very limited downtown. Just past the Safeway you will see the Visitor Information Center on the right. They can give you a map of the town with directions for finding some of the more interesting older buildings.

PORT TOWNSEND

Continuing straight ahead you will soon find yourself in the **historic waterfront district** of town along Water Street. The handsome old buildings in this part of town are filled with shops and restaurants, this is the place to do some poking around.

The third business area in Port Townsend is up on the bluff overlooking the waterfront. This was once the "sophisticated" shopping area, a place to shop for ladies who didn't want to have to visit the rowdy waterfront area below. To get there you'll probably drive. While you are doing that take the time to wend your way to the north and take a look at **Fort Warden**. The fort occupies a commanding position near Point Wilson. Now a state-owned conference center, the fort was once one of three that guarded the entrance to the sound. The **Coast Artillery Museum** at the fort will show you how it all worked. Fort Warden also has an excellent campground, just the place if you don't mind being outside walking range of the downtown area.

Port Townsend celebrates a **Rhododendron Festival** in May and a **Wooden Boat Festival** in September.

You will notice that there is a ferry dock in Port Townsend. Using it you can make the short crossing to Whidbey Island. Our Tour 5 passes nearby. It is also possible to take a passenger ferry (no vehicles) from Port Townsend to either Victoria, B.C. or to Seattle.

Port Townsend Area Campgrounds

Point Hudson Resort and Marina 🔲 MED 🔲🔲🔲🔲🔲🔲   103 Hudson St., P.O. Box 1180, Port Townsend, WA 98368; 360 385-2828 or 800 826-3854 for reservations; http:// portofporttownsend.dst.wa.us/marine/pthudson.html; 60 sites, open all year - For convenience it is hard to beat this little campground. It is located right on Point Hudson which is at the north end of Port Townsend's waterside business area. From this campground you can easily stroll over to shop or visit a restaurant in the evening. The resort was once a Coast Guard station and the tidy white-painted buildings maintain the atmosphere. So does the location on the point where you can keep an eye on all the passing ships, ferries, and yachts. The campground is not difficult to find. The main drag along the waterfront is known as Water Street. As you approach the end of the street you will see the RVs directly ahead. You must jog left one block to find the entrance road at the end of Washington Street.

Fort Warden State Park and Conference Center 🔲 MED 🔲🔲🔲🔲🔲🔲🔲🔲   200 Battery Way, Port Townsend, WA 98368; 360 385-4730 for reservations; http:// www.olympus.net/ftworden/; 80 sites, open all year - This is a huge state park on the grounds of a former military base. The RV sites are in two areas: those near the ocean have full hookups while those up the hill have electricity and water with a nearby dump station. This is a scenic and interesting place, the only drawback is that the downtown area is some two miles south. Although this is a state park it is not on the state reservation system, you must make reservations directly with this campground. To find Fort Warden follow signs north from town, the distance is about two miles (3 km).

Jefferson County Fairgrounds 🔲 LOW 🔲🔲🔲🔲   70 sites, open all year - There are 70 pull-through sites with parking on grass. Each site has 20-amp. power and water hookups. The restroom building has flush toilets and hot showers. This is a good back-up facility for the area, other campgrounds are often full. The campground is located west of town, follow the fairgrounds signs.

DAY 3 - DESTINATION THE PORT ANGELES AREA
46 miles (74 km), 1.5 hours (to Port Angeles)

Along the Way - The direct route to Port Angeles doesn't take long, the distance is very short. You'll retrace your steps back to Highway 101, then follow that highway for 35 miles (56 km) west to Port Angeles. Between Port Townsend and Port Angeles you'll find yourself driving though the town of **Sequim**, a popular retirement town due to a well-publicized annual rainfall that is far less than that of most of Western Washington due to the "rain-shadow effect" of the Olympic Mountains to the southwest. Since Sequim is so close to Port Angeles that it is almost a suburb, see below for some attractions in the area.

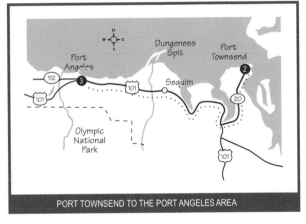

PORT TOWNSEND TO THE PORT ANGELES AREA

PORT ANGELES

With a natural harbor in a very convenient location at the mouth of Puget Sound it is no wonder that Port Angeles (population 18,000) is a fishing and ferry port. You can join a fishing charter for salmon or bottom fish or take a ferry across the Strait of Juan de Fuca to Victoria for a day trip or to join our Vancouver Island tour. For a view of the city and the mountains in the park to the south drive out **Ediz Hook**, the sand spit which forms the harbor. Port Angeles hosts the **Clallam County Fair** the third weekend of August.

The big attraction of Port Angeles is, of course, access to the northern reaches of **Olympic National Park**. The 17-mile (27 km) road up to **Hurricane Ridge** actually begins in Port Angeles. This is an excellent drive for those desiring views of the park's high country without much hiking. Thirty miles (48 km) east from Port Angeles on Highway 101 the **Sol Duc Road** also gives access to the park and hot springs there. You'll find hiking trails from both roads.

The presence of the park might make you forget the southern coastline of the Strait of Juan de Fuca. Don't let it, there are many coastal destinations in the region. Among them are the **Dungeness National Wildlife Refuge** on **Dungeness Spit**, the **Salt Creek Recreation Area**, and **Neah Bay** out near Cape Flattery. While you are out near Neah Bay you might want to follow the road that leads south to **Ozette Lake** 15 miles (24 km) east of town and hike the convenient (and essential in this wet country) boardwalks out to **Sand Point** and **Cape Alava** on the isolated Pacific Coast.

The retirement community of **Sequim** and the **Dungeness Valley**, 17 miles (27 km) east of Port Angeles, offers a surprising number of things to do. The **Dungeness Spit** is directly north of town, this is a national wildlife refuge. The 5.5-mile (8.9 km) spit is the longest natural one in the world and an excellent place to see seabirds. There is also a campground at the base of the spit in Clallam County's Dungeness Recreation Area. In town you might want to visit the **Museum and Arts Center** which houses exhibits related to mastodons dug up nearby. The find was unusual because there was a spear point found between the ribs of one of the beasts, evidence that they were hunted by early Americans. For more active animals there is the **Olympic Game Farm** located north of town, it is home to many that starred in TV and movies and has a large collection of endangered and unusual animals as well as a petting farm and aquarium. There are also a couple wineries in the area, the **7 Cedars Casino**, and a golf course.

Port Angeles Area Campgrounds

This is a big area with a fine choice of campgrounds. For those with big rigs who must have full hookups there are a number of fine commercial campgrounds near Sequim and outside Port Angeles. If you do not require hookups you will find that several of the larger Olympic National Park campgrounds are easily accessible from Port Angeles but that most are older national park campgrounds not really suitable for really large modern rigs. The first campground listed below has hookups and an enviable location while the second is inside the park but still offers hookups.

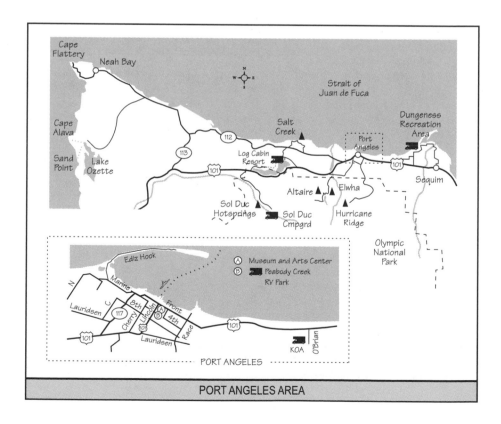

PORT ANGELES AREA

Log Cabin Resort `HIGH` 3183 East Beach Road, Port Angeles, WA 98363; 360 928-3325; www.logcabinresort.net; 40 sites, open April 1 through October 31 - About 15 miles (24 km) west of Port Angeles is beautiful Lake Crescent. On the north shore is an old resort, originally established in 1895. There is a small lodge with restaurant and cabins, swimming and fishing out front, and a fine but rustic little RV park. To reach the resort start at the junction of Hwy. 101 and Hwy. 112 which is about 3 miles west of Port Angeles. Drive west 10.8 miles (17.4 km) on Hwy. 101 Just before you reach the east end of the lake East Beach Rd., a well-marked little paved road, goes right. Follow the road behind cabins along the lake shore for about three miles (5 km) to the resort.

Sol Duc Campground `MED` P.O. Box 2169, Port Angeles, WA 98362; 360 327-3583; www.northolympic.com/solduc; 20 sites, open mid-May to mid-October, varies - There are two choices for campers near the hot springs at Sol Duc. There is a park campground with medium-sized unserviced sites and also a commercial campground for self-contained rigs with room for very large rigs offering electrical hookups. The icon information above is for the commercial campground. The park service campground facilities are much like those at Mora and the Hoh Valley described elsewhere in this guide, it has 80 sites. To reach the campgrounds drive west from the junction of Hwy. 101 and Hwy. 112 about 3 miles west of Port Angeles for 26 miles (42 km) to the Sol Duc entrance road, then south 13 (21 km) miles to the hot springs and campground.

Port Angeles KOA `HIGH` 80 O'Brien Rd., Port Angeles, WA 98362; 360 457-5916 or 800 KOA-7558 for reservations; 90 sites, open

SOL DUC HOT SPRINGS

April 1 to Nov 1 - This campground is convenient to both the Sequim area and Port Angeles because it is between the two. It has just what you would expect from a full-service KOA. Drive east from Port Angeles for 7 miles (11 km) to O'Brian road, turn south and in a half-block you'll see the campground on the right.

🚐 **Peabody Creek RV Park** 127 S Lincoln, Port Angeles, WA 98362; 360 457-7092 or 800 392-2361 for reservations; http://members.tripod.com/peabodyrv/; 41 sites, open all year - If you want to be right in town this is the campground for you. To get there turn inland from Front Street on Lincoln and drive two blocks.

🚐 **Dungeness Recreation Area** 65 sites, open February 1 through Octobert 1 - A convenient place to stay to explore the Dungeness Spit and Dungeness Valley-Sequim area. It is within easy walking distance of the spit. To get there drive 4 miles (6 km) west from Sequim on Hwy. 101, turn right on Kitchen Road and follow it 4 miles (6 km) north to the campground.

DAY 4 - DESTINATION FORKS, HOH VALLEY AND RIALTO BEACH
56 miles (90 km), 1.5 hours (to Forks)

Along the Way - As you head west from the intersection of the Sol Duc road with Highway 101 you will cross one of the less interesting regions of the loop around the Olympics. The highway passes through an area of privately held forest land, much of it has been logged and replanted.

After 15 miles (24 km) you'll reach a town, really a populated intersection, called **Sappho**. Highway 113, which joins the highway here, will take you north to join Highway 112 as it connects Port Angeles with **Neah Bay**. This can be an interesting side trip if you have the time, plan on at least 3 hours even if you only drive out to Neah Bay and back.

Finally, 11 miles (18 km) from Sappho you'll pass the road out to La Push and Mora and in another 2 miles (3 km) enter Forks.

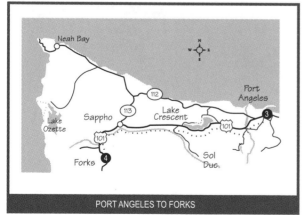

PORT ANGELES TO FORKS

FORKS, THE HOH VALLEY, AND RIALTO BEACH

When logging was going full blast Forks (population 2,900) was known as the logging capital of the Olympic Peninsula. It probably still is the logging capital but the tourist industry is getting more and more important to the local economy. This might seem surprising since Forks is the wettest town in the state with an annual rainfall of over 100 inches. Forks is the center of an interesting region on the western border of the Olympic National Park. From Forks there is good access to an otherwise isolated coastal section of the park as well as the rain forests on the western slope of the Olympic Mountains.

The town of **Forks** lines both sides of Highway 101. You'll find several restaurants as well as a couple of good-sized supermarkets, the best places to get supplies on the northwest side of the peninsula. On the east side of the highway you'll spot a **National Park Information Center**, recently moved from a location at the ranger station a few miles north of town. South of town is the **Forks Visitor's Center** and next door the **Forks Timber Museum**. Forks holds an annual celebration during the week ending with the **Fourth of July**, it has traditional logging contests as well as a fun run and other activities.

From Highway 101 just north of Forks a 14-mile (23 km) paved road runs west to the coast. At the end of the road is the Quileute Indian town of **La Push**. Just before reaching La Push you'll see parking areas for the National Park's **Third Beach** and **Second Beach**. You must hike to these beaches, 1.3 miles (2 km) to Third and .5 miles (.8 km) to Second. **First Beach** is accessible from La Push itself.

About 11 miles (18 km) along the road from Forks to La Push you'll reach **Mora Junction**. If you turn north here you'll be able to follow a road leading past the big national park campground called Mora to **Rialto Beach**. Rialto Beach is located just across the Quillayute River outlet from LaPush, it is one of the most scenic of all

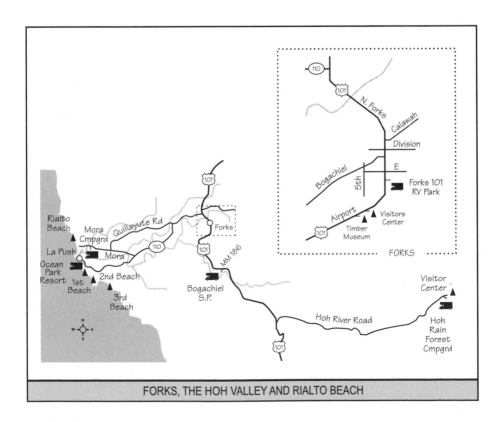

FORKS, THE HOH VALLEY AND RIALTO BEACH

RIALTO BEACH

Washington State beaches and is known for its accumulation of driftwood.

Also easily accessible from Forks is the Olympic National Park's **Hoh Valley Rain Forest**. Drive south from Forks for 12 miles (19 km), then turn east on the Hoh River Road. This 18-mile (29 km) paved road leads to the Hoh Valley Rain Forest Visitor Center. There is a large national park campground near the visitor center and there are several very good hiking trails allowing you to wander through one of the very few temperate rain forests in the world.

Forks Area Campgrounds

Mora Campground `LOW` 94 sites, open all year - This large Olympic National Park campground sits in a grove of huge hemlocks and Sitka spruces along the Quillayute River some two miles (3 km) from the coast at Rialto Beach. The park service worries about big rigs here but there are several sites where they will fit. Give up the hookups for a night to appreciate the lush vegetation and huge trees of this part of the state. It is located right off the road to Rialto Beach, you can't miss it.

La Push Ocean Park Resort `LOW` 770 Main Street, P.O. Box 67, La Push, WA 98350; 360 374-5267 or 800 487-1267 for reservations; 52 sites, open all year - This RV park sits behind First Beach in the town of La Push. Just drive to La Push, you'll see it on the left as you reach town.

Forks 101 RV Park `MED` 901 Hwy. 101 South, P.O. Box 1041, Forks, WA 98331; 360 374-5073 or 800 962-9964 for reservations; 50 sites, open all year - This is a commercial campground right in Forks. If you want to be in town, this is the place. It's on the east side of the highway near the center of town.

🚐 **Hoh Rain Forest Campground** [LOW] 🔺 ⬛ 🚰 89 sites, open all year - Another national park campground, this one is located in one of the most interesting places in the park, right near the Hoh Valley Visitor Center. This campground has plenty of longer RV sites for modern rigs.

🚐 **Bogachiel State Park** [MED] 🔺 ♿ ⬛ 🚰 🎣 🔥 💧 42 sites, open all year - This campground is right next to the highway but is protected somewhat by being in a grove of hemlocks next to the Bogachiel River. Only 6 of the sites have hookups. The campground is located six miles (10 km) south of Forks on Hwy. 101.

DAY 5 - DESTINATION LAKE QUINAULT AND THE KALALOCH COAST
67 miles (108 km), 1.5 hours (to Lake Quinault)

Along the Way - From the Hoh River Valley inersection, Highway 101 soon curves west to the coast. For about 12 miles (19 km) it runs along the ocean with frequent parking areas and trails leading short distances down the hill to the beach. **Ruby Beach**, the farthest north, is a good place to stop and walk down to the beach. Those red pebbles on the beach are not rubies, they're garnets. The island offshore is Destruction Island, it has its own lighthouse.

Watch for the **Kalaloch Lodge** above the beach just off the road, the Kalaloch Campground is nearby, so is **Kalaloch Visitor Information Center**. Consider taking a break here and looking around, you might decide to stay. The highway soon turns inland and passes through Queets. The gravel **Queets River Road** leads inland for 14 miles (23 km) from an intersection about 8 miles (13 km) east of Queets on Hwy. 101 giving access to trails and also a primitive campground inside the park.

Twenty-five miles (40 km) southeast of Queets along Hwy. 101 you reach the small community of Amanda Park. Quinault Lake is nearby, roads lead along both the north and south shores of the lake and on into the park.

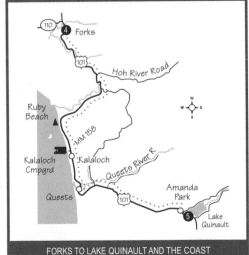

FORKS TO LAKE QUINAULT AND THE COAST

LAKE QUINAULT AND THE COAST

The Lake Quinault area provides visitors with very accessible rain forest access. The lake itself is actually part of the Quinault Indian Reservation but south of the lake is Olympic National Forest land and the north is Rainier National Park land. There are several campgrounds along the south shore of the lake and the **Quinault National Recreation Trail System** on the hillside

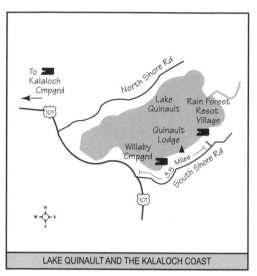

LAKE QUINAULT AND THE KALALOCH COAST

above provides an excellent way to get out in the rain forest among the tall trees on trails that are fun but not too challenging. The south shore is also home to the venerable **Lake Quinault Lodge**, built in 1926 and certainly worth a walk-through.

You can actually drive a 30-mile (48 km) loop that passes around the lake and about 14 miles (23 km) up the Quinault Valley into the park. Quite a bit of this road is gravel, it is not recommended for larger RVs.

For aggressive hikers there are a number of much longer trails that lead up the Quinault River drainage into the interior of the park and into the Colonel Bob Wilderness on the south shore of the Quinault River.

Lake Quinault Area Campgrounds

Campgrounds for big rigs with hookups are scarce in this region. Smaller rigs not needing hookups will find a wealth of places to spend the night however. Our primary campground choice is a private one on the south shore of Lake Quinault suitable for any rig. Several USFS campgrounds are nearby and there is a large national park campground on the coast.

Rain Forest Resort Village [MED] 516 South Shore Road, Lake Quinault, WA 98575; 360 288-2535 or 800 255-6936 for reservations; http://home.earthlink.net/~rfrv/RV_Park/rv_park.html; 31 sites, open all year - This resort has been here on the south shore of beautiful Lake Quinault for many years. It is located just down the road from famous Lake Quinault Lodge. All spaces are back-in ones with room for big rigs. A word of warning about winter camping at this campground. The sites sit very near the lake and in winter the lake level sometimes rises to cover them. This is unpredictable and if the lake is up the campground is closed. It is best to call ahead to check. To reach the campground just follow the South Shore Road from Mile 125 of Highway 101. The resort is about 3.5 miles (5.6 km) from the highway.

Willaby USFS Campground [LOW] South Lake Quinault Road; 21 sites, open mid-April to early September - This small Forest Service campground on the south shore of Lake Quinault has room for a few medium but not large RVs. Just follow the South Shore Road from the intersection with Hwy. 101 and you'll soon see the campground.

Kalaloch Campground [LOW] 175 sites, open all year - This Olympic National Park campground has a desirable location above a wild beach. It has a few spaces large enough for big rigs and is very convenient to the highway. The campground is located within walking distance of the Kalaloch Inn and park service information center. It is near Mile 158 of Hwy. 101.

DAY 6 - DESTINATION OCEAN SHORES AND THE NORTH BEACHES
57 miles (92 km), 2 hours (to Ocean Shores)

A long the Way - Back on Highway 101 and headed south you have a choice of routes. The main highway will take you directly to **Hoquiam** with little delay. From there you can cut west to the North Beaches. This is the route to take if you are in need of supplies, there is a better choice of stores in Hoquiam than you will find in the little towns along the coast.

A more direct route, all on paved roads, takes you west on back roads to Moclips at the north end of the North Beaches coastal strip. From there you can follow the coast road south. This back road leaves Highway 101 at **Humptulips** near Mile 109 of Highway 101. Drive west 12 miles (19 km) to Copalis Crossing, then at the T intersection turn right and follow signs for Moclips north 10 miles (16 km) to a point on the coastal Highway 109 just south of **Pacific Beach**. From there you can drive south on Highway 109 to **Copalis** (8 miles (13 km)), **Ocean City** (11 miles (18 km)) or **Ocean Shores** (16 miles (26 km)).

OCEAN SHORES AND THE NORTH BEACHES

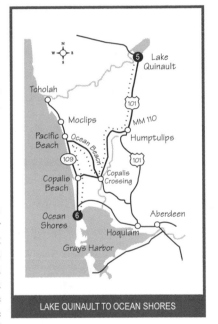

LAKE QUINAULT TO OCEAN SHORES

The **North Beaches** stretch from Ocean Shores on the north point of the entrance to Grays Harbor for about 30 miles (48 km) north to the Quinault Indian Reservation. The name North Beaches refers to the fact that these beaches are north of the mouth of Grays Harbor, there are also fine beaches south of Grays Harbor, we visit them on Tour 6 when we visit the Westport area. The North Beaches are the closest Pacific beaches to Seattle, they can be reached in about 3 hours by freeway, so you will find much more activity here than on the more remote beaches to the north.

There are a number of small towns along the coast. From south to north they are Ocean Shores, **Ocean City**, **Copalis Beach**, **Pacific Beach**, **Moclips**, and finally, inside the Quinault Indian Reservation, **Taholah**. The towns north of Ocean Shores are small, most have little more than a few motels, campgrounds, and restaurants. The beaches out front are wide and solid, driving is allowed on many of them. One of the big attractions is the razor clams, there are beds of clams in front of the towns, when the tide is particularly low and the season open you'll usually find hundreds of folks digging clams on the beach. The beaches are great when the tides aren't out too, you can ride a bicycle, fly a kite, fish, or just comb the tide line.

Ocean Shores is a different story. It's much bigger with a population of around 2,500. This town was developed during the 1960s as a resort and retirement haven. It

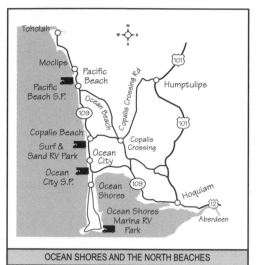

OCEAN SHORES AND THE NORTH BEACHES

has big beachside motels, a golf course, restaurants and shops, and even a lake and canals that offer decent fishing. Ocean Shores has a marina just inside the mouth of Grays Harbor, the commercial campground is located at the marina. You can arrange a fishing charter here or, during the summer, catch a small walk-on only passenger ferry across the mouth of Grays Harbor to Westport.

Ocean Shores hosts a large number of events. These include the **Beachcombers Fun Fair** in early March, the **Festival of Colors** in May, the **Ocean Shores International Kite Challenge** in June, and the **Dixieland Jazz Festival** in November.

Two larger towns, **Hoquiam** (population 9,000) and **Aberdeen** (population 16,600), are about 20 miles (32 km) east of Ocean Shores. These larger towns make a good place to pick up supplies. They also have their own attractions. The **Lady Washington** is based and often moored here, it is a replica of one of the ships in which an expedition led by Captain Gray discovered both the Columbia River and Grays Harbor in 1788.

Just south of Hoquiam, near the airport, you'll find the entrance road for **Bowerman Basin**. This is a wildlife refuge, during late April and early May it is a wonderful place to view thousands of shorebirds.

Ocean Shores and the North Beach Area Campgrounds

Copalis Beach Surf and Sand RV Park MED ▲ ⚹ ⊞ ⊟ ⚹ ⚹ ⊞ ⊟ 8 McCullough Road, P.O. Box 208, Copalis Beach, WA 98535; 206 289-2707 or 800 867-2707 for reservations; 54 sites, open all year - This is one of several campgrounds in or near Copalis. This one has an associated restaurant and lounge. It is located right along the beach, you can walk 100 yards through the beach grass to arrive at the water's edge. To find the campground follow the road toward the beach from the coastal road passing inland of Copalis. There's a big sign on the main road, the campground is on the left after two blocks.

Ocean City State Campground MED ▲ ⚹ ⊞ ⊟ ⚹ ⚹ 800 452-5687 for reservations; 178 sites, open all year - This is a very large state campground located next to the beach. Only a small number (29) have hookups, but the sites are large with room for big rigs. The entrance to the campground is a half-mile south of the intersection of Hwy. 109 and Hwy. 115 (the Ocean Shores access highway).

Ocean Shores Marina and RV Park MED ▲ ⚹ ⊞ ⊟ ⚹ ⚹ ⊞ ⊟ 1098 Discovery Ave. SE, Ocean Shores, WA 98569; 360 289-0414 or 800 742-0414 for reservations; 102 sites, open all year - This campground is located next to the marina where the ferry to Westport docks. That means that it is quite a distance south of the central business district but convenient to both Damon Point State Park and the Oyhut

State Game Refuge at the far south end of the peninsula. To reach the campground follow signs to the marina. As you arrive in Ocean Shores on Hwy. 115 take Point Brown Avenue (to the left after the sharp right turn as you arrive in town) and follow it south for 5.5 miles (8.9 km).

Pacific Beach State Park [MED] [▲] [♿] [🚐] [🚻] [🚿] 800 452-5687 for reservations; 64 sites, open all year - This is a state campground on a small piece of ground, there is less spacing between sites than is normal in a state campground. However, the sites are right next to the beach and about half of them offer electrical hookups. Big rigs are fine. The campground is located right in the town of Pacific Beach and is well signed from the entrance road to town.

DAY 7 - DESTINATION SEATTLE
130 miles (210 km), 2.5 hours

The drive back to Seattle is quick and easy. Follow Highway 109 through Hoquiam and Aberdeen. You'll hit 4-lane highway on the far side of Aberdeen and never really have to slow down much, except during rush hours, as you travel east to an intersection with Highway 5 just south of Olympia, then north through Tacoma to Seattle.

Information Resources

See our Internet site at www.rollinghomes.com for Internet site addresses.

Destination Belfair and Kitsap Peninsula

North Mason Visitor Information Center, East 22871 Hwy. 3, P.O. Box 1419, Belfair, WA 98528; 360 275-5548

Theler Wetlands - Mary E. Theler Community Center, East 22871 Hwy. 3, P.O. Box 1445, Belfair, WA 98528; 360 275-4898

Destination Port Townsend

Port Townsend Visitors Center, 2437 E Sims Way, Port Townsend, WA 98368; 360 385-2722 or 888 365-6978

Destination Port Angeles

Sequim-Dungeness Valley Chamber of Commerce and Visitor Center, 1192 E Washington, P.O. Box 907, Sequim, WA 98382; 360 683-6197 or 800 737-8462

Dungeness National Wildlife Refuge, 33 S Barr Road, Port Angeles, WA 98362; 360 457-8451

Port Angeles Chamber of Commerce, 121 E Railroad, Port Angeles, WA 98362; 360 452-2363 or 877 456-8372

North Olympic Peninsula Visitor & Convention Bureau, P.O. Box 670, Port Angeles, WA 98362; 360 452-8552 or 800 942-4042

Olympic National Park, 600 E Park Avenue, Port Angeles, WA 98362; 360 452-0300

Destination Forks and Hoh Valley

Forks Chamber of Commerce, P.O. Box 1249, Forks, WA 98331; 360 374-2531 or 800 44-FORKS

Destination Ocean Shores and North Beaches

Ocean Shores Chamber of Commerce, P.O. Box 382, Ocean Shores, WA 98569; 800 762-3224

Grays Harbor Chamber of Commerce, 506 Duffy Street, Aberdeen, WA 98520; 360 532-1924 or 800 321-1924

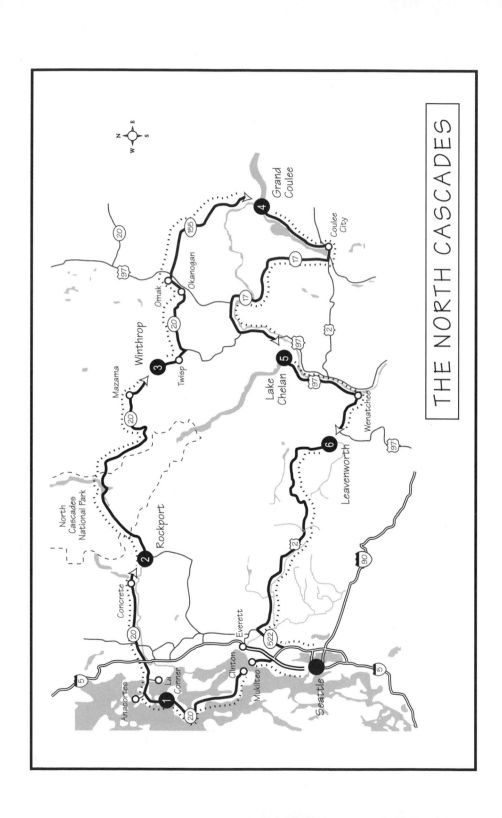

THE NORTH CASCADES

The North Cascades Loop

Top Attractions

+ Ferry to Whidbey Island
+ Deception Pass
+ North Cascades National Park
+ Winthrop and the Methow Valley
+ Grand Coulee Dam
+ Lake Chelan
+ Leavenworth Alpine Village

General Description

The well-known Cascade Loop is one of the most heavily promoted tourist destinations in the state of Washington. Deservedly so, this tour is definitely a great way to spend a week or two. You'll have a chance to enjoy a variety of landscapes: islands and seashores, rugged evergreen-clad mountains, piney ranchland, and the dry coulee country of Eastern Washington. The total distance is 601 miles (969 km), total driving time about 17 hours.

You'll start your journey with a short ferry ride to Whidbey Island. The ferry runs from Mukilteo, which is just north of Seattle, to Clinton. The drive up the island offers several interesting side trips and stops. You don't have to use a ferry to get off Whidbey Island, the bridge at Deception Pass at the north end of the island not only brings you back to the mainland, it offers you one of the most scenic views in the state. Actually, this bridge doesn't really take you to the mainland, it takes you to Fidalgo Island, from there it is easy to travel onward since this so-called island is really only separated from the mainland by what is little more than a wide canal.

From Fidalgo Island you'll travel on Highway 20 up the Skagit Valley to the

North Cascades National Park. After spending a night in or near the park you drive on eastward descending into the Methow Valley. Winthrop is the center of activity in the Methow, it's a friendly little town with a western theme.

Your route continues eastward the next day, you cross Loup Loup Pass, drive through the Colville Indian Reservation, and stop for the night at one of the world's man-made wonders, Grand Coulee Dam. The Grand Coulee area has more than just the dam, it's also a water-sports paradise.

If you liked Grand Coulee you'll probably also like Lake Chelan. It too offers a lot for water-oriented RVers, but there's more. The apple orchards on the surrounding hills give the valley its own unique flavor.

From Chelan you'll start back through the mountains toward Seattle. Your route takes you down the Columbia River and then up the Wenatchee River Valley through fruit orchards and past fruit stands. You'll spend the night in Leavenworth, an unabashedly tourist-oriented town with a Bavarian motif.

Finally, to return to Seattle you'll follow Highway 2 across Stevens Pass. At 4,061 feet this pass is about 1,400 feet lower than Washington Pass on the North Cascades Highway, it stays open all winter long.

The Roads

This tour almost exclusively follows two-lane highways. All are suitable for any rig.

Highway 20, the North Cascades Highway, is only open in the summer. Crews do not clear it of snow so when the snow starts falling in November the road is closed from Mile 134 near Diablo to Mile 171. It doesn't open again until about mid-April, the date depends upon how much snow fell the preceding winter.

Highway 2, which you will follow to return back across the Cascades from the east side is also a two-lane road. This is a well-traveled highway, you'll share the road with lots of others because many people like to drive this scenic route as an alternative to the massive freeway that crosses Snoqualmie Pass to the south.

Practical Tips

Like almost all the tours in this book this one is long if you really only have a week to do it. Fortunately you can easily bypass some of the stops and spend time in the ones that have the most appeal to you. A quick look at our route map will show you that it is particularly easy to bypass the stops at Whidbey Island and Grand Coulee, and thereby save yourself some driving miles too.

If you decide that the ferry ride to Whidbey Island isn't particularly appealing because of the expense or time involved you can easily bypass it by driving north on Hwy. 5 to Mount Vernon and then driving westward a relatively short distance on Hwy. 20 to the tour's first-night campgrounds. You'll retrace only a short part of this route the following day on your way to the North Cascades National Park.

As we mentioned above this is definitely a summer-and fall-only route since the North Cascades Highway (Hwy. 20) is not open during the winter. Let the opening dates for the highway define proper season for this tour, all of the other destinations visited have excellent weather for the entire time that the North Cascades Highway is open.

DAY 1 - DESTINATION DECEPTION PASS, FIDALGO ISLAND, SKAGIT RIVER DELTA

78 miles (126 km), 2.5 hours (to Deception pass excluding ferry)

Along the Way - For the first day's drive of this tour you have a choice of routes. If you have the time and feel like taking a ferry ride you can take the ferry from Mukilteo to Whidbey Island and then drive up the island to the evening's destination. If you want to save the ferry toll you can drive farther north and then cut west to the same destination. We'll describe both routes.

For the leisurely ferry route drive north on I-5 for about 12 miles (19 km) to Exit 182 and follow the signs northwest to Mukilteo. A ferry from there provides frequent service to the town of Clinton on the south end of Whidbey Island. A good two-lane highway runs all the way up the center of the island past the towns of **Coupeville** and **Oak Harbor**. Both deserve a stop for a look around, as does **Fort Casey** near Coupeville. At one time the fort's batteries provided coastal defense, batteries were also located directly across the channel near Pt. Townsend. A ferry runs from Keystone, near the fort, across the channel to Pt. Townsend.

If you don't want to take the ferry just drive north on I-5 for about 60 miles (97 km) to Exit 230. Drive west on Hwy. 20 to reach the campgrounds listed below.

DECEPTION PASS, FIDALGO ISLAND, AND THE SKAGIT RIVER DELTA

SEATTLE TO DECEPTION PASS

This area is a popular day or weekend destination for folks from Seattle. There are quite a cluster of attractions easily accessible from the campgrounds below. A tow car or small RV is a real advantage for visiting them.

Deception Pass is the narrow channel that separates the north end of Whidbey Island from Fidalgo Island. Two soaring bridges span the gap, they provide opportunities for some great pictures. The water in the passage below runs pretty fast, it is fun to watch boats riding the current. The pass is within Deception Pass State Park, you can walk beaches within the park on both the Whidbey Island and Fidalgo Island shores.

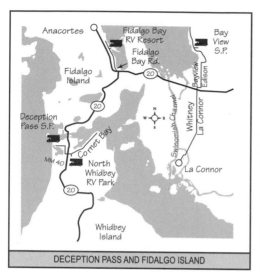

DECEPTION PASS AND FIDALGO ISLAND

Ferries run from the town of **Anacortes** on Fidalgo Island into the **San Juan Islands**. It can be hard to get a vehicle onto these ferries (service is chronically inadequate to the San Juans) but there is usually plenty of room for walk-on passengers. The islands are very scenic, we suggest the ride out to Friday Harbor on San Juan Island. You can easily explore Friday Harbor on foot, have a nice meal, and then catch another ferry back to Anacortes. This is definitely a day-long trip.

The **Swinomish Casino** is conveniently located just west of where Hwy. 20 crosses the Swinomish Channel.

The little town of **La Conner** attracts hordes of visitors from Seattle on any sunny weekend. It sits next to the Swinomish Channel separating Fidalgo Island from the mainland and has lots of little shops and restaurants. This is a particularly popular destination during the **Skagit Valley Tulip Festival** during the first half of April each year. Acres and acres of tulips and daffodils fill the fields of the Skagit delta between La Conner and Mount Vernon.

Deception Pass, Fidalgo Island, and Skagit Delta Area Campgrounds

🚐 **Deception Pass State Park** [MED] [icons] 800 452-5687 for reservations; 230 sites, open all year - This large state park has a very impressive location offering views of Deception Pass, trails, fishing and swimming in a nearby lake, and excellent beaches. Driving north on Hwy. 20 on Whidbey Island watch for the Mile 40 marker. Turn left at the stop light which is .8 miles (1.3 km) from the marker. From Deception Pass just drive south on Highway 20 for a mile (1.6 km) to the stop light, the campground will be on the right.

🚐 **North Whidbey RV Park** [MED] [icons] [GS] 565 W Cornet Bay Rd, Oak Harbor, WA 98277; 360 675-9597 or 888 462-2674 for reservations; http://www.whidbey.net/rvpark/nwrvpark.html; 101 sites, open all year - Located just a mile (1.6 km) from Deception Pass and right across from the entrance to Deception Pass State Park this campground is a nice commercial alternative to the state campground. Driving north on Hwy. 20 on Whidbey Island watch for the Mile 40 marker. Turn right on Cornet Bay Road at the stop light which is .8 miles (1.3 km) from the marker, the campground will be on the right immediately after the turn. From Deception Pass just drive south on Highway 20 for a mile (1.6 km), turn left on Cornet Bay Road, the campground will be on the right.

🚐 **Fidalgo Bay RV Resort** [HIGH] [icons] [GS] 1107 Fidalgo Bay Road, Anacortes, WA 98221; 360 293-5353 or 800-727-5478 for reservations; http://www.fidalgobay.com/; 187 sites, open all year - A very nice RV park next to Fidalgo Bay just outside Anacortes. Some sites are beachfront. To find it drive .3 mile (.5 km) northwest on the Highway 20W spur toward Anacortes from its intersection with

Highway 20S as it comes north from Oak Harbor and Deception Pass. Turn right onto Fidalgo Bay Road and follow it 1.2 miles (1.9 km) to the resort.

🚐 **Bay View State Park** [MED] [icons]   800 452-5687 for reservations; 76 sites, open all year - A good campground for birders, just down the road is the 2.2-mile (3.5 km) Padilla Bay Shore Trail which runs along a dike overlooking a tidal estuary. Also nearby is the Breazeale-Padilla Bay Interpretive Center. To reach the campground turn north from Highway 20 on the Bayview-Edison Road, the intersection is 2.4 miles (3.9 km) east of the Swinomish Channel bridge. Drive north 3.7 miles (6 km) to the campground.

DAY 2 - DESTINATION NORTH CASCADES NATIONAL PARK
57 miles (92 km), 2 hours (to Rockport)

A **long the Way** - From Deception Pass continue following Hwy. 20 northeast. After a few winding miles there's a stop sign where our Highway 20 meets what appears to be a major highway. Here a spur of Hwy. 20 (known as 20W) goes left to Anacortes, we go right following what is still the same Hwy. 20 we have been following up Whidbey Island. The road passes over the Swinomish Channel as a four-lane road, crosses farming country for a few miles, narrows to two lanes, and passes under I-5 and into the strip malls on the outskirts of Burlington. You'll soon see a sign for Hwy. 20 that jogs you north for about a mile before you are directed east on Avon Ave.

You are now established on the North Cascades Highway, still called Hwy 20. For the next 143 miles (231 km), until you reach a junction just south of Twisp, you won't have to make many route choices. The highway is well supplied with mile markers, you'll soon see Milepost 61 and then a sign telling you that Winthrop, on the far side of the Cascade Mountains, is 131 miles (211 km) ahead.

You'll want to make a stop at the **North Cascades National Park Service Complex Headquarters** just ahead near Sedro-Woolley. It's at about Mile 64 and located right next to the road. They can give you information about activities in the park

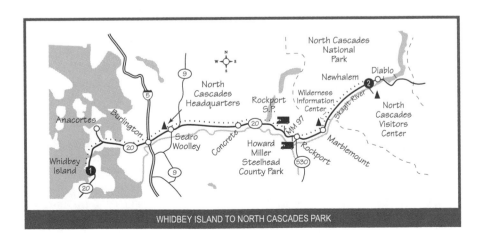

WHIDBEY ISLAND TO NORTH CASCADES PARK

ahead. They can also give you the status of campgrounds in the park and tell you whether any sites remain empty, no reservations are taken for camping sites in the park so this information is invaluable in making your plans for the evening stop.

Driving east from Sedro-Woolley you will be following the Skagit River Valley and pass through the towns of Concrete, Rockport, and Marblemount. Near Rockport Highway 530, which forms a loop from the south that starts near Arlington, joins the highway. If you want hookups when you stop for the night the two campgrounds near Rockport make a good place to stop. One is a state park and the other a county park. They are listed under campgrounds below. These campgrounds are outside the national park.

The stretch of road eastward to Marblemount closely follows the **Skagit River**. The Skagit has been designated a **Wild and Scenic River** and during the winter hosts one of the largest gatherings of **bald eagles** in the lower 48 states. The section of river between Rockport and Newhalem is a prime viewing area from mid-December through February. Eagles perch in trees overlooking the river or munch on decaying salmon along the gravel bars.

The town of Marblemount, at Mile 106, is your last chance for gas on this side of the mountains. Don't forget to check your gauge. Marblemount is also home to the park's **Wilderness Information Center** where you get back-country permits for the park.

At about Mile 111 you actually enter the park. Before you know it you will be entering the Seattle City Light company town of Newhalem. Before you really reach the town, at about Mile 120, you'll see the sign for the right turn into the **North Cascades Visitor Center** and Newhalem Campground. The visitor center is well worth a stop. It is the most important park service facility in the park, there are exhibits and a very well done slide show.

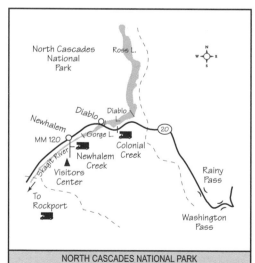

NORTH CASCADES NATIONAL PARK

NORTH CASCADES NATIONAL PARK

You may be surprised at the nature of this national park. Although we usually call it a national park in this book it is technically a national park complex. The **North Cascades National Park Service Complex** is actually composed of three parts: **North Cascades National Park**, **Ross Lake National Recreation Area**, and **Lake Chelan National Recreation Area**. Hwy. 20 actually never enters the national park itself, instead the park is split by the Ross Lake N.R.A., and the road passes through this N.R.A.

The reason for this is that long before the park was established three dams were built here by Seattle City Light to provide Seattle with power. They form three lakes: little Gorge Lake, larger Diablo Lake, and huge Ross Lake. There are also two Seattle

City Light company towns inside the N.R.A.: Newhalem and Diablo. The park itself lies to the north and south and has little in the way of man-made disturbances. Only trails and boats provide access.

Newhalem itself presents a very neat and well-tended appearance. Seattle City Light employees who work at the dams live here. Seattle City Light maintains a **visitor center**, it's a good place to check for information about local sights and hikes since most short ones are related to City Light facilities. Just a few miles further along, on a side road from near Mile 126, is another Seattle City Light town, **Diablo**.

Seattle City Light offers **tours** of its dams. There is a short tour that starts in Diablo and includes a ride up an incline railroad for a look at the top of the dam and the facilities there. No reservations are required for this tour. You need reservations for a second tour which starts in Diablo and includes a ride up the incline railway to the top of Diablo Dam, a boat ride up Diablo Lake to Ross Dam, and a chicken dinner after the tour in Diablo.

There are a wealth of **hiking opportunities** in this park. Passenger boats ply both Diablo and Ross Lake, you can catch a ride to the beginning points for many wilderness hikes. Register with the back-country ranger station in Marblemount or at the ranger stations in Sedro-Woolley or Winthrop (if you are coming the other way) before your hike if you plan to camp overnight. Also, you should be aware that if you park at a trail head in the national forests to the west and east (not the park complex though) you need a Trail Park Pass available at forest service offices.

Shorter hikes from the road that do not require registration include the River Loop Trail, Newhalem Rockshelter Trail, To Know a Tree Trail, Trail of the Cedars,

DIABLO LAKE

and Ladder Creek Falls Trail, all in the Newhalem area. There's also the Thunder Woods trail at Mile 131, the Ross Dam Trail (Mile 134), Happy Creek Forest Walk (Mile 135), and Ruby Creek Trail (Mile 138).

For us, however, the main attraction is the road. It has long reached as far as the town of Diablo. In 1972 a new portion opened that continued on over the Cascades. The road is spectacular because it travels through true wilderness. There are no towns, just mountains everywhere. This new road is only open in the summer, during the winter it is closed from Mile 134 to Mile 171. Open dates depend upon the snow, usually the road is open from mid-April to some time in November. Highlights of this new portion of road are the **overlooks** at **Diablo Lake (Mile 131)** and **Ross Lake (Mile 135)**, and **Rainy Pass (4,855 feet at Mile 157)** and **Washington Pass (5,277 feet at Mile 162)**.

North Cascades National Park Campgrounds

None of the campgrounds in the park offer hookups, and room for larger rigs is pretty scarce. Your best bet if you have a large rig is to stay at a campground outside the park. There are two good ones near Rockport.

Howard Miller Steelhead County Park P.O. Box 127, Rockport, WA 98283; 360 853-8808; 49 sites, open all year - This campground is in the town of Rockport. Our guess is that when the campground is full Rockport's population doubles. There's a small store and a tavern above the campground for limited necessary supplies. This is a large open grassy campground right next to the Skagit River. Sites are large and there are no trees to block your slide-out. You might not even notice Rockport from the main road. It is near Mile 98 and inside the angle formed by the intersection of Hwy. 20 and Hwy. 530. There are two entrance to the campground, one signed off Hwy. 20 which brings you down through the village, the other off 530 just north of the bridge.

Rockport State Park 800 452-5687 for reservations; 50 sites, open April 1 to October 31 - This state park campground is set in a grove of 300-year-old Douglas firs and cedars. It is located just a mile west of Rockport on Hwy. 20.

Nehalem Creek National Park Campground 111 sites, open mid-April through October and weekends in the winter - This is the nicest, if not the largest, of the campgrounds in the park. Access roads and sites are paved, sites that will accommodate larger rigs are limited. There are no hookups but there is a dump station. A beautiful National Park Service information center is part of the complex. The campground is on the western edge of Nehalem near Mile 120.

Colonial Creek Campground 163 sites, open early May to October - This campground is on both sides of the road at the point where Highway 20 crosses an arm of Diablo Lake. Roads are paved and sites are gravel, there are a few sites suitable for larger rigs in the south-side section of the campground. It is located near Mile 130.

DAY 3 - DESTINATION WINTHROP
94 miles (152 km), 3 hours

Along the Way - We'll begin this day's drive in Newhalem although you may have spent the night farther west in Rockport or east at Colonial Creek.

Gorge Lake, behind **Gorge Dam**, is the smallest of the three dam-created lakes. It covers 210 acres. The dam here was built in the 1920s. You can see most of Gorge Lake from the highway which passes along its northern shore.

At the east end of Gorge Lake the road crosses to the south side of the Skagit River. The original road goes on in to **Diablo**, the new road passes south of **Diablo Lake** which is the second largest of the lakes and covers an area of 910 acres. The road dips down to the shore of the lake at Colonial Creek at Mile 130. There is a large campground here as well as a boat launch. There is an excellent view of this lake from the **overlook** at Mile 131, just up the hill past the campground.

Ross Lake behind **Ross Dam** is the largest of the lakes. There is no road access to Ross Lake, the best view is from the **Ross Lake Overlook** at Mile 135.

Before you know it you will be past the lake area and climbing toward Rainy Pass. Once you leave the lakes you also leave the N.R.A., you're now in the Okanogan National Forest. **Rainy Pass** is 4,860 feet high (Mile 157). There's a picnic area and trails there. In fact, the Pacific Crest National Scenic Trail crosses the road at the pass.

Five miles farther along is **Washington Pass**, 5,477 feet (Mile 162). A stop here is essential, the view from the overlook is spectacular. You look across the valley at **Liberty Bell** and the **Early Winter Spires**, also straight down at the highway climbing from the east side of the pass.

From Washington Pass the road descends steeply for a few miles, then follows the Methow Valley on in to Winthrop.

WINTHROP

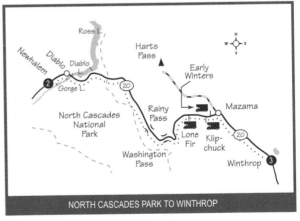

NORTH CASCADES PARK TO WINTHROP

Since the opening of the North Cascades Highway the little town of **Winthrop** (population 400) has become a four-season tourist Mecca. The town rebuilt itself as a western town by building false fronts on the buildings and covering the sidewalks with boardwalks. In the winter this is one of the top cross-country skiing areas in the state, and the surrounding hills are filled with summer hiking trails. There are a number of annual events celebrated in Winthrop including **49ers Days** during the second weekend of May, **Winthrop Rodeo Days** on Memorial Day weekend, **Winthrop Rhythm and Blues Festival** in mid-July, the **Labor Day Rodeo** and the **Methow Valley Moun-**

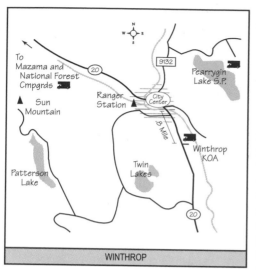

WINTHROP

tain Bike Festival in the first part of October.

Two miles (3 km) north of town is **Pearrygin Lake**. In the summer the lake offers a welcome respite from the relatively hot and dry countryside. There is a very popular state campground at the lake.

If you have a smaller vehicle you might want to drive the 19-mile (31 km) road up to **Harts Pass** and Slate Peak which at 7,448 feet is the highest point that can be driven to in Washington State. Consider yourself warned that much of this road is gravel and some sections have steep drop-offs and no guard rails. Trailers are not allowed on the latter portion of the drive beyond Ballard Campground. The road leaves Hwy. 20 at Mazama which is about 14 miles (23 km) west of Winthrop.

Winthrop can get very crowded, particularly on weekends in the summer. The best way to handle it is to play along and enjoy it. There are many restaurants and small shops and the weather is usually great here on the dry side of the Cascades. There are a fine selection of nearby campgrounds to use as a base.

The surrounding countryside is mostly within the **Okanogan National Forest**. There is a ranger station on Hwy. 20 just west of town where you can pick up information about destinations and hikes in the national forest.

Winthrop Campgrounds

You have the full range of campground types to choose from here in Winthrop. There are good commercial campgrounds, an excellent state campground, and even some federal campgrounds not too far out of town. The state park and several commercial campgrounds are located at Lake Pearrygin, about 2.5 miles (4 km) out of town to the north.

Winthrop KOA 1114 Hwy. 20, P.O. Box 305, Winthrop, WA 98862; 509 996-2258 or 800 KOA-2158 for reservations; www.methownet.com/koa; 110 sites, open April 15 to November 1 - This is a very pleasant KOA located on the banks of the Methow River about a mile south of Winthrop. 50-amp. power and large pull-through sites are available. There's a courtesy shuttle in to town. To find the campground just head out of Winthrop on Hwy. 20 to the south. You'll see it on the left exactly .8 miles (1.3 km) after crossing the bridge.

Pearrygin Lake State Park 800 452-5687 for reservations; 83 sites, open mid-April to October 31 - A very nice state park with big sites, some pull-throughs, full hookups, and lots of well-tended grass on the lake shore. To reach the campground drive north on E Chewuch Road for 1.6 miles (2.6 km), turn right on Bear Creek Road and drive 2 miles (3.2 km) to the entrance of the park.

🚐 **National Forest Campgrounds** [LOW] [△] [⛺] open May to mid-October - There are three campgrounds along Hwy. 20 west of Winthrop: Early Winters (16 miles (26 km) out), Klipchuck (19 miles (31 km) out), and Lone Fir (27 miles (44 km) out). Klipchuck is by far the largest with 46 sites. These campgrounds are suitable only for small to medium sized rigs and have no hookups. They have vault toilets.

DAY 4 - DESTINATION GRAND COULEE
99 miles (160 km), 2.5 hours

Along the Way - From Winthrop head south on Hwy. 20. You'll pass through Twisp and about 2 miles (3 km) south find the intersection where Hwy. 20 heads west over Loup Loup Summit. Watch carefully so that you do not miss the turn, although you would expect that WA 20 would be the main road it really appears to be a minor side road.

It is 29 miles (47 km) from the intersection near Twisp to the twin towns of **Okanogan** and **Omak**. Loup Loup Summit at 4,020 feet presents no real problems even for large rigs, there are two forest service campgrounds near the summit. While it is possible to bypass Okanogan and Omak by jogging south to Hwy. 97 near the western edge of Okanogan it is really not worth the bother, just head straight ahead through the towns, it is more interesting.

In Omak you will see the direction signs pointing right for Hwy.155. You'll pass across a fairly narrow bridge and then enter the **Colville Indian Reservation**. As you follow the highway the 50 miles (81 km) across the reservation to Grand Coulee Dam you'll pass across one more pine-clad summit, **Disautel Summit** at 3,252 feet, and also pass through **Nespelem**, the burial place of Chief Joseph, famous chief of the Nez Percé. Visits to his grave are discouraged. Just south of Nespelem you can stop at the **Coleville Indian Agency** for information about the reservation. You may also want to visit the **Coleville Tribal Museum** in the town of Grand Coulee.

GRAND COULEE

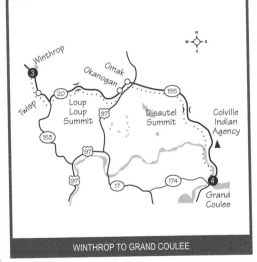

WINTHROP TO GRAND COULEE

As you drive into the town of Coulee Dam from the north you couldn't possibly miss the huge dam spanning the river valley ahead. **Grand Coulee Dam** was one of the big government programs of the 1930s. It was a huge project with several aims. It was to provide work for thousands of men. It was to provide irrigation water for a huge area. And it was to provide lots of electricity. Today there are 11 dams on the Columbia south of the Canadian border. This is the largest of them and by far the most

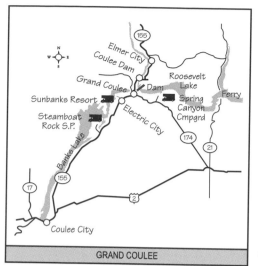

GRAND COULEE

impressive. It also provides a benefit that may not have been deemed to be very important by its planners and builders, the dam has created two huge lakes that are recreation areas in a region that almost always has beautiful weather during the summer.

The large lake behind the dam is known as **Roosevelt Lake**. Access to this lake from the Grand Coulee Dam area is limited. There is one federal campground on the lake near the dam with road access, but road access to the remainder of Roosevelt Lake requires that your travel eastward and detour away from the lake.

There is a second more convenient lake, however. **Banks Lake**, created as part of the Grand Coulee irrigation scheme, dominates recreation in the area. It stretches some 30 miles (48 km) south from Grand Coulee's towns, and is shallow enough to become quite warm in the summer. Banks Lake attracts water sports lovers from all over the state.

There are actually four towns surrounding the dam. **Coulee Dam** (population 1,100) is situated below the dam, **Elmer City** is downstream along the Columbia (north), **Grand Coulee** and **Electric City** are just above the dam along the shore of Banks Lake (south).

The dam provides the focus for many tourist activities in the area. The first stop is the U.S. Bureau of Reclamation's **Visitor Arrival Center**. It is located just below the dam on the left bank (as you face downstream). Coming from the north as we do you'll pass it as you follow the highway up the right side of the canyon to pass around the dam. Stop here to find out about the tours and evening laser light show.

During the summer there is a nightly **laser light show** projected on the face of the dam. It's a fun evening activity and takes about 35 minutes. The time of the show varies during the year from 10 p.m. to 8:30 p.m. depending upon when it gets dark.

There are **two tours of the dam** available, both are interesting. One tours the huge **Third Powerhouse** on the right side of the dam (facing downstream) and focuses on the power generation aspect of the dam, the other tours the **power and pump station** on the left bank and focuses on the irrigation aspects of the dam.

Grand Coulee Campgrounds

Grand Coulee has a fine set of campgrounds. Once again there is a selection of commercial, state and federal campgrounds.

Sunbanks Resort MED 🏕 P.O. Box 116, Grand Coulee, WA 99133; 509 633-3786; 152 sites, open all year - This large resort-style RV park occupies a peninsula projecting into Banks Lake just south of Electric City. This means that it is away from the highway, a fortunate circumstance. There are a variety of site types at this campground, you'll want to choose the right one for your lifestyle. There are a line of large sites designed for big rigs located just in front of the huge log main building. These have full hookups with 50-amp. power and are the only real choice if you have a big rig. They're good sites with views across a lawn to the lake. The rest of the RV sites in the resort have only electricity and water hookups, there is a dump station however. Many sites are on grass along the lake, you can tie your boat up in front of your rig. There are also quieter sites on the hill overlooking everything, choose one of these for a little more seclusion. The resort has a large log main lodge. It houses the reception office, a small store, a small restaurant offering breakfasts and hamburgers, and the restroom facilities. There's a sandy beach, a boat launch, and a dock area with rental boats of various kinds. To reach the resort head south just a short distance along the east shore of Banks Lake from Electric City.

Steamboat Rock State Park MED 800 452-5687 for reservations; 126 sites, open all year - One of the most modern and popular campgrounds in the Washington State park system, this campground occupies a scenic location below Steamboat Rock on the shore of Banks Lake. Reservations are essential all summer long. The campground is located 12 miles (19 km) south of Grand Coulee on Hwy. 155.

Spring Canyon Campground LOW 87 sites, open all year - A large federal campground with room for big rigs overlooking Roosevelt Lake about 3 miles (5 km) east of Grand Coulee on the south shore of the lake. There are no electric hookups but there is a boat launch and a beach as well as very nice big sites with great views.

GRAND COULEE DAM

Day 5 - Destination Chelan
106 miles (171 km), 2.5 hours

Along the Way - Today's route is rather convoluted, but it passes by and through some interesting sites and scenic country.

From the Grand Coulee Dam head south on Hwy. 155 along the eastern shore of Banks Lake. Basalt-topped cliffs dominate the landscape along most of the length of the lake. **Steamboat Rock**, almost an island, is impressive and hard to miss. At the south end of the lake you will join Hwy. 2 and pass through Coulee City and across the top of the low Dry Falls Dam which forms the south end of Banks Lake. A few miles beyond the dam take the side trip south for 2 miles (3 km) to the **Dry Falls** overlook. There is a small but interesting visitor center describing the unusual geological history of the region.

Back on Hwy. 2 watch for the intersection with Hwy. 17 in about two miles (3 km). You want to turn north here. Hwy. 17 goes north through farm land studded with scattered rocks. Eventually, after 21 miles (34 km) you will join Hwy. 174 and drive west to the Columbia at Bridgeport. **Chief Joseph Dam** is located here, you can take a tour or stop for the night at little Bridgeport State Park, there is a nearby golf course.

Follow the Columbia downstream toward Brewster. After a few miles you will see the sign pointing left for **Fort Okanogan**. Here you'll find another state information center which overlooks the confluence of the Columbia and Okanagan Rivers. Fort Okanogan was a fur-trading station located near the confluence during the 1800s. The actual sites (there were two of them) of the forts are far below near the rivers, you can look through a couple of sighting contraptions at the center to see where they once were.

Continuing south along the river you'll pass through Brewster and Pateros, and pass little Wells Dam. Finally you'll spot Hwy. 97 Alt branching right to climb the hill to Chelan.

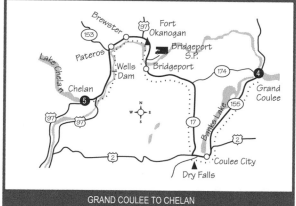

GRAND COULEE TO CHELAN

Chelan

The town of Chelan (population 3,000) occupies a moraine at the south end of 55-mile-long (89 km) **Lake Chelan**. Chelan is mostly known for two things in Washington state, its apples and the lake which is a popular recreation destination for folks from far around. In fact, most weekends during the summer find Chelan packed with visitors, many from west of the mountains.

During spring, summer, and fall the valley's **apple orchards** are hard to miss. There are about 10,000 acres planted in Red Delicious, Golden Delicious, and other varieties. One of the best things about Chelan is that popular as it is with tourists, the orchards remain an important part of the economy and the atmosphere here. Chelan apples are thought to be better than those grown in many other locations because the lake tends to moderate the temperatures in the valley.

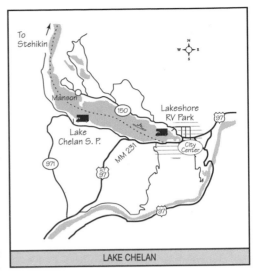

LAKE CHELAN

One of the best places to see apples is on the slopes above **Manson**, located about 8 miles (13 km) up the east shore of the lake from Chelan. The town promotes a 16-mile (26 km) **scenic driving loop** that offers views of the lake, orchards, and surroundings. It's also an excellent bicycle route. Manson hosts two apple-related festivals during the year: the **Manson Apple Blossom Festival** is in early May and the **Manson Harvest Festival** in the middle of October. There's also a **casino**.

The deep and narrow lake winds its way back into the Cascades, the far north end is actually inside the North Cascades National Park Service Complex. One of the popular things to do in Chelan is to take a ferry ride to **Stehekin** which is at the north end of the lake. These ferries do not carry vehicles. At least one boat each day leaves in the morning and returns in the afternoon, in summer more boats operate and there is even a high-speed catamaran making two trips each day. A one-way trip on the cat takes only an hour and 15 minutes. In Stehekin you can wander around the isolated little town or take one of several tours offered to visitors. Stehekin is an important access point to the North Cascades National Park, there is a park information center and a shuttle bus to help you access nearby campgrounds and trails.

Chelan itself offers a full plate of both sports and cultural related attractions. During the year the town hosts events related to arts and crafts, hang gliding, music, mountain biking, fine arts, hydro racing, running and fishing. There should be something for everyone

At the south end of the lake near Chelan the main focus on the lake is water sports. You have a choice of personal water craft, water skiing, even sailing. The water is a little chilly, even in the middle of the summer, but the air is warm so no one seems to mind.

Chelan Campgrounds

Lakeshore R.V. Park [HIGH] City of Chelan, P.O. Box 1669, Chelan, WA 98816; 509 682-8023; 160 sites, open March 1 through November 1 - The largest and most convenient of the Chelan campgrounds is located right in town on the shore of the lake. This is a city campground, it's very nice. The park has restrooms with hot showers, a swimming beach, tennis courts and a playground. Best of all, it's just a short stroll to the center of town as well as a nearby Safeway. The campground is on the lake shore near where the road heads out to Manson. If you follow signs for Manson from any of the entrances to Chelan you'll see it on your left as you start out of town.

🚐 **Lake Chelan State Park** [MED] [⛺] [♿] [🚐] [🍴] [♨] [🛶] [⛽] [🛏] 800 452-5687 for reservations; 144 sites, open mid-May to October 31 and weekends in winter - This state campground has lots of camping sites but very few have hookups. There's a swimming beach and a boat launch here, the campground is located 9 miles (15 km) from Chelan up the western shore of the lake. It is an extremely popular campground, reservations are a must all summer long.

DAY 6 - DESTINATION LEAVENWORTH
53 miles (85 km), 1.25 hours

A long the Way - From Chelan follow Hwy. 97 Alt west along the south shore of the lake and then south through scenic Knapp Coulee and down to the Columbia. The highway follows the river past **Rocky Reach Dam** toward Wenatchee.

As you approach the northern outskirts of **Wenatchee** watch for signs for Hwy. 2. Just before you reach the intersection you will see a sign pointing right for **Ohme Gardens.** These hillside gardens are well worth a stop.

Once established on Hwy. 2 you will follow the Wenatchee River Valley westward through fruit tree orchards. After passing **Cashmere** the valley narrows and the evergreens take over, before long you'll find yourself approaching Leavenworth.

CHELAN TO LEAVENWORTH

LEAVENWORTH

Like the town of Winthrop, visited earlier in this circuit, Leavenworth (population 1,700) is a small out of the way town that has re-created itself as a tourist destination. Beginning in the early 60s Leavenworth's business community began to build and rebuild using a Bavarian theme. Today the town, together with a stunning location surrounded by mountains, actually does look somewhat Bavarian.

Best of all, at least in the view of the businesses in town, some 1.5 million people each year visit Leavenworth to shop, dine, and enjoy the events scheduled throughout the year. It would be hard to drive through town on Hwy. 2 and not stop for at least a quick look around. A better plan is to stay at one of the nearby campgrounds and spend at least an evening.

Leavenworth is full of shops, restaurants, and art galleries. They provide a lot to keep you busy any day of the year. But the town also hosts special events. These include **Fasching** in early February, **Maifest** in early May, **Leavenworth Summer Craft Fair** in early June, **Kindrfest** at the middle of June, a **Summer Theater** in July, August and September, a **Chamber Music Festival** in July, **Wenatchee River Salmon Festival** in the middle of September, an **Autumn Leaf Festival** in late September, **Oktoberfest** in the first half of October, **Christkindlmarkt** in late November, and lots more. Check with the Chamber of Commerce for exact dates and information about additional events.

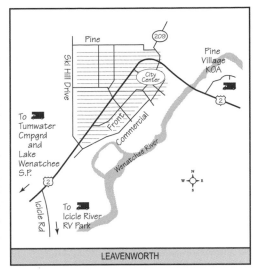

LEAVENWORTH

Leavenworth Area Campgrounds

The area offers a good selection of campgrounds. For easy access to the town you will want to stay in one of the commercial campgrounds, but there are also state and forest service campgrounds nearby.

Pine Village KOA Kampground 11401 River Bend Dr., Leavenworth, WA 98826; 509 548-7709 or 800 KOA-5709 for reservations; 135 sites, open March 20 through November 1 - This is the handiest place to stay if you are interested in visiting the village for shopping or to visit a restaurant. The large campground sits in tall evergreens above the Wenatchee River. There's a shuttle bus to take you in to town, the distance is less than a mile. This is a large KOA with a full list of amenities. Sites are mostly back-in although there are a few pull-throughs. Full hookups with power to 50-amps. are available as is cable TV. There is a swimming pool and hot tub, a small store, a game room, trails to the river, a playground, and all the other normal KOA features. The campground is located on the east side of town. You'll see signs pointing north just east of the bridge, the campground is .6 mile (1 km) up the road, the entrance is on the right.

Icicle River RV Park 7305 Icicle Rd., Leavenworth, WA 98826; 509 548-5420; 98 sites, open April through October. - Farther from town than the KOA (about 3 miles (5 km) out), this campground has beautiful sites and is not as busy. To reach the campground drive 1 mile (1.6 km) west on Hwy. 2 to Icicle Road. Turn left here and drive 3 miles (5 km) to the campground which is on the left.

Lake Wenatchee State Park 800 452-5687 for reservations; 197 sites, open mid-April to late October - This is a very large state campground in two different sections separated by a mile or so. The nearby lake is the attraction here, there's a popular swimming beach. To reach the campground drive west from Leavenworth on Hwy. 2 for 16 miles (26 km), then turn north on Hwy. 207. The entrance to the first campground is in 3.5 miles (5.6 km), the second is another mile (1.6 km).

🚐 **Tumwater Forest Service Campground** ⬜ 🔺 🔲 🔲   84 sites, open Memorial Day to late October - Conveniently located right off Hwy. 2 Tumwater Campground has large paved sites and is set in pine trees and situated next to Chiwaukum Creek. To reach the campground drive west on Hwy. 2 for 10 miles (16 km) from Leavenworth.

Day 7 - Return to Seattle
114 miles (184 km), 3 hours

From Leavenworth Hwy. 2 leads eastward and over **Stevens Pass**. The pass is 4,061 feet and located 33 miles (53 km) from Leavenworth. Stevens Pass Ski Area at the top of the pass is a popular destination during the winter for Seattle-area skiers.

Once past the summit the road descends steeply to the Skykomish River Valley and passes through a string of little towns: Skykomish, Index, Gold Bar, Startup, Sultan, and finally, Monroe. In Monroe watch for signs for Hwy. 522 once you reach the west side of town. Hwy. 522 will take you southwest to Hwy. 405, the Seattle ring road on the east side of Lake Washington.

Information Resources

See our Internet site at www.rollinghomes.com for Internet site addresses.

Destination Deception Pass, Fidalgo Island, and the Skagit Delta

Central Whidbey Chamber of Commerce, 302 North Maine, P.O. Box 152, Coupeville, WA 98239; 360 678-5434

Greater Oak Harbor Chamber of Commerce, 890 SE Bayshore Dr., P.O. Box 883, Oak Harbor, WA 98277; 360 675-3755

Oak Harbor Visitor Information Center, 32630 Hwy. 20, Oak Harbor, WA 98277; 360 675-3535

Anacortes Chamber of Commerce, 819 Commercial Ave. #G, Anacortes, WA 98221; 360 293-7911

Swinomish Casino and Bingo, Swinomish Casino Dr., Anacortes, WA 98221; 360 293-2691

La Conner Chamber of Commerce, P.O. Box 1016, La Conner, WA 98257; 888 642-9284 or 360 446-4778

Destination North Cascades National Park

Sedro-Woolley Chamber of Commerce, 714B Metcalf St., Sedro-Woolley, WA 98284; 360 855-1841

North Cascades NPS Complex, 2105 State Route 20 (Mile 64), Sedro-Woolley, WA 98284; 360 856-5700

North Cascades Chamber of Commerce, P.O. Box 175, Marblemount, WA 98267; 360 873-2210

Wilderness Information Center, North Cascades National Park, 7280 Ranger Station Road, Marblemount, WA 98267; 360 873-4500, ext. 39

North Cascades Visitor Center, Mile 120, Newhalem, WA; 206 386-4495

Seattle City Light Skagit Tours; 206 684-3030

Destination Winthrop

Winthrop Chamber of Commerce, 202 Riverside Ave, P.O. Box 39, Winthrop, WA 98862; 888

463-8469 or 509 996-2125

Wenatchee National Forest Winthrop Visitor Information Center, Building 49, Highway 20, 24 West Chewuch Road, P.O. Box 579, Winthrop, WA 98862; 509 996-4000

Destination Grand Coulee

Grand Coulee Dam Area Chamber of Commerce & Visitor Information Center, Box 760, 306 Midway, Hwy. 155, Grand Coulee, WA 99133; 509 633-3074 or 800 268-5332

Grand Coulee Power Office, Information Center, Code 1400, P.O. Box 620, Grand Coulee, WA 99133-0620; 509 633-9265

Destination Chelan

Lake Chelan Chamber of Commerce, 102 E Johnson Ave., P.O. Box 216, Chelan, WA 98816; 509 682-3503 or 800 424-3526

Lady of the Lake, 1418 W. Woodin Ave., Chelan, WA 98816; 509 682-4584

Wenatchee National Forest, Chelan Ranger District, 428 W Woodin Ave, Chelan, WA 98816; 509 682-2576

Mill Bay Casino; 509 687-2102 or 800 648-2946

Destination Leavenworth

Ohme Gardens County Park, 3327 Ohme Rd, Wenatchee, WA 98801; 509 662-5785

Leavenworth Chamber of Commerce, 894 Hwy. 2, P.O. Box 327, Leavenworth, WA 98826; 509 548-5807

Wenatchee National Forest, Leavenworth Ranger District, 600 Sherbourne, Leavenworth, WA 98826; 509 548-6977

Wenatchee National Forest, Lake Wenatchee Ranger District, 22976 State Hwy. 207, Leavenworth, WA 98826; 509 763-3103

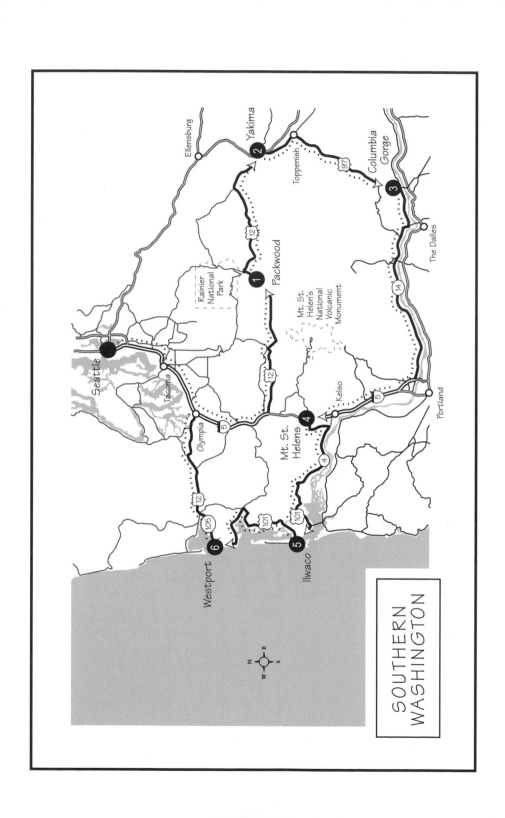

SOUTHERN WASHINGTON

Chapter 10

Tour 6

Southern Washington

Top Attractions

✦ Mt. Rainier National Park

✦ Yakima Wine Country

✦ Columbia Gorge

✦ Mt. St. Helens National Monument

✦ Long Beach Peninsula and Willapa Bay

✦ Grays Harbor

General Description

This one-week tour will take you to a large variety of landscapes and climates. In seven days you'll visit mountains, productive farmlands, dry grasslands, an active river corridor, and even the Pacific Coast. Of the three Washington state tours in this book this one visits areas that are probably a little less well-known than the others, yet in many ways it is the best of the three. You'll visit a national park, a national scenic area, and a national volcanic monument. The total distance covered is 767 miles (1,237 km) or an average of about 110 miles (177 km) each day, not at all an uncomfortable distance. Total driving time should be about 19.5 hours.

From Seattle you'll drive south on I-5 and then east to spend the night near (or in) Mt. Rainier National Park. The next day you cross the Cascades through White Pass to the Yakima Valley. From there you head southward to spend the night on the shores of the Columbia River. Traveling westward you will visit Mt. St. Helens National Monument and then continue westward along the lower Columbia River to the river mouth at Ilwaco and the Long Beach Peninsula. Finally, you'll circle north around Willapa Bay to Westport and then return to Seattle.

The Roads

All of the roads that you will travel on this tour are paved and fairly heavily traveled, big rigs will find no particular obstacles. Almost all of the roads are two-lane although about 200 miles (323 km) of the trip are on the I-5 Interstate or four-lane roads between Aberdeen and Olympia.

About the only places you might have some concern if you are driving a big rig would be the side-trips up the mountain in Mt. Rainier National Park and again up the mountain at Mt. St. Helens National Volcanic Monument. Tow cars are handy at these destinations.

Practical Tips

There is a lot to see and do on this trip. Although the tour is laid out as a 7-day trip you will probably find that you could use more time in the schedule to enjoy the various destinations. It is very easy to cut two or three days from the itinerary by traveling I-5 back to Seattle from Mt. St. Helens rather than making a visit to the coast. It would also be possible to spend an enjoyable week just visiting the beaches and not even crossing the Cascades.

If you have a lot of time it is also easy to combine this tour with several of the others. When you examine the maps you will see that a combination with the Olympic Peninsula tour makes a lot of sense. You could also combine with Tour 1 of the Oregon coast or Tour 3 of northern Oregon.

Day 1 - Destination Packwood and Mt. Rainier National Park
168 miles (271 km), 3.5 hours (To junction of Hwys. 12 and 123)

Along the Way - From Seattle head south on I-5. Avoid the rush hour, traffic between Seattle and Tacoma can be bad. Take Exit 68 south of Chehalis and follow US 12 eastward through Morton and Randle to Packwood

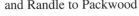

Mt. Rainier National Park

Packwood is near the southeastern entrance to Rainier National Park. This is the least-used access route to this popular park, a good thing since it means that the campgrounds here tend to fill up later in the day than those nearer Seattle and Tacoma.

Think of the park as having two centers of interest for vehicle-based visitors. One centers around the visitor center at **Paradise** on the south side of the moun-

SEATTLE TO MT. RAINIER NATIONAL PARK

tain, the other centers around the visitor center at **Sunrise** on the northeast side of the mountain. Of course, if you are willing to hike the entire park is open to you. From Packwood the drives to Paradise and Sunrise both make excellent day trips.

The **Stevens Canyon Road** access route to Paradise and **Cayuse Pass** access route north to Sunrise are both closed by snow during the winter. They usually open some time during May, depending upon the amount of snow that has fallen during the winter. No gas is available in the park. Make sure you gas up before leaving Packwood.

The drive to Paradise from the intersection of Hwy. 12 and Hwy. 123 some 7 miles (11 km) northeast of Packwood is about 25 miles (40 km). You'll probably want to continue on to Longmire, a distance of 9 miles (15 km), and then return. Combined with a few stops and short hikes this can make for a full day's drive. Leaving Packwood you follow US 12 northeast to the junction with Highway 123 where you head north into the park. Four miles (6 km) from the junction the Stevens Canyon Road to Paradise goes left. Near the junction is the **Ohanapecosh** Campground. Turn in to the campground, there is a **visitor center** here that makes a good place to introduce yourself to the park's attractions.

This region of the park is largely old-growth evergreen forest. An excellent way to enjoy the trees is a hike on the 1.5-mile (2.4 km) **Grove of the Patriarchs interpretive trail**.

From Ohanapecosh the highway climbs over Backbone Ridge, descends to cross the Muddy Fork of the Cowlitze River at Box Canyon, and then climbs through Stevens Canyon to reach the high country at Paradise.

Paradise sits at the 5,400-foot level of the mountain. Most people who climb the mountain start from the huge Paradise parking lot. There is a year-round visitor center here. You'll also want to visit the old Paradise Inn. If the weather allows you can follow trails through the surrounding meadows and enjoy the wildflowers and the views.

MT. RAINIER NATIONAL PARK

The traditional route to Paradise climbs the mountain from **Longmire**. You may want to drive down the mountain to take a look at the **National Park Inn** and the **Longmire Museum**. The short and easy **Trail of the Shadows** lets you explore the immediate area.

A good second day's drive will take you from Packwood along the east side of the park to **Sunrise**, a 33-mile (53 km) drive one way from the intersection of Hwy. 12 and Hwy. 123. En route highway 123 climbs the valley of the Ohanapecosh River to **Cayuse Pass** at 4,694 feet. From there you might want to make a short side trip east on Hwy. 410 to **Lake Tipsoo** just below **Chinook Pass** for great views back westward to the mountain (assuming good weather). Returning to Hwy. 123 you'll descend into the White River Valley a few miles until you reach the road to Sunrise.

It's 15 miles (24 km) from Hwy. 410 up to Sunrise. The road passes White River

Campground, the Frying Pan Creek Trailhead, and then loops its way up the side of the mountain to the meadows around Sunrise. You'll find a visitor's center here, also the **Sunrise Lodge**, and lots of trails. Sunrise is as high as you can get on the mountain in your car, 6,400 feet, and is only assessable and open from July to early September.

Mt. Rainier Area Campgrounds

Packwood RV Park and Campground MED A r ☕ ⛽ 🎒 🔥 ⏣ P.O. Box 309, Packwood, WA 98361; 360 494-5145; 89 sites, open all year - Located in the middle of Packwood, this RV park is a relaxed place in a relaxed town. You can stroll across the street to a restaurant or the grocery store, things couldn't be more convenient. The campground is set under large trees providing lots of shade. Parking is on grass with room for any size rig. Full hookups (50-amp.) are available, as are sites with electricity and water only. Some sites are pull-throughs. There is a restroom with flush toilets and hot showers, a laundry, and a dump station. The campground sits near the center of town, it is well-signed and hard to miss.

Ohanapecosh Campground LOW A ☕ ⛽ 🔥 800 365-2267 for reservations; 205 sites, open late May to mid-October - A large national park service campground set in big trees near the southeast entrance of Rainier National Park. It has 205 sites, no utility hookups, all sites can be reserved from June 28 to Labor day and reservations are recommended for this period. Very large rigs (over about 35 feet) will not fit in this campground, slightly smaller large rigs will find just a few useable spots. There is a very convenient National Park Service information facility in the campground. You can make reservations for Rainier National Park campgrounds up to five months in advance. To make them call 800 365-CAMP or use the internet at reservations.nps.gov/. Do not enter www before this address.

La Wis Wis Campground LOW A ⛽ 🔥 100 sites, open mid-May through September 30 - This is a forest service campground (Gifford Pinchot National Forest) set in cedars, hemlocks and firs along a river. Most sites are short, a few will allow the use of medium-sized rigs. To reach the campground drive northeast on Highway 12 from Packwood for 7 miles (11 km), the campground entrance is on the left.

DAY 2 - DESTINATION YAKIMA VALLEY
65 miles (105 km), 2 hours

A long The Way - Highway 123 into the park branches off Highway 12 about 7 miles (11 km) northeast of Packwood. Highway 12 continues east over 4,500 foot **White Pass**. This road is open year round and presents no problems for larger rigs. The crest of the pass is occupied by the White Pass ski area which is probably best known for the Mahre brothers, these two Olympic skiers grew up skiing here. The climb from the intersection to the pass is 13 miles (21 km), have someone keep an eye on the back window for views of Mt. Rainier. Watch for **The Palisades** turn out, a good place to stop for the view and to see the interesting basalt cliff-side columns.

After the pass the road descends through dryer country, pines begin to appear. You pass Rimrock Lake behind Tieton Dam and follow the Tieton River through canyons rimmed by basalt cliffs. There are several small forest service campground along the way. Thirty-four miles (55 km) from the pass Highway 12 meets Highway 410, a summer-only route over 5,430-foot Chinook Pass, and together they soon become a 4-lane highway and continue the 17 miles (27 km) east to Yakima. Highway 12 meets the I-82 freeway just north of Yakima.

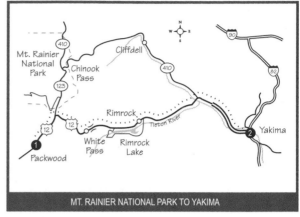

YAKIMA VALLEY

You'll probably be amazed by the many things to do and see in the Yakima Valley. The valley, stretching southeast from Yakima itself, includes the towns of Union Gap, Wapato, Toppenish, Zilah, Granger, Grandview, Sunnyside and Prosser. The Yakima Valley can be hot in the middle of the summer, spring and summer visits are great. Here are just a few of the offerings.

In Yakima (population 55,000) the **Yakima Valley Museum** is excellent, it has displays covering the Oregon Trail, Yakama Indians, Chief Justice William O. Douglas, and horse-drawn vehicles. Another good museum is in Union Gap, this is the

CAMP IN A TEEPEE AT THE YAKAMA NATION RV RESORT

Central Washington Agricultural Museum. It does a good job on the agricultural aspect of the valley's history. It's big with farm machinery, a tool museum, and 18 display buildings.

You might consider a drive north through the **Yakima River Canyon**. Highway 821 leaves the I-82 freeway about four miles (6 km) north of Yakima and follows the river for 27 miles (44 km) north to Ellensburg. The river is a favorite of fly fishermen and summer river rafters.

The irrigated Yakima Valley has long been an important fruit-growing center and in recent years has also become the wine center of Washington state. There are many **wineries with wine tasting rooms** and gift shops throughout the valley. The best way to visit is in your own vehicle, pick up a wine tour pamphlet and map at any visitor center or commercial campground. An added bonus is that throughout the valley you'll find stands offering fresh fruits and vegetables. Offerings vary, it just depends upon what is in season.

There's a large Latin population in the Yakima valley making this a great place for **Mexican food and specialties**. One favorite seems to be the El Ranchito complex just south of Zilah. They have inexpensive food, a bakery, Mexican groceries and crafts, and even a tortilla factory. There's good parking for big rigs across the street.

The huge 1.4 million-acre **Yakama Nation Reservation** stretches westward from

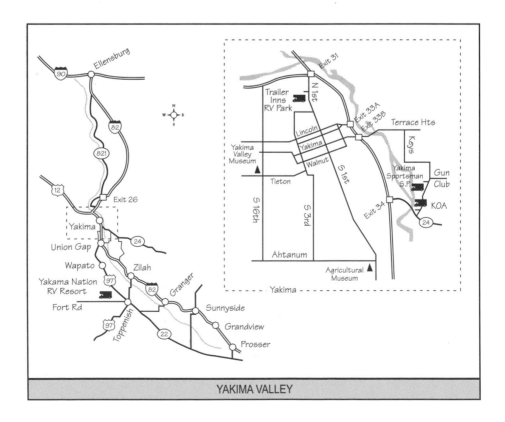

YAKIMA VALLEY

the Yakima Valley all the way to Mt. Adams. Near Toppenish you'll find a cluster of Yakama Nation-owned attractions including the **Yakama Nation Cultural Center** and restaurant, the **Yakama Nation Legends Casino**, and the **Yakama Nation Resort RV Park**.

The town of **Toppenish** (population 7,500) is the commercial center for the reservation. It is known for the outdoor murals painted on the buildings around town, some fifty of them in all. There's also the **American Hop Museum** with everything you ever wanted to know about hops.

The most popular annual event in the valley is probably the **Central Washington State Fair** in the latter part of September and first part of October, it offers a rodeo and the other things you would expect of a large state fair.

Yakima Area Campgrounds

Yakama Nation RV Resort 280 Buster Road, Toppenish, WA 98948; 509 865-2000 or 800 874-3087 for reservations; 95 sites, open all year - This large modern campground (opened in 1992) is conveniently located for visiting the wine tasting rooms in the Zilah area. A bonus is that both the Yakama Nation Cultural Center and Legends Casino are nearby. The spacious campground has 95 full-hookup RV spaces, tent sites, and even rental teepees. Parking is on paved back-in and pull-through sites surrounded by well-clipped grass and electricity is 30- and 50-amp. Facilities include swimming pool and spa, a weight room, basketball and volleyball courts, and a very popular one-mile walking and jogging track around the campground. Just next door is the Yakama Nation Cultural Center. It has a restaurant offering buffets and cultural favorites like salmon, buffalo, and fry bread. There is also a theater, a museum, a library, and a gift shop. The Legends Casino is about a half-mile from the campground. The campground is some 17 miles (27 km) south of Yakima along Hwy. 82. Driving south on I-84 from Yakima, take the Highway 97 Exit (Exit 37) and watch for the cultural center on the right in 14 miles (23 km) just north of Toppenish. It is well signed and located just west of the highway with excellent access.

Yakima Sportsman State Park 800 452-5687 for reservations; 65 sites, open all year - A medium-sized and heavily used campground due to its location near the city, this park offers the normal excellent state campground amenities in a convenient location. From I-84 in Yakima (Exit 34) take Hwy. 24 (also known as E. Nob Hill Blvd) east .7 mile (1.1 km), turn north on Keyes Rd. The campground is 1 mile (1.6 km) north on the left.

KOA RV, Tent & Kabin Resort 1500 Keys Rd., Yakima, WA 98901; 509 248-5882 or 800 KOA-5773 for reservations; 143 sites, open all year - Located very near Yakima Sportsman State Park, this campground has a pleasant out of town ambiance yet is near central Yakima. It offers 50-amp. power and the normal KOA amenities. Take Exit 34 from I-84, drive east .7 mile (1.1 km), turn north on Keyes Road, you'll see the campground on your left immediately.

Trailer Inns RV Park 1610 North First Street, Yakima, WA 98901; 509 452-9561or 800 659-4784 for reservations; 154 sites, open all year - This commercial campground has an urban Yakima location with bus service and convenient access to the Yakima green belt bike trail nearby. Take Exit 31 from I-82 and drive .2 miles (.3 km) south on First Street, the entrance is on the right.

DAY 3 - DESTINATION MARYHILL AND THE COLUMBIA GORGE
79 miles (127 km), 2 hours

Along The Way - Highway 97 branches off I-82 just south of Union Gap. For the first 15 miles (24 km) it is a four-lane highway with some side road access.

Just outside Toppenish after passing the Yakama Nation Heritage Center, the road branches to the right and becomes a two lane highway. This part of the drive, from Union Gap until crossing Satus Pass about 34 miles (55 km) south of Toppenish, is on the Yakama Indian Reservation. It is mostly grasslands with the occasional wooded drainage. As the road climbs you will encounter more trees.

After crossing Satus Pass (3,107 feet) and entering Klickitat County don't be surprised if you encounter a good cross-wind. The Columbian Gorge is famous for its winds, and they often extend far inland from the river.

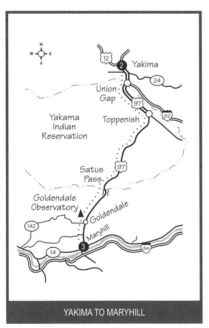

YAKIMA TO MARYHILL

Sixteen miles (26 km) south of the pass you'll pass the town of **Goldendale**, a good place to gas up. Goldendale is home of the **Goldendale Observatory**. In the evening visitors are allowed to use the telescope here to view the planets and stars. The observatory is located in Goldendale Observatory State Park just north of town, a good spot for views of mounts Hood, St. Helens, Adams, and Rainier.

After passing Goldendale you'll soon start descending into the Columbia gorge. Highway 97 meets Highway 14 which follows the river's north shore. Follow the signs for Highway 97 as it jogs down the steep hillside to the river.

MARYHILL AND THE COLUMBIA GORGE

The Columbia Gorge actually extends from Maryhill west for about 90 miles (145 km). The region we've chosen for our stop is one of the more interesting on the Washington side. There are several unusual sights nearby, it is a small fruit-growing region, and the river offers both interesting dams and windsurfing.

In the immediate vacinity are two sights connected with the eccentric railroad heir Sam Hill. Hill was the son-in-law of railroad baron James J. Hill, builder of the Great Northern Railway. Hill's story is too involved to relate here, but you'll become familiar with it as you take a look at the two structures he built nearby.

The first is a concrete replica of Stonehenge in England. This **Northwest Stonehenge** sits on a site which might have been more appropriate to a replica of the

Athens Parthenon. It overlooks the gorge from a hilltop just above the campgrounds mentioned below. To reach it you just follow the small paved road through fruit-tree orchards and the historic village of Maryhill, then up the hillside, a distance of about two miles (3 km) from the campgrounds. During the season you will find fruit stands between the campgrounds and the village.

Another nearby Sam Hill edifice is the **Maryhill Museum of Art**. Hill built the place as a mansion but didn't live there, reportedly because his wife refused to live in such an remote and windy place. At first glance you may think that Hill was hardpressed to find exhibits for the museum, the collection is very eclectic. However,

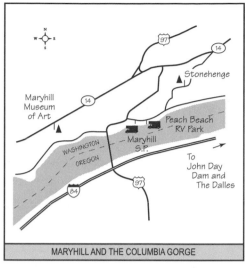

MARYHILL AND THE COLUMBIA GORGE

you'll find the varied exhibits well worth the stop, this museum draws a lot of people, especially considering its very remote and out-of-the-way location. The exhibits include an excellent collection of American Indian artifacts, memorabilia related to Queen Marie of Romania (a family friend), French fashion from the 1940s, and pho-

THE NORTHWEST STONEHENGE

tos of Sam's work with road building in the Northwest during the early part of the century. The museum is located a few miles west of the campgrounds along Highway 14.

You'll have a chance to see much more of the Columbia Gorge as we drive west to our next destination. Also take a look at Tour 3 for details about the south side of the gorge.

Maryhill Area Campgrounds

Maryhill State Park ☑☑☑☑☑☑☑☑ 800 452-5687 for reservations; 67 sites, open all year - This state campground is located right on the banks of the Columbia. It is very popular with windsurfers, expect it to fill up early on summer weekends. There are about 50 sites with water, sewer, and electrical (30-amp.) hook-ups. Large grassy areas separate the rigs and there is lots of shade. Restrooms have flush toilets and hot showers, there is a dump station, a swimming beach, and a boat launch. You'll spot the campground next to the river as you descend the hill on Highway 97. It is just upriver from the Sam Hill Memorial Bridge where 97 crosses the Columbia.

Peach Beach RV Park ☑☑☑☑☑☑ 89 Maryhill Hwy., Goldendale, WA 98620; 509 773-4698; 81 sites, open all year - Located right next to the state campground on the east side, this RV Park is so similar to the state park that it might be an extension. The major difference is that many sites have 50-amp. power and the price is slightly lower than the state campground.

DAY 4 - DESTINATION MT. ST. HELENS NATIONAL VOLCANIC MONUMENT
160 miles (258 km), 4 hours (to Silver Lake)

A long The Way - From the eastern end of the Columbia Gorge you can drive along the Washington shore on Highway 14. This is a two-lane highway and not nearly as busy as I-84 on the Oregon shore of the river.

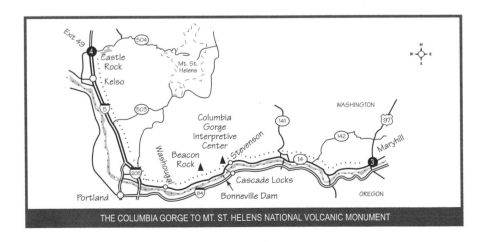

THE COLUMBIA GORGE TO MT. ST. HELENS NATIONAL VOLCANIC MONUMENT

The distance from Maryhill to the I-205 freeway at Vancouver Washington is 95 miles (153 km). Along the way you'll have excellent views of the far side, the river traffic and the windsurfers.

This is a long day's drive and there are several good places to stop and stretch your legs.

About 55 miles (89 km) west of the Maryhill Museum about a mile west of the town of Stevenson you might enjoy a visit to the new **Columbia Gorge Interpretive Center**. It is architecturally impressive and houses a variety of objects from the area including a fish wheel, a steam engine, and the largest collection of rosaries in the world.

A few miles farther west you reach **Bonneville Dam**. You can either cross the river on the **Bridge of the Gods** to Cascade Locks and visit the main visitor center (described in Tour 3) or visit the newer Second Powerhouse on the Washington side.

Back on the road you won't get far before you reach **Beacon Rock State Park**. The huge Beacon Rock is 848 feet high. It's the core of an ancient volcano and has a path (with railings) all the way to the top, a distance of about a mile and pretty steep.

Finally, 10 miles (16 km) before you reach Highway I-205 at Vancouver, Washington you pass through Washougal. The attraction here is a **Pendleton Woolen Mills factory store**, you'll see the signs from the highway. Take the 15th Street Exit.

When you reach I-205 head north toward Seattle, you'll soon merge onto I-5 and after driving a little less than an hour reach Exit 49, your turnoff for Mt. St. Helens.

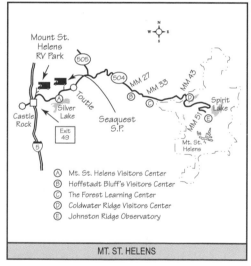

MT. ST. HELENS

When Mt. St. Helens blew on May 18, 1980 it created a unique tourist attraction. The thousands of square miles of devastated landscape make an impressive destination, and a lot of effort has been expended to make the mountain accessible. It is now the **Mount St. Helens National Volcanic Monument**.

While it is possible to approach the mountain from the north and the south the easiest access for motorized travelers is from the west. A new parkway, The **Spirit Lake Memorial Highway**, has been built which leads from Exit 49 of I-5 some 51 miles (82 km) eastward toward the mountain. Most of the parkway was built after the eruption, it is wide and beautiful, suitable for any rig. The only problem is that after the Hoffstadt Bluffs Visitor Center at Mile 27 the road climbs rather steeply, sometimes with seven percent grades. You can leave trailers or big rigs at the visitor center and use the tow car to drive on up.

Along the road there are now no less than 5 information centers. This must be the highest concentration of such places in the world and a trip to the mountain for most people is largely a drive from one center to the next. If you do want to get off the road and explore however, you can do so. There are a number of hiking trails accessible from the parkway.

The first stop is **Mount St. Helens Visitor Center**. It is some 5 miles (8 km) from I-5 and run by the Forest Service. It has exhibits that make a great introduction to your drive up to the mountain with background information about the eruption. The mountain is not visible from this center.

Stop number two is **Hoffstadt Bluffs Visitor Center** at Mile 27. This center is the most commercial of the five, it seems to be dedicated mostly to selling souvenirs and services. From here you can take a helicopter tour, have a meal in a large restaurant, or buy a souvenir.

The third center is called **The Charles W. Bingham Forest Learning Center** and is at Mile 33. This one is a Weyerhaeuser operation and explores the timber and logging aspects of the eruption. A huge amount of timber was blown down, much was destroyed but a lot was salvaged. Weyerhaeuser is now doing a lot of replanting. Don't miss this stop, we found it the most interesting of all the centers, it is very well done.

At Milepost 43 is **Coldwater Ridge Visitors Center**. This Forest Service facility has a great view of the mountain and exhibits about the impact of the eruption on the plants and animals nearby. There's also a cafeteria and a souvenir store.

Finally, at Mile 51, is **Johnston Ridge Observatory**. This new center is very close to the mountain, just 5 miles (8 km) from the crater. You can actually see the new swelling lava dome inside the crater because the crater walls on this side were blown out during the eruption. Johnston Ridge overlooks the devastated Sprit Lake and gives you the best idea of the massive devastation caused by the eruption.

Mt. St. Helens Area Campgrounds

Mount St. Helens RV Park MED ▲ ⌀ ⚏ ⚐ ⚑ ☐ ⊙ GS   167 Schaffran, Castle Rock, WA 98611; 360 274-8522; 88 sites, open all year - This modern RV park, not far from I-5 Exit 49, makes an excellent base for your visit to Mt. St. Helens. The sites are arranged on a terraced hillside. You'll find a variety of site types, the largest rigs will fit although sites do not have a lot of separation. Full hookups including cable and telephone are available. The campground can provide information and advice about a trip up the mountain. Amenities include a laundry, recreation hall, and playground. Nearby is an Imax theater offering a film about the eruption. To find the campground take Exit 49 from I-5. Drive east on Hwy. 504 for 2 miles (3 km). Turn left on Tower Road, you'll see the campground entrance on the right soon after the turn.

Seaquest State Park LOW ▲ ⌀ ⚏ ⚐ ⚑ ⚘ ☐   800 452-5687 for reservations; 92 sites, open all year - This state park offers sites set in huge evergreens. It is just off Hwy. 504 and a convenient location for a visit to the monument. From Exit 49 on I-5 follow Hwy. 504 east toward the mountain for 6 miles (10 km), the entrance is on the left.

DAY 5 - DESTINATION ILWACO AND LONG BEACH
90 miles (145 km), 2.5 hours

A long The Way - To reach the Long Beach Peninsula from Mt. St. Helens National Monument you will follow Hwy. 4, the Ocean Beach Hwy., which runs westward on the north shore of the Columbia River. This is not as fast a route as Hwy. 30 on the south side of the river. If you are in a hurry you can cross the river into Oregon at Longview and then return when you reach Astoria but you really won't save a lot of time.

From the Mt. St. Helens campgrounds near Castle Rock drive south on I-5 a few miles to Exit 39. This is marked as the exit for Hwy. 4. Follow the signs through Longview and soon you'll be leaving town and spot the river off to the left. The highway follows the river until it reaches Cathlamet, then it jogs inland for a short distance, returns to the river at Skamokawa, and then goes inland to climb over a range of hills. Near Naselle take the left onto Hwy. 401 which will take you back to the river. You'll pass the **Astoria-Megler Bridge** and spot Astoria on the far shore of the river. Ilwaco is just 11 miles (18 km) ahead.

ILWACO AND THE LONG BEACH PENINSULA

MT. ST. HELENS TO ILWACO

During the late 1800s the Long Beach Peninsula, like Seaside in Oregon to the south, was a beach resort frequented by folks from Portland. During the middle 1900s the peninsula was almost forgotten, but lately it has begun to be noticed again.

There are actually two centers of interest here. First there's the area near the mouth of the Columbia near Ilwaco. Second is the Long Beach Peninsula itself which starts just a few miles north of Ilwaco and runs northward for 28 miles (45 km). The peninsula forms the western border of Willapa Bay, famous for its oysters.

Ilwaco is a fishing town. It is located a few miles east of the mouth of the Columbia on the north shore. In addition to serving fishermen, the town also hosts the Cape Disappointment Coast Guard Station. This is the Coast Guard's lifeboat school, it is located here because there are lots of opportunities to practice in the wild surf of the Columbia bar. The Coast Guard station is actually right next to one of the nicest Washington state parks, **Fort Canby**. This park, in addition to a fine campground, has **two lighthouses**, a nice beach, miles of trails, and the excellent **Lewis and Clark Interpretive Center**. There's also a great view of the mouth of the Columbia, complete with ships crossing the bar, from the interpretive center or the nearby lighthouse.

Historically the **Long Beach Peninsula** (also sometimes called the North Beach

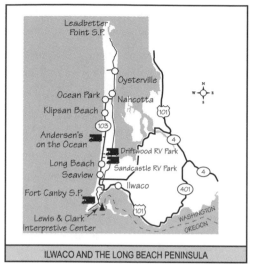

ILWACO AND THE LONG BEACH PENINSULA

Peninsula) was connected to the river port at Ilwaco by a narrow-gauge railroad. Today the rail lines have been replaced by a road, Hwy. 103. As you drive up the peninsula you'll find a number of small towns: Seaview, Long Beach, Klipsan Beach, Ocean Park, Surfside, Nahcotta, and Oysterville. Most of the tourist activities center around the town of Long Beach, that's where you'll find the majority of the restaurants and shops. The real attraction is out of sight to the west, it's the longest beach in the continental U.S. The peninsula finally ends at Leadbetter Point State Park, an excellent birding location. As you return (and if you are an oyster fan) stop in Nahcotta to buy oysters and other seafood at the wharf (in season).

Long Beach is definitely a tourist town, it hosts several annual events. Early in the season, in April, there's the **Ragtime Rhodie Dixieland Jazz Festival**. There's also a Fourth of July event called **Fireworks on the Beach**. Biggest of all it the **Washington State International Kite Festival** the third week of August.

Long Beach Area Campgrounds

You'll find a large number of commercial campgrounds along the Long Beach Peninsula in the towns of Seaview, Long Beach and Ocean Park. The ones below are just a start.

Fort Canby State Park [MED] 800 452-5687 for reservations; 245 sites, open all year - This is a large state campground. It is probably the best place to say in the area because it offers nice large sites with hookups near a beautiful beach, two lighthouses, trails, the north Columbia River jetty, and the Lewis and Clark Interpretive Center. It is easy to explore nearby Ilwaco and the Long Beach Peninsula using your car. Sixty sites have electricity, water, and sewer hookups while another 26 have electricity and water. Restrooms have flush toilets and hot showers. Near the entrance to the park there is a small store with groceries. Two miles (3 km) from the park entrance, in Ilwaco there are larger stores and other services. To find the park follow signs west from Ilwaco. There are actually two entrance roads, one going west from Ilwaco and the other following the water in a generally southwesterly direction.

Sandcastle RV Park [MED] 1100 N Pacific Hwy., Long Beach, WA 98631; 360 642-2174; 48 sites, open all year - Located just north of the central area of Long Beach so you can stroll into town. From central Long Beach drive north to 11th Street.

Driftwood RV Park [MED] [GS] P.O. Box 296, 1512 N Pacific Hwy., Long Beach, WA 98631; 360 642-2711; www.driftwood-rvpark.com; 55 sites, open March through October - Just slightly farther north than the Sandcastle, also convenient to town. From central Long Beach drive north to 14th Street.

🛏 **Andersen's on the Ocean RV Park**  1400 - 138th Street, Long Beach, WA 98631; 360 642-2231 or 800 645-6795 for reservations; www.aone.com/~andersen; 75 sites, open all year - Three miles (5 km) north of Long Beach but nearer to the beach than other Long Beach area campgrounds. You can walk through the dunes to the beach directly from the campground.

DAY 6 - DESTINATION WESTPORT
80 miles (129 km), 2.5 hours

Along The Way - To reach Westport you follow Hwy. 101 east from Seaview and then north around the eastern shore of Willapa Bay. At Raymond, just past South Bend and 45 miles (73 km) from Seaview, turn westward toward the coast again and follow the highway through North Cove and Grayland. You'll reach an intersection where the stub road to Westport meets Hwy. 105 and, continuing north three miles (5 km), soon find yourself in Westport.

WESTPORT

Although Westport (population 1,900) is just across the entrance of Grays Harbor from Ocean Shores the atmosphere is entirely different. Westport is very devoted to fishing, both charter and commercial. During the off season it seems almost derelict, but when the fish are running it is another story. The thing to do in Westport is take a charter fishing trip to catch salmon, halibut, tuna, or bottom fish. Also popular these days are boat trips out to the "whale hole" to watch the gray whales as they pause during their spring migration to Alaska during March, April, and May.

When you aren't out on the ocean there are other things to do in Westport. Along the waterfront next to the harbor there are a number of tourist shops and restaurants. Tourist sights include the **Westport Maritime Museum** and the privately owned

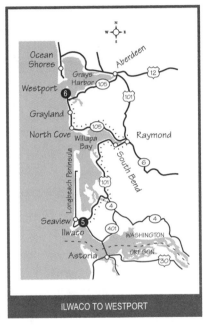

ILWACO TO WESTPORT

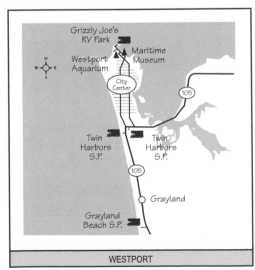

WESTPORT

Westport Aquarium. There is also a boat during the summer that ferries walking passengers across to Ocean Shores.

Westport hosts its share of events, there's something almost every weekend during the summer months. Among them are a **Kite Festival** in early July, the **International Nautical Chainsaw Carving Competition** in early August, the **Annual Longboard Surf Contest** about the middle of August and **The Westport Seafood Festival** is on Labor Day. Check with the Chamber of Commerce for more events and exact dates.

Westport Area Campgrounds

▣ **Grizzly Joe's RV Park and Boat Moorage** [MED] [⌇] [⊡] [⊵] [⊞] [⊡] 743 Neddie Rose Dr., P.O. Box 1755, Westport, WA 98595; 360 268-5555; 35 sites, open all year - There are several campgrounds in the town of Westport. Some are a block or so back from the docks in town, some overlook the north side of the marina. This is one of those overlooking the marina. It is well-maintained and well-run. A few sites are pull-throughs but the best sites overlook the marina, RVs drive forward into these and pay a few dollars more for the view. There is room for the largest rigs at this campground. All sites have full hookups with 30-amp. power. There is a spotless restroom and laundry. The campground has its own dock To reach the campground find your way to the north end of the business district and then follow the signs onto the point around the north side of the harbor. You'll see the campground on your right toward the end of the road.

▣ **Twin Harbors State Park** [MED] [△] [⌇] [⊡] [⊵] [⊞] [♨] 800 452-5687 for reservations; 298 sites, open mid-February to October 31 - This is a very large state campground about 3 miles (5km) south of town. There is good access to the beach. Only 49 sites have hookups and these are all closely grouped. The campground is located right at the junction where the stub road north to Westport meets Hwy. 105. The entrance is on the road toward Aberdeen.

▣ **Grayland Beach State Park** [MED] [△] [⌇] [⊡] [⊵] [⊞] [♨] 800 452-5687 for reservations; 60 sites, open all year - Farther south than Twin Harbors but nicer with the sites arranged off 6 rings. The campground has 60 campsites with full hookups suitable for 40-foot rigs. There is a nature trail through the dunes to the beach. From the intersection south of Westport where Hwy. 105 from the south and Hwy. 105 from Aberdeen meet drive south 4.5 miles (7.3 km) to the entrance which is just south of the small town of Grayland.

Day 7 - Destination Seattle
128 miles (206 km), 3 hours

The drive back to Seattle is an easy one, most roads are limited access highways. Follow Highway 105 east to Aberdeen. Turn eastward on Hwy. 12. You'll soon hit 4-lane highway and never really have to slow down much, except during rush hours, as you travel east to an intersection with Highway 5 just south of Olympia, then north through Tacoma to Seattle.

Information Resources

See our Internet site at www.rollinghomes.com for Internet site addresses.

Destination Rainier National Park

Mt. Rainier National Park, Star Route, Tahoma Woods, Ashford, WA 98304; 360 569-2211

Ohanapecosh Visitor Center; 360 494-2229

Gifford Pinchot National Forest, Packwood Information Center, 13068 US 12, Packwood, WA 98361; 360 494-0600

Destination Yakima Valley

Yakima Valley Visitors & Convention Bureau, 10 North 8th Street, Yakima, WA 98901; 509 575-3010 or 800 221-0751

Yakima Valley Museum, 2105 Tieton Dr., Yakima, WA 98902; 509 248-0747

Central Washington Agricultural Museum, 4508 Main Street, Union Gap, WA 98903; 509 457-8735

American Hop Museum, 22 S B Street, P.O. Box 230, Toppenish, WA 98948; 509 865-4677

Destination Maryhill

Klickitat County Tourism, 131 W Court, Goldendale 98620; 509 773-3466

Maryhill Museum of Art, 35 Maryhill Museum Drive, Goldendale, Washington 98620; 509 773-3773

Destination Mt. St. Helens

Columbia Gorge Interpretive Center, 990 SW Rock Creek Dr., Stevenson, WA 98648; 509 427-8211 or 800 991-2338

Pendleton Woolen Mills, Washougal Weaving Mill, #2 - 17th Street, Washougal, WA 98671; 800 760-4844 or 360 835-1118

Mt. St. Helens National Volcanic Monument, 42218 NE Yale Bridge Road, Amboy, WA 98601; 360 247-3900

Mt. St. Helens National Volcanic Monument Visitors Center; 360 274-2100

Mt. St. Helens Cinedome, 1239 Mt. St. Helens Way, Castle Rock, WA 98611; 360 274-8000

Destination Ilwaco and Long Beach

Long Beach Peninsula Visitor's Bureau, P.O. Box 562, Long Beach, WA 98631; 360 642-2400 or 800 541-2542

Lewis and Clark Interpretive Center; 360 642-3029

Destination Westport

Westport/Grayland Chamber of Commerce, 2985 Montesano St., P.O. Box 306, Westport, WA 98595; 800 345-6223 or 360 268-9422

Westport Maritime Museum, 2201 Westhaven Dr., Westport, WA 98595; 360 268-0078

Westport Aquarium, 321 Harbor St, Westport, WA 98595; 360 268-0471

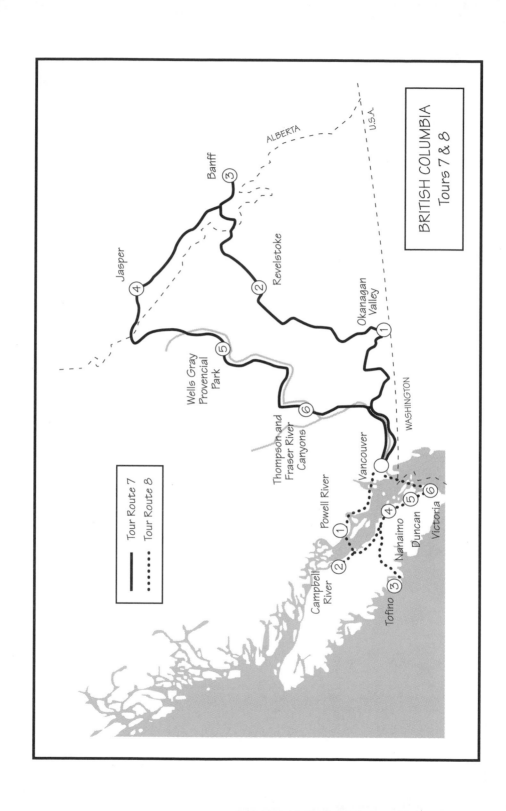

BRITISH COLUMBIA
Tours 7 & 8

Tour Route 7
Tour Route 8

ALBERTA

U.S.A.

Banff ③

Jasper ④

Revelstoke ②

Okanagan Valley ①

Wells Gray Provencial Park ⑤

Thompson and Fraser River Canyons ⑥

WASHINGTON

Powell River

Campbell River

Vancouver

① ② Nahaimo ④ Duncan ⑤ Victoria ⑥

③ Tofino

Chapter 11

Vancouver

Top Attractions

✦ Stanley Park

✦ Gastown

✦ Chinatown

✦ Capilano Suspension Bridge

✦ Granville Island

General

Like the other two gateway cities in this book, Vancouver is the major population center for its Province. With about 1,500,000 people in the metropolitan area Vancouver is also close to the same size as Portland and Seattle.

The city is probably best known for its spectacular location. Mountains rise nearby both to the north and east, the ocean is not only to the west in the form of Howe Sound, but also, as Burrard Inlet and False Creek, to the north and south. To top it off there's the spectacular Lions Gate Suspension Bridge spanning the mouth of Burrard Inlet between Stanley Park and North Vancouver.

Vancouver is a transportation center so it serves well as a gateway to British Columbia. The Vancouver International Airport has many international connections and is easy to get to by air from almost anywhere.

Highway access to Vancouver is decent but not great. Highway 1 from eastern Canada is a multi-lane freeway that enters the city from the east. Unfortunately, it does not connect with major highways from the U.S. so access from the south can be a little confusing. Most folks cross the border at the north end of the U.S. Hwy. I-5 in Blaine, Washington. From there you can follow what appears to be the main road,

Hwy. 99, north into Vancouver. You will soon find yourself on boulevards and then cross into the downtown area, not the best place to be in a big RV. A better plan is to follow signs from the border that lead you up Hwy. 15 (not a freeway but also not heavily trafficked) to connect with Hwy. 1 to the east of Vancouver. From there you can use the freeway to get to Vancouver campgrounds to the north and east of downtown, travel north to Horseshoe Bay, or travel eastwards for the Mainland Tour detailed in this book.

History

Probably not too surprisingly, Vancouver got its start at about the same time as Portland and Seattle. The first European settlers to the area were fur trading companies that established forts along the Fraser River just to the east. Serious settlement of what is now Vancouver began in the 1850s, the large area now covered by Vancouver actually encompassed more than one small settlement. One of these was Granville, also called Gastown, today it is considered the place where Vancouver began.

In the beginning the city of Victoria, on Vancouver Island to the west, grew faster than Vancouver. Concern that Vancouver Island might be incorporated into the U.S. resulted in a concentrated British effort to develop the island, and gold discoveries up the Thompson and Fraser Rivers in the mountains east of Vancouver only gradually moved the center of population growth over to the mainland.

Other early events either precede or echo the histories of Portland and Seattle. Vancouver had its own serious fire in 1886, rebuilding resulted in many of the Gastown buildings you see today. The railroad reached Vancouver in the next year, and, just like Portland and Seattle, a direct and relatively easy to travel connection with the east really caused the city to take off.

As Canada's major West Coast port Vancouver grew rapidly and continues to do so today. More freight passes through Vancouver than any other Canadian port, and by some measures Vancouver is considered the largest port on the west coast of North America.

Layout

The original Gastown settlement is at the base of a peninsula and didn't have a great deal of area for growth because it is hemmed in by water. As a result the city has spread off the peninsula to the north and south and today continues to grow to the east up the wide Fraser Valley.

The downtown peninsula is bounded on the north by Burrard Inlet and on the south by False Bay. Just south of Gastown is the city's Chinatown. To the west of these is the modern downtown area and farther to the west a primarily residential area known as the West End and also Stanley Park. Visitors from the U.S. will be impressed with Vancouver's cosmopolitan air, and also with the number of people who live near the center of town.

North of the peninsula, across Burrard Inlet, is North Vancouver, you reach it via the scenic Lions Gate Bridge. South of the Peninsula is a large residential area known as Central Vancouver which is also the location of the University of British Columbia.

More remote suburbs include Richmond, to the south, New Westminster, to the southeast, and Burnaby and Port Coquitlam to the east. You can go even farther and

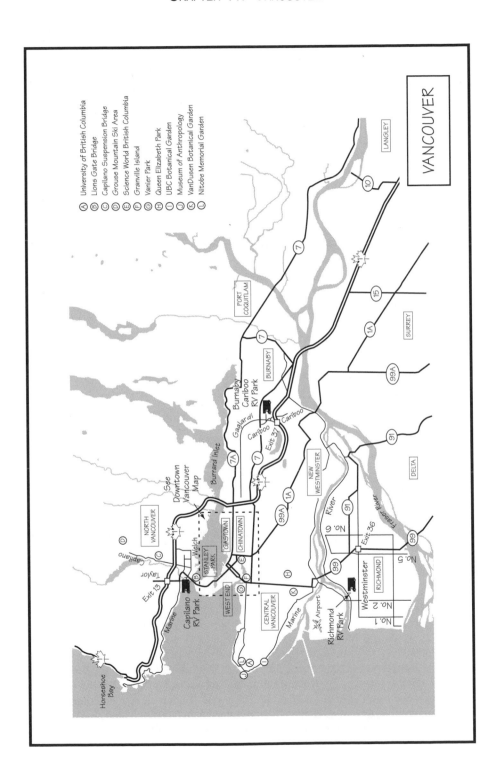

VANCOUVER

Ⓐ University of British Columbia
Ⓑ Lions Gate Bridge
Ⓒ Capilano Suspension Bridge
Ⓓ Grouse Mountain Ski Area
Ⓔ Science World British Columbia
Ⓕ Granville Island
Ⓖ Vanier Park
Ⓗ Queen Elizabeth Park
Ⓘ UBC Botanical Garden
Ⓙ Museum of Anthropology
Ⓚ VanDusen Botanical Garden
Ⓛ Nitobe Memorial Garden

still consider yourself in the Vancouver metropolitan area. Delta and Surrey are to the south toward the U.S. border and to the east up the Fraser Valley are Langley and Abbotsford.

Transportation

Vancouver has an excellent public transportation system. The system's name has recently been changed from BC Transit to Translink. There are several different arms of this organization. Pamphlets with details about service are available at the many info centres in Vancouver and on approaches to the city.

The Coast Mountain Bus Company is the bus arm. It provides excellent bus service throughout the greater Vancouver area.

Vancouver has a light rail transportation system too. This is known as SkyTrain. There is one line, it is underground downtown and above ground elsewhere. It runs southeastward from downtown and provides service to Burnaby, New Westminster, and Surrey. Trains run every 5 minutes or so.

SeaBus passenger ferries connect downtown Vancouver with North Vancouver. The Vancouver terminal is near Canada Place, the North Vancouver terminal is Lonsdale Quay. From the quay there is bus service to many North Vancouver destinations.

There are also tiny passenger ferries that chug around False Creek and are appropriately known as the False Creek Ferries. There are docks at many tourist destinations including Granville Island, Vanier Park, and Science World.

When you arrive in Vancouver on public transportation you will probably find yourself in the central business district. The new center of attraction for visitors is **Canada Place**. Now a combination cruise ship dock, convention center, hotel, shopping center, and theater, the very modern soaring tent-like building on a pier was originally build as a pavilion for the Expo86 fair. Canada Place is served by the SkyTrain light rail system.

Up the hill from Canada Place **Granville Street** has been closed to most traffic to become a European-style pedestrian mall. Along or near Granville you'll find lots of shopping. From its intersection with Granville you can follow Robson Street northwestward toward the West End and Stanley Park. Robson is lined with restaurants and boutiques.

Stanley Park is Vancouver's jewel. This huge park covers the entire tip of the peninsula occupied by Vancouver. It is a big place, there are miles and miles of trails as well as roads allowing you to tour the park in an automobile. A **Seaside Promenade** runs along the entire coastline of the park. Stanley Park is also home to the excellent **Vancouver Aquarium**. The Golden Gate-like **Lions Gate Suspension Bridge** makes a scenic jump from Stanley Park to North Vancouver.

If you head eastward from Canada Place you'll soon find yourself in historic **Gastown**. Cobblestone streets and well-maintained 19th-century buildings make the neighborhood stand out, and because it is a designated historic district the shops are open on Sundays.

Just southeast of Gastown is **Chinatown**. This is the second largest such area on the West Coast, only San Francisco's Chinatown is larger. In addition to the usual shops and restaurants you might want to visit the **Dr. Sun Yat-sen Classical Chinese Garden** which is located on Carrall Street between W. Pender and Keefer.

You can easily visit **North Vancouver** as a pedestrian by taking a ferry across Burrard Inlet. The SeaBus terminal is just east of Canada Place, ferries dock in North Vancouver at Lonsdale Quay. There's a farmers market at the quay as well as restaurants and shops. Busses to the sights in North Vancouver also depart from the quay.

Two popular attractions lie up the mountain. The first is the **Capilano Suspension Bridge**. This dizzying suspension foot bridge crosses the Capilano River at a height of 70 meters (230 feet). Higher on the same road is **Grouse Mountain** ski area. You can ride the gondola up to the ski slope for magnificent views of the city and hiking trails.

There are a number of attractions south of downtown also. One of the closest and most easily accessible is **Science World British Columbia**. This is a science/technology museum housed in a 17-story ball originally built for Expo86. There is also an Omnimax theater. It is served by SkyTrain and also by the False Creek Ferries.

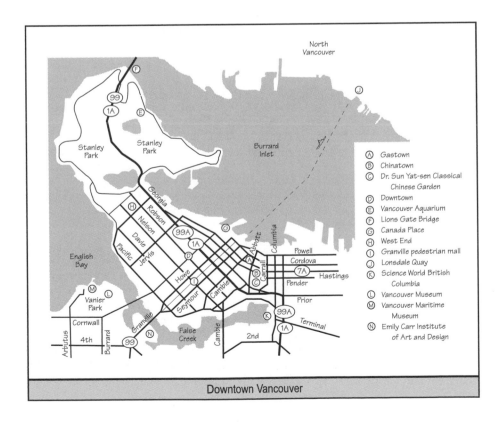

Downtown Vancouver

From Science World you can use the ferry to hop over to **Granville Island**, also accessible by car or bus. Not long ago this was little more than an area of old warehouses but it has been completely redone. Now there's a visitor information centre, a public market, the **Emily Carr Institute of Art and Design**, a marina, shops, restaurants, and theaters.

The area on the south side of False Bay is known as Central Vancouver. Attractions there are mostly grouped in Vanier Park and on the University of BC Campus although there are also two excellent gardens. The first of these is **Queen Elizabeth Park**, a 130-acre park located on Little Mountain which offers views of the city. The **Bloedel Floral Conservatory** in the park is a dome-style greenhouse housing tropical plants and birds. The **VanDusen Botanical Garden** is nearby and offers 55 acres of beautiful gardens.

Vanier Park is located on the south shore of English Bay just west of Granville Island. In the park you'll find two museums. The **Vancouver Museum** is a regional history museum much more interesting then most of this genre, probably because Vancouver's history includes the coastal Indian cultures and also the European exploration of the Northwest. There's much more of the latter at the nearby **Vancouver Maritime Museum**. The park also has a planetarium and an astronomical observatory.

West of Vanier Park and occupying 1,900 acres on Point Grey is the **University of British Columbia**. The **Museum of Anthropology** here is excellent and covers, of course, the Pacific Northwest Indian cultures. The university campus has miles of hiking trails and beaches. Also on campus are the **Nitobe Memorial Garden**, a traditional Japanese garden and the **UBC Botanical Garden**.

Vancouver Area Campgrounds

Capilano RV Park `MED` 295 Tomahawk Avenue, North Vancouver; B.C. V7P 1C5; 604 987-4722; http://capilanorvpark.com/; 208 sites, open all year - This campground is conveniently located in North Vancouver just north of the Lions Gate Bridge and near Hwy. 1. It is also within easy walking distance of the Park Royal Shopping Centre. There is good bus service into Vancouver from near the campground. To most easily drive to the campground leave Hwy. 1 at Exit 13 (Taylor Way-Vancouver). Drive south .9 miles. You will cross Marine Drive and drive into the shopping centre access road and under an overhead crossing (height 4.5 meters). Take a left just after the overhead on Bridge Road, you'll see the campground on your left in .2 miles.

Burnaby Cariboo R.V. Park `MED` 8765 Cariboo Place, Burnaby, B.C. V3N 4T2; 604 420-1722 or 800 667-9901 for reservations; www.bcrvpark.com; 217 sites, open all year - This is a convenient campground for folks approaching Vancouver from the east. It is located just off Hwy. 1 and is near Burnaby Lake which has good hiking trails. There's an indoor swimming pool and Jacuzzi. The Lougheed Shopping Center is a short drive away. To find the campground take Exit 37 (Cariboo Rd.). You'll be on Gaglardi Way. Drive only a short distance and turn right at the Cariboo Rd sign. Again drive only a short distance and turn left on Cariboo Road. Now drive about 2 kilometers (1 mile) north and turn right on Cariboo Place, this is the entrance road to the campground. The route is signed so it is easier to drive than to read.

⇆ Richmond RV Park Campground `MED` `▲` `ƒ` `☐` `☐` `☐` `☐` `GS` 6200 River Road, Richmond, B.C. V7C 5G1; 604 270-7878 or 800 755-4905 for reservations; http://travel.bc.ca./r/richmondrv/; 254 sites, open all year - This campground isn't quite as upscale as the two listed above, but it tends to be less crowded and has a nice location across the street from the river. There is a little aircraft noise from the nearby float plane base and the international airport on the island to the north. There's also a nice bike trail and promenade running for miles along the river. This campground has no sewer hookups, instead they have a mobile dump station vehicle as well as several fixed dump stations. To reach the campground take Exit 36 (Westminster Hwy.) from Hwy. 99 between the border and Vancouver. Drive west on Westminster for 5.6 kilometers (3.5 miles) to No. 2 Road. Turn right and drive 1.6 kilometer (.1 mile) to River Road. Again turn right and drive .6 kilometer (.4 miles), you'll see the campground on the right.

Information Resources

See our Internet site at www.rollinghomes.com for Internet site addresses.

Vancouver Tourist Info Centre, Plaza Level, 200 Burrard Street, Vancouver, B.C. V6C 3L6; 604 683-2000

Capilano Park and Suspension Bridge, 3735 Capilano Road, North Vancouver, B.C. V7R 4J1; 604 985-7474

Grouse Mountain, 6400 Nancy Greene Way, North Vancouver, B.C. V7R 4K9; 604 984-0661

Science World British Columbia, 1455 Quebec St., Vancouver, B.C. V6A 3Z7; 604 443-7443

Queen Elizabeth Park, 33rd Avenue and Cambie St,, Vancouver, B.C.; 604 257-8400

VanDusen Botanical Garden, 5251 Oak St., Vancouver, B.C. V6M 4H1; 604 878-9274

Vancouver Museum, 1100 Chestnut St, Vancouver, B.C. V6J 3J9; 604 736-4431

Vancouver Maritime Museum, 1905 Ogden Avenue, Vancouver, B.C. V6J 1A3; 604 257-8300

UBC Museum of Anthropology, 6393 NW Marine Drive, Vancouver, B.C. V6T 1Z2; 604 822-5087

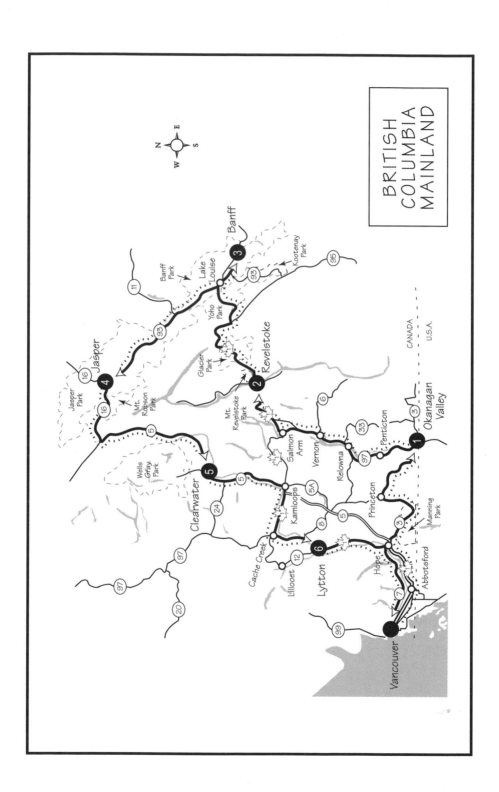

British Columbia Mainland

Top Attractions

✦ Okanagan Valley

✦ Canadian Rockies including Yoho, Banff, and Jasper National Parks

✦ Lake Louise

✦ Icefields Parkway and the Columbia Icefield

✦ Mt. Robson

✦ Wells Gray Provincial Park and Helmcken Falls

✦ Fraser River Canyon

General Description

Inland British Columbia represent one of the premier RVing destinations in North America. This is a spectacularly beautiful region, you'll see more impressive mountain scenery here than anywhere else you are likely to ever take an RV.

This is a huge area. While it would theoretically be possible to make this entire tour in one week we definitely would not recommend that you try to do so. At the end of your trip you would be exhausted. You would also feel like you had missed more than you had seen. The distances are long but the miles are packed with things to see while several individual destinations offer plenty to keep you busy for several days. Our advice, plan on at least two weeks if you want to do this entire trip. Driving distance for the tour is 2,094 km (1,298 miles), approximate driving time is 31.5 hours.

The route starts at the coast in the province's largest city, Vancouver. As you drive up the Fraser River Valley you will be crossing a cultivated area of farms and small towns. However, when you reach Hope you leave all this and immediately begin climbing into a much more sparsely populated region. Highway 3 crosses both the Hozamen and Okanagan Ranges and passes through Manning Provincial Park before descending into irrigated fruit-growing country in the Okanagan Valley.

After spending some time in the valley this tour heads north to Salmon Arm where it joins the transcontinental Highway 1 and turns eastward. After stopping for a night near Revelstoke in the Columbia River Valley you'll climb to cross through Glacier National Park and the Dogtooth Range, descend to cross over the Columbia River once again, and then ascend into the Canadian Rockies through Yoho National Park to Banff National Park.

When you've had a chance to see all there is to see in Banff you can head north along the Icefields Parkway past the Columbia Icefield to Jasper National Park. Jasper too has a lot to offer, but after a couple of days it is time to begin the drive back toward Vancouver. During the day you'll pass through Mt. Robson Provincial Park and then spend the night either in or near Wells Gray Provincial Park.

Continuing southward you'll follow a slightly out-of-the-way route to thread your way down the impressively scenic Thompson and Fraser River Valleys. You'll spend the night in the canyons and then continue south to meet the expressway near Hope and retrace your way to Vancouver.

The Roads

Virtually all of the roads on this tour are of the two-lane variety. On the other hand, although they are two-lane roads they are in excellent condition with good shoulders and frequent passing lanes and rest areas. This is a mountainous route, it starts at sea level and travels over many passes reaching its highest altitude on the Icefields Parkway in Banff National Park, 2,067 meters (6,787 feet). If you have toured Colorado this may not seem high but rest assured that you will be more than satisfied by the mountains you find along this route.

Practical Tips

Since this tour traverses fairly high mountain country, particularly in Banff and Jasper National Parks, it is a summer trip. Plan to start no earlier than May and to be out of the mountains before the end of September. Even within these boundaries it is very possible that you might receive a dusting of snow during the night.

In this chapter you'll find lots of ways to make a one-week tour into a two or three-week one. Here's one way to shorten things a bit. One way to make more time is to use the new Highway 5, also known as the Coquihalla Highway. Using the Coquihalla from Hope to Merrit and then the Okanagan Connector from Merrit to Kelowna you can cut the first day's 8-hour drive down to only 4 to 5 hours. On your way home, if you've overstayed along the way, you can drive directly from Clearwater to Vancouver and cut an entire day from your itinerary by following the Coquihalla Highway from Kamloops to Hope.

DAY 1 - DESTINATION THE OKANAGAN VALLEY
524 kilometers (326 miles), 8 hours (to Kelowna)

Along the Way - From Vancouver point your rig's nose east and follow the Trans-Canada Highway to the town of Hope. The entire 188 kilometer (117 mile) distance is along a multi-lane limited access freeway. You have a reasonably long day ahead of you but there are a number of worthwhile stops along this section of the route in case you feel the need to pause.

There are a number of attractions near Bridal Falls, B.C. at Exit 135. Good signage makes finding them pretty easy. **Minter Gardens** is north of the freeway. Here you'll find a number of different types of gardens set on 27 acres with wheelchair assessable paths. **Bridal Veil Falls Provincial Park** is south of the freeway. Short trails take you to overlooks to view the falls. There are a couple of campgrounds at this exit, these might be handy if you have some children along and they spot the signs for **Dusty's Dinotown**, a dinosaur theme park.

Hope forms a kind of transportation crossroads. In or near the town three major routes intersect. Highway 1 heads north from town up the Fraser Canyon. Highway 5, also called the Coquihalla Highway, provides a quick and direct toll route north to Kamloops. And finally, Highway 3 , the Crowsnest Highway, winds it's scenic way east. You'll be following Highway 3 but first you might want to stop and take a look at Hope.

Movie fans already know Hope, it was the location for the filming of Sylvester Stallone's first Rambo film, *First Blood.* As a result you may find that the town looks vaguely familiar, even if you've never been there. The **Hope Museum** is a good stop if you want to know more about the town, the town info centre is located at the same place. You might also enjoy a look at the **chain saw sculptures** nearby.

Highway 3 is a fine two-lane highway, but it does cross some healthy mountains. From Hope to Osoyoos at the south end of Canada's section of the Okanagan Valley is a distance of 246 kilometers (153 miles). The highest point along the route is Allison Pass in Manning Provincial Park with an altitude of 1,352 meters (4,416 feet).

The road climbs steeply out of Hope. The first point of interest comes pretty quickly. Sixteen kilometers (10 miles) east of Hope pull off at the **Hope Slide** view-point. You'll see that the entire face of the mountain to the north has slid into the valley. This happened fairly recently, on January 9, 1965. Four people were killed by the slide.

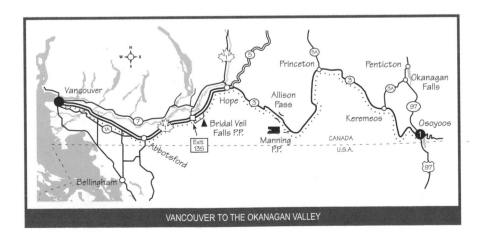

VANCOUVER TO THE OKANAGAN VALLEY

Deep in the Cascades the highway enters **Manning Provincial Park**. There are four campgrounds in the park, all are suitable for RVs. The campgrounds, a visitor center, and the Manning Park Resort with a restaurant and other services are all located near each other about 42 kilometers (26 miles) east of Hope. You'll note signs for several hiking trails as you drive through the park, some have decent parking areas for big rigs.

Continuing east you'll begin to notice that the countryside is becoming much dryer. You'll pass through the ranch and lumber town of Princeton and then, 198 kilometers (123 miles) from Hope enter **Keremeos**. You can't miss the huge number of fruit stands along the highway in this town, you're entering British Columbia's fruit country. A combination of warm sunny weather and abundant water from irrigation make this Canada's fruit basket. Expect to find cherries by the end of June, apricots in July, peaches just a little later, pears toward the end of August, and apples in September. Fruit ripens first in the southern Okanagan and later in the north because the south is warmer.

Just 48 more kilometers (30 miles) along Hwy. 3 and you will arrive in Osoyoos, the south end of Canada's Okanagan Valley, almost on the U.S. border.

The Okanagan Valley

Canada's portion of the Okanagan River Valley stretches 200 kilometers (125 miles) north from the U.S. border. The outstanding feature here is probably the weather, the average rainfall is only 9 inches per year because the North Cascades shelter the valley from storms coming from the Pacific.

When you add the valley's water to the weather the Okanagan becomes a perfect playground. Several lakes dominate the valley, the largest by far is Okanagan Lake, it's 170 kilometers (105 miles) long. In summer they're plenty warm enough for swimming and have many very popular beaches. Boating of all kinds is extremely popular.

There are a number of small towns and three good-sized cities in the valley. Most are arranged off Highway 97 which runs up the center of the valley.

Farthest south of the three cities is **Penticton** (population 33,000). The town sits between two lakes: to the south is Skaha Lake and to the north is Okanagan Lake. There are excellent beaches on both lakes, several RV parks are located on the Skaha Lake shore. Penticton attracts a lot of visitors and has all the facilities they require. You can't miss the **SS Sicamous**, an old sternwheeler beached on the shore of Okanagan Lake, it is now a museum and there are hopes of restoring it to operating condition. The town has an excellent **museum** covering all aspects of the town's history. The **Okanagan Game Farm** is located about eight kilometers south of town on Highway 97, it has a good selection of animals from around the world. You'll also find no shortage of golf courses, water slides, and vineyards offering tours. Penticton hosts several celebrations including a **Peach Festival** during the second week of August and also celebrate the **Okanagan Wine Festival** in October.

From Penticton Highway 97 follows the west side of Okanagan Lake to the north for 58 kilometers (36 miles). There are a number of small towns on this side of the lake, as well as a number of good campgrounds. Connecting the West Side to Kelowna is a Seattle-style floating bridge.

Kelowna is the province's fourth largest city with a population of about 100,000 people. Like Penticton, Kelowna caters to visitors, there are many attractions devoted to them. Tours of vineyards and fruit-growing and packing operations are very popular, just check with the infocentre to see what is available. The city is surprisingly pleasant with a number of excellent lake-side parks offering good beaches and a nice central downtown area. Kelowna helps celebrate the **Okanagan Wine Festival** during the first week of October.

About 50 kilometers (36 miles) north of Kelowna is the region's third large city, **Vernon**, with a population in the neighborhood of 35,000. Along the way watch for the signs for **Ellison Provincial Park** about 16 kilometers (10 miles) south of Vernon, it is a fresh-water underwater park for snorkeling and scuba.

Vernon has fewer visitor attractions than the cities farther south. The **O'Keefe Ranch** is located 13 kilometers (8 miles) to the north on Hwy. 97 toward Kamloops. It is an early cattle ranch and is open to the public as a non-profit historic site, there is a mansion and several other buildings, also a restaurant.

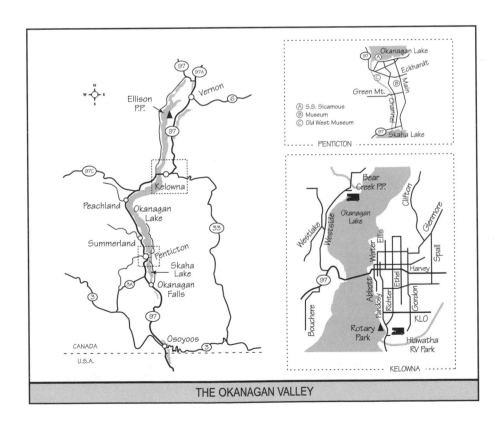

THE OKANAGAN VALLEY

Okanagan Valley Campgrounds

You'll find no shortage of campgrounds in the Okanagan Valley. During the summer they can all fill up so make sure you make reservations in advance. Both of the following campgrounds are in the Kelowna area but you'll also find many in Penticton and other places along the various lakes.

Hiawatha RV Park 3787 Lakeshore Rd., Kelowna. B.C. V1Y 1X2; 250 861-4837 or 888 784-7275 for reservations; www.hiawatharvpark.com; 85 sites, open March 1 to October 15 - The RV park is located in southern Kelowna almost directly across the street from the beachside Rotary Park. To reach the campground from the floating bridge drive to the second traffic light, Pandosy Street, and turn right. Drive 4.4 kilometers (2.7 miles) south on Pandosy St., it will become Lakeshore Road, and the campground is on the left.

Bear Creek Provincial Park 800 689-9025 for reservations; 121 sites, open April 1 to October 31 - This is a beautiful lake-side park with a large campground. There is a beach and extensive hiking trails. To reach the campground head west from Kelowna on Highway 97. After leaving the bridge travel 2 kilometers (1.2 miles) and turn right on Westside Road. Follow the road for 9 more kilometers (6 miles) and you'll reach the campground.

SS SICAMOUS

DAY 2 - DESTINATION REVELSTOKE
192 kilometers (119 miles), 3 hours

A long the Way - From the Okanagan Valley follow Hwy. 97 north to intersect the Trans-Canada Highway (Hwy. 1) near Salmon Arm and Sicamous. Both of these towns are on the shore of Shuswap Lake. This is a very large, x-shaped lake. Many visitors rent houseboats in Sicamous so they can RV on the lake.

As you head east on Highway 1 you might want to keep an eye open for a few roadside attractions that have been developed with travelers in mind. A good rest stop is **Craigellachie** where the last spike of the transcontinental rail line was driven. This is really just a rest stop with plenty of parking and restrooms as well as a display. Then the commercial stops start including **Beardale Castle Miniatureland**, **Enchanted Forest**, and a reconstructed ghost

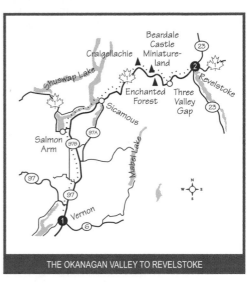

THE OKANAGAN VALLEY TO REVELSTOKE

town called **Three Valley Gap**. The distance from Salmon Arm to Revelstoke through the Monashee Mountains is only 104 kilometers (64 miles) so you'll soon find yourself approaching Revelstoke.

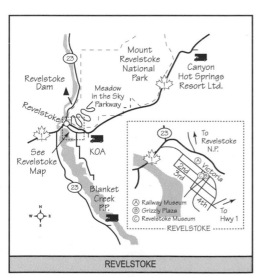

REVELSTOKE

REVELSTOKE

You'll probably be surprised at what this little town (population 6,500) on the Columbia River has to offer. The historic downtown area is well preserved and pleasant with restaurants, shops and even frequent evening entertainment in **Grizzly Plaza**. The town has the excellent **Revelstoke Railway Museum** as well as a local historical museum called the **Revelstoke Museum**.

As you might expect of a town in such a spectacular mountainous location, several of the best attractions are in the surrounding area. **Mount Revelstoke National Park** is right outside town. You can drive the **Meadows in the Sky Parkway** which climbs steeply for 26 kilometers (16 miles) and about 1,100 meters. Near the end of the road there's a parking lot and a shuttle bus will carry you another kilometer to the top for spectacular views. Because the road is steep with switchbacks trailers are not permitted. There is a small parking lot where you can leave your trailer near the entrance at the bottom.

There are two dams on the Columbia River above Revelstoke. The nearest to Revelstoke is called **Revelstoke Dam**. It is located 8 kilometers (5 miles) north of town on Highway 23 and has a good self-guided tour of the facility including a trip to the top of the dam for the view.

Revelstoke Area Campgrounds

🚐 **KOA Revelstoke** [MED] [icons] P.O. Box 160, Revelstoke, BC V0E 2S0; 604 837-2085 or 800 KOA-3905 for reservations; 230 sites, open May 1 to October 1 - This conveniently-located KOA is located about 5 kilometers (3 miles) east of town on Highway 1.

🚐 **Blanket Creek Provincial Park** [LOW] [icons] 800 689-9025 for reservations; http://revelstokecc.bc.ca/blanket.htm; 64 sites, open May to October - The park is located along the shore of Arrow Reservoir just south of the mouth of Blanket Creek. There's a scenic waterfall, fishing, and an old homestead site to explore. To reach the campground just drive south along the west shore of the reservoir from Revelstoke about 25 kilometers (15 miles).

🚐 **Canyon Hot Springs Resort Ltd.** [MED] [icons] P.O. Box 2400, Revelstoke, BC V0E 2S0; 250 837-2420; http://www.revelstokecc.bc.ca/canyhot.htm; 200 sites, open May 15 to September 30 - If you feel like driving a few more miles when you reach Revelstoke consider driving on to this campground. It is a hot springs with both a hot pool and a swimming pool. The campground has a few electricity and water hookups but has mostly unserviced sites. To reach the campground drive east on Highway 1 from Revelstoke for 35 kilometers (22 miles), the campground is on the right.

Day 3 - Destination Banff National Park
233 kilometers (145 miles), 3 hours (to Lake Louise)

A long the Way - From Revelstoke to Banff National Park Highway 1 follows the original route of the Canadian Pacific Railway. This portion of the railroad was one of the most problematic when it was being built in the 1880s because of the terrain it crosses. Today, for highway travelers, that translates into a scenic and interesting day of driving.

East of Revelstoke just 72 kilometers (45 miles) the highway crosses **Rogers Pass** (1,387 meters, 4,563 feet) in the middle of **Glacier National Park**. You might want to pull off at the Rogers Pass Information Centre to see what the park has to offer. Be advised that there is a fee for use of the park unless you just drive through. The scenery through the park is spectacular, in winter avalanches often close the highway, but summer travelers shouldn't have to worry about that. There are two campgrounds suitable for RVs in the park: Illecillewaet Campground (60 sites) is 3 kilometers west of Rogers Pass and Loop Brook Campground (20 sites) is 5 kilometers west of Rogers Pass. Neither has hookups.

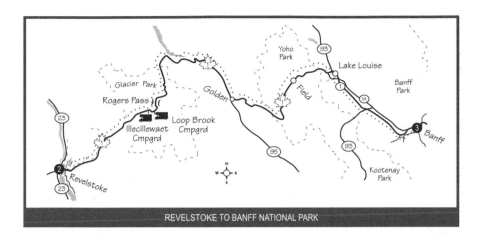

REVELSTOKE TO BANFF NATIONAL PARK

Continuing eastward the highway descends to the Columbia River at the town of Golden. Here the river is flowing north, not south. From Golden the road ascends the valley of the Kicking Horse River and soon enters **Yoho National Park**. From Field to the Continental Divide just west of Lake Louise the railway builders had a real challenge. The last 10 kilometers of the grade were called the "**Big Hill**", there is a grade of about 4.5%. Since the normal maximum grade for a railroad is about 2.2% there were lots of problems, eventually two "Spiral Tunnels" were built to reduce the grade. From the Spiral Tunnel Viewpoint, 7.4 kilometers (4.6 miles) east of Field, you can take a look at the entrances to the Mount Ogden Spiral Tunnel as well as enjoy a great view of the Yoho Valley which extends to the north.

Once you pass the Continental Divide at the top of the hill you have entered Alberta, Banff National Park, and the watershed of the Bow Valley. The Trans-Canada Highway follows the Bow Valley toward the southeast. This section of Banff National Park, roughly from Lake Louise to the town site of Banff, is the most frequented part of the park and offers plenty to keep a visitor busy for a long time. It is also truly beautiful because it is ringed by some of the highest and most spectacularly rugged peaks in the world. A second and much smaller road, the **Bow Parkway**, offers a scenic and quiet alternative to the four-lane highway, and follows pretty much the same route except that it is on the east side of the Bow River instead of the west. You'll want to traverse the Bow Parkway at least once so you can stop occasionally and enjoy the valley. The distance between Banff and Lake Louise along the Bow Parkway and a short section of Hwy. 1 near Banff is 56.6 kilometers (35.1 miles).

When you arrive on Hwy. 1 from the west you'll almost immediately see the exit for **Lake Louise**. This is the smaller of the two population centers of the park. Just off the highway to the west is what is known as the village of Lake Louise, it is really little more than a shopping center offering a tourist info centre, small stores, tourist services, and gasoline. Just past the village is a turn to the left for the giant Lake Louise Campground. If you go straight instead you will wind up the hillside for about 4 kilometers (2.5 miles) to beautiful Lake Louise. There are big parking lots here but it is best not to try to take a very large rig or a trailer, the lots are big but still crowded. At the foot of the lake you'll see a huge hotel, the **Chateau Lake Louise**, it has been there in one form or another since 1890. You'll no doubt be part of a huge throng of visitors, you can walk through the hotel lobby and take some pictures from the lawn of the spectacular view featuring the emerald-colored lake and the glacier at the far end. Then you can explore part of the trail network along and above the lake, there are even a couple of teahouses where you can stop for refreshments.

At the lower end of the valley is the town of **Banff** with a population of about 7,500. We'll call it the Banff town site to distinguish it from the park in general. This is the major population, business, and tourist center of the park. In addition to many park-type wonders in the area you'll find a wealth of shops and restaurants that rival any resort town. You'll also find a supermarket and other services required by RVers including some huge government-owned campgrounds. This is the largest town to be found inside any national park in either Canada or the U.S.

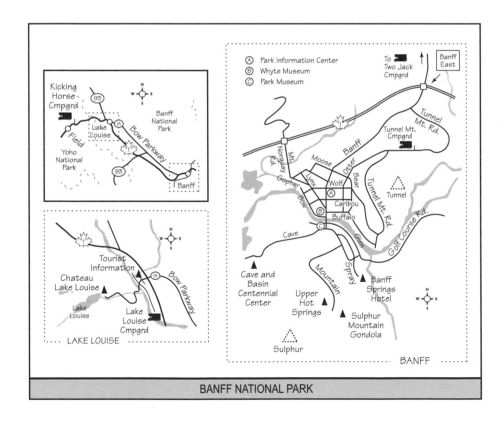

BANFF NATIONAL PARK

LAKE LOUISE

There are several interesting sights in the town site area. It would be a good idea to make your first stop at the downtown **Park Information Centre** for local maps and information. The **Banff Springs Hotel** is one of the early Canadian Pacific Railways resort hotels and remains a fascinating place to visit. Just off the entrance road to the hotel is the road to the golf course, it leads past **Bow Falls** to a loop route through the golf course and can be a good place to see **elk**, they favor the course as a place to graze and relax. The original reason Banff was established was the hot springs, you can visit the **Cave and Basin Centennial Center** built at the site of the original hot springs, you can't swim there any more but you will find lots to see. The Sundance Canyon Trail starts at the center and takes you along the Bow River to Sundance Canyon, about 7 kilometers (4.4 miles) round trip. If you do want to swim you can do so at **Upper Hot Springs**. Near Upper Hot Springs is the **Sulphur Mountain Gondola Lift** which takes you up to an observatory and restaurant high on Sulphur Mountain. There are two worthwhile museums in Banff town site, the **Whyte Museum of the Canadian Rockies** and the **Park Museum**.

There are several excellent drives in the Banff town site area in addition to the one up to the Sulphur Mountain Gondola Lift. You can drive to an excellent viewpoint overlooking the town site by following **Mt. Norquay Drive**. It is on the far side of Highway 1 at the West Banff Exit and climbs about 300 meters in 5.8 kilometers (3.6 miles). From the East Banff Exit you can follow **Lake Minnewanka Road** to visit the ghost town of **Bankhead**, view **Lake Minnewanka** or take a commercial boat tour, then return on a loop drive past **Two Jack Lake** and **Johnson Lake**.

Banff National Park Area Campgrounds

The campgrounds in the national parks are very popular, and they don't take reservations. During July and August it is important to get to the parks at about check-out time at 11:00 a.m. (particularly those which offer hookups) to insure that you will get a good site. The campgrounds mentioned below are the main ones, there are a number of other smaller campgrounds without hookups. There are also overflow camping areas without hookups for when things are **really** crowded.

Lake Louise Campground LOW △ ♦ 🖳 🖥 🦌 🔥 405 sites, open all year - There are really two sections to this campground. The largest has 216 unserviced sites attractively arranged in a forested area, the second has electrical and water hookups and has 189 sites, all pull-throughs. The campground is located near Lake Louise Village. Turn left just past the village and drive 1.6 kilometer (1 mile) to the campground entrance. Showers were added to the campground in 1999, only the trailer portion of the campground is open year round, the tent section is open May 14 to October 3.

Tunnel Mountain Campgrounds MED △ ♦ 🖳 🖥 🦌 🔥 1,127 sites, open all year - There are actually three campgrounds in this complex near Banff town site. Village I has 618 unserviced sites, Trailer Court has 321 sites with full-hookups, and Village II has 188 sites offering only electricity but arranged to allow easy snow removal and open all year long. To reach the campgrounds without driving through the crowded town make sure to take the East Banff Exit (also called Minnewanka Loop). The route is well signed. Drive toward the town from the highway for 1 kilometer (.6 miles), turn left onto Tunnel Mountain Road. In 3 kilometers (1.8 miles) you'll see the entrance for Village I Campground, after another 1.5 kilometers (.9 miles) is a second entrance that serves both Village II and Trailer Court Campgrounds.

Two Jack Campground LOW △ 🖳 🖥 🦌 🔥 455 sites, open June to early September - This is a second large campground fairly close to Banff town site. No hookups here but the campground serves as an excellent backup during the busy July, August period. To reach the campground take the East Banff Exit from Highway 1 and drive away from Banff town site toward Lake Minnewanka. In 1.2 kilometers (.7 mile) turn right at the intersection and in another 5.3 kilometers (3.3 miles) you'll see the campground.

Kicking Horse Campground LOW △ 🖳 🖥 🦌 🔥 92 sites, open May to early October - Here's an alternative in the Lake Louise area, actually this campground is in Yoho National park not far from Highway 1. To get to the campground take the Yoho Valley Road Exit, it is 3.7 kilometers (2.3 miles) east of Field and 22.3 kilometers (13.9 miles) west of the Lake Louise Exit. Follow Yoho Valley Road for 1.1 kilometers (.7 miles) to the campground.

DAY 4 - DESTINATION JASPER NATIONAL PARK
232 kilometers (144 miles), 4 hours (to Jasper townsite)

Along the Way - The route to be followed today is entirely along the 230 kilometer (143 mile) **Icefields Parkway** stretching from an intersection on the Trans-Canada Highway near Lake Louise north through the mountains to Jasper. Don't hurry along this highway, there is plenty of magnificent scenery and many places to stop, enjoy the view, and even take some hikes.

Like most Canadian National Parks there is a day fee for the use of Banff and Jasper National Parks. It is possible to drive through Banff Park on Highway 1 without paying the fee, but not the Icefield Parkway. There are kiosks on both ends of the Icefields Parkway to collect the fee.

Some 35 kilometers (21 miles) from the start of the Parkway you'll come to **Bow Lake**. From here you'll see no more of the Bow River. There's a viewpoint where you can look across the turquoise-colored lake and see **Num-Ti-Jah Lodge** and the **Bow Glacier** beyond.

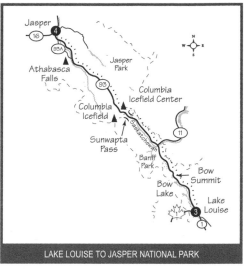

LAKE LOUISE TO JASPER NATIONAL PARK

Six kilometers (4 miles) beyond Bow lake the highway crests **Bow Summit** at 2,067 meters (6,787 feet). This is the highest point on the Parkway.

Seventy-five kilometers (47 miles) north of the intersection with Highway 1 the Parkway crosses the North **Saskatchewan River**. To the west is the Howse Valley.

RVERS VISITING THE COLUMBIA ICEFIELD CENTER

The North Saskatchewan River and the Howse Valley were one of the early passes used by explorers and fur traders to cross the Rocky Mountains. Highway 11 heads east from here to Rocky Mountain House and Red Deer.

Sunwapta Pass (2,035 meters, 6,675 feet) marks the boundary between Banff National Park and Jasper National park. A few kilometers north of the pass is the huge **Columbia Icefield Center**. This is an observatory with great views across the valley to the **Athabasca Glacier** and the **Columbia Icefield**. It also serves as the embarkation point for bus tours onto the glacier. Busses leave the Center and drive to the edge of the glacier, there passengers change to special busses with huge tires called snocoaches to actually drive out onto the glacier. As an alternative you can drive to the foot of the glacier yourself and take a short hike for a close look. The Icefield Center also houses a Parks Canada visitor centre.

It is well worth a short side trip off the highway to take a look at **Athabasca Falls**. The access road is actually a short section of Highway 93A which was an older version of today's highway that runs north along the western side of the valley parallel to today's road for about 25 kilometers. The turn for Athabasca Falls is well marked, it is 73 kilometers (45 miles) north of the Columbia Icefield Center. The Athabasca River drops over a ledge and tumbles through a narrow canyon. Overlooks and a pedestrian bridge offer excellent views, a great place for pictures.

Thirty kilometers (19 miles) beyond the falls the Icefield Parkway intersects Highway 16 which crosses the Rockies through Yellowhead Pass. If you continue straight on across the highway you will find yourself in Jasper town site.

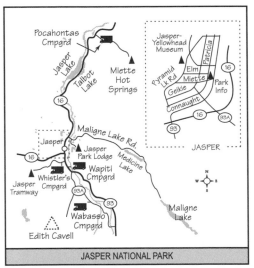

JASPER NATIONAL PARK

JASPER NATIONAL PARK

Jasper town site serves as the service and administration center of Jasper National Park just as Banff town site does for Banff National Park. Jasper, however, definitely reflects its roots as a division town on the Grand Trunk Pacific and Canadian Northern Railways. The town, with a population of about 5,500, has a number of worthwhile sites to visit. The **Park Visitor Centre** is near the center of town. There's also a museum, the **Jasper-Yellowhead Museum**, with exhibits about the history of the park.

The Jasper area has its own mountain tram. The **Jasper Tramway** climbs The Whistlers Mountain to a terminal at 2,285 meters (7,516 feet). From there you can climb a trail to the summit at 2,464 meters (8,085 feet). Jasper also has its own old hotel, the **Jasper Park Lodge**, located east of the town site on Lac Beauvert and accessible off Maligne Lake Road. The lodge also has an 18-hole golf course.

There are some interesting drives in the Jasper region. **Maligne Lake Road** leads eastward from the Jasper town site area for 44 kilometers (28 miles) to the very scenic Maligne Lake. Along the way you can take a look at Maligne Canyon and Medicine Lake. At Maligne Lake you can either rent your own canoe or take a commercial boat cruise on this 22-kilometer-long mountain lake.

When you drove north to Jasper you followed Highway 93. Athabasca Falls was near the south entrance to Highway 93A. This 24-kilometer (15-mile) road provides access to some interesting sights and locations. One of them is **Mt. Edith Cavell Road**. This narrow road climbs 14.5 kilometers (9 miles) to the foot of **Mount Edith Cavell** and the **Angel Glacier**. Trailers are not allowed on the road so if you have one you'll probably want to make this drive as a side trip once you are established in a campground. Also worth a look is the **Athabasca Trail Exhibit** at the picnic area at the mouth of the Whirlpool River. The Athabasca Trail was another one of those

ATHABASCA FALLS NEAR JASPER

cross-Rockies routes used by explorers and fur traders, it ascended the Athabasca River to this point from the east, then climbed the Whirlpool River through Athabasca Pass before descending to the Columbia River Valley.

Another interesting drive is to follow Hwy. 16 to the north as it follows the Athabasca River on its descent to the eastern plains. Along the way the highway passes between two large lakes: Jasper and Talbot. Forty-four kilometers (27 miles) from Jasper townsite is the junction with Miette Hot Spring Road. Turn right here, and in just 1.3 kilometers (.8 miles) stop at the **Punchbowl Falls** pull-off and take the short walk to the overlook for the very scenic falls. If you continue along the road you will reach **Miette Hot Springs** some 17 kilometers (10.5 miles) from the highway, Parks Canada operates a swimming pool complex here.

Jasper National Park Campgrounds

Whistler's Campground MED ▲ ⌂ ⛺ 🚻 🚿 ♨ 🔥   781 sites, open May 5 to October 10, varies slightly – This is the largest of the campgrounds near Jasper, and the nearest to the town site. It is the only one to offer full hookups, as well as electricity-only and unserviced sites. The campground is located just 2.5 kilometers (1.5) from the town site along Hwy. 93 toward Lake Louise.

Wapiti Campground LOW ▲ ⌂ ⛺ 🚻 🚿 ♨   362 sites, open all year except May 23 to June 17 and Sept. 12 to Oct. 10, varies slightly - Only a little farther south than Whistler's Campground, Wapiti has mostly unserviced sites but a few also offer electrical hookups. To reach the campground drive south on Hwy. 93 from Jasper town site, the campground is on the left after 4.4 kilometers (2.6 miles).

Wabasso Campground LOW ▲ ⌂ ⛺ 🚻 🚿 ♨ 🔥   228 sites, open May 19 to May 22 and June 25 to September 6, varies slightly - Wabasso is located on the Hwy. 93A loop, but you can consider it a Jasper town site-area campground since it is only 17 kilometers (11 miles) from the town site. It is a convenient campground for visits to Mt. Edith Cavell. Most sites are unserviced but a few offer electricity. To reach the campground follow Hwy. 93A from it's junction with Hwy. 93 which is 6.8 kilometers (4.3 miles) south of the junction of Hwy. 93 and Hwy. 16 near Jasper townsite. Drive 9.2 kilometers (5.7 miles) from the junction to the campground.

Pocahontas Campground LOW ▲ 🚿 ♨   140 sites, open May 19 to October 10, varies slightly - If you would like to stay away from the Jasper townsite area this campground in the northeast end of the park is a good choice. It is located on Miette Hot Springs road just 2.2 kilometers (1.4 miles) from Hwy. 16. It is very convenient to Punchbowl Falls

---

DAY 5 - DESTINATION WELLS GRAY PROVINCIAL PARK
371 kilometers (231 miles), 5.5 hours (to Clearwater)

A long the Way - From the Jasper town site area we'll follow Hwy. 16 westward across Yellowhead Pass (1,131 meters, 3,711 feet), and into **Mt. Robson Provincial Park**. You'll be driving along the upper Fraser River Valley and pass Yellowhead and Moose Lakes. **Mt. Robson** is the highest mountain in the Canadian Rockies (3,954 meters, 12,972 feet). You can stop at the visitor center near the western border of the park some 62 kilometers (39 miles) west of Yellowhead Pass. From the visitor center you have a spectacular view of the mountain. The reason it is so impressive is that the visitor center sits at an altitude of only about 850 meters (2,800 feet) and is only 11 kilometers from the mountain, you definitely get the full effect.

From Mt. Robson Provincial Park the highway continues westward until it meets Highway 5 near Tête Jaune Cache. Turn south here toward Kamloops. The highway climbs over a low pass and then follows the North Thompson River Valley through the small town of Blue River and eventually reaches Clearwater.

WELLS GRAY PROVINCIAL PARK AND CLEARWATER

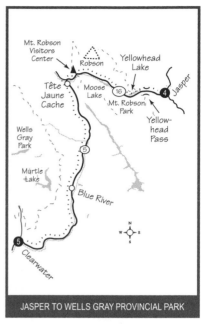

JASPER TO WELLS GRAY PROVINCIAL PARK

Clearwater (population 1,700) serves as the gateway to Wells Gray Provincial Park. The small town stretches along the highway and offers a few restaurants, stores and campgrounds. There is also an info centre at the junction with Wells Gray Park Road, a good place to pick up information about facilities and conditions in the park.

Wells Gray Provincial Park is very large but much of it is pretty hard to reach. The southern portion of the park near Clearwater is the most accessible for RVers. This park is known for its waterfalls, you can see three of them by taking an easy three hour drive north from Clearwater. The road that leads from Clearwater into the park is not a major highway but also no particular challenge. It is paved all the way to Helmcken Falls, a distance of 47 kilometers (29 miles). From a junction just before you reach the falls an unpaved road continues on into the park to Clearwater Lake, another 28 kilometers (17 miles).

Spahats Falls is really in another park, **Spahats Creek Provincial Park**. It takes about 10 minutes to walk to the viewpoint where you see Spahats Creek fall about 60 meters out of an impressive gorge and then flow into Clearwater Creek. The falls are 10 kilometers (6 miles) from the junction in Clearwater.

35 kilometers (22 miles) from the junction in Clearwater you enter Wells Gray Provincial Park. In just another few kilometers you'll see the parking area for the

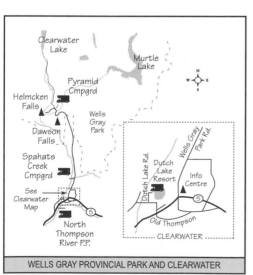

WELLS GRAY PROVINCIAL PARK AND CLEARWATER

Dawson Falls viewpoint. A short walk takes you to a viewpoint where you can see the Murtle River flow over a 20-meter drop.

The most famous of the falls in the park is undoubtedly **Helmcken Falls**. This is the fourth highest waterfall in British Columbia and an unusually impressive sight due to the volume of water and the massive amounts of spray rising into the air. The water falls into a fairly restricted bowl causing strong updrafts and heavy mists. The falls are 47 kilometers (29 miles) from the junction in Clearwater.

Wells Gray Provincial Park and Clearwater Area Campgrounds

🚐 **Dutch Lake Resort and RV Park** [MED] [icons] P.O. Box 2160, RR2 361 Ridge Rd., Clearwater, BC V0E 1N0; 250 674-3351 or 888 884-4424 for reservations; 65 sites, open April 15 to October 3 - This is a pleasant commercial campground with sites near a lake, it is in the community of Clearwater. From the info centre at the junction of the Wells Gray Park Road and Hwy. 5 continue southwest on the highway for 1 kilometer (.6 miles). Turn right on the Old Thompson Highway and drive 1.1 kilometers (.7 miles) to Dutch Lake Road. Turn right here and drive through a subdivision, you'll soon see the campground entrance on your right.

🚐 **North Thompson River Provincial Park** [LOW] [icons]   61 sites, open April through October - This large provincial campground is near Clearwater just off the highway. The Clearwater and Thompson Rivers meet here, some sites are right on the Thompson River. From the junction of the Wells Gray Park Road and Highway 5 drive southwest 4.8 kilometers (3 miles), the campground entrance is on the left.

🚐 **Pyramid Campground** [LOW] [icons]   50 sites, open May through September - This campground is inside Wells Gray Provincial Park about 4 kilometers from Helmcken Falls. Sites are large and there is a trail from the campground that leads 14 kilometers to Majerus and Horseshoe Falls on the Murtle River. You can't miss this campground, the entrance is right at the junction of the paved road to Helmcken Falls and the gravel road to Clearwater Lake. It is 43 kilometers (27 miles) north of Clearwater.

🚐 **Spahats Creek Campground** [LOW] [icons]   20 sites, open April through October - Located right next to Spahats Creek Falls about 10 kilometers (6 miles) from the junction of Highway 5 and the Wells Gray Park access road.

DAY 6 - DESTINATION THOMPSON AND FRASER RIVER CANYONS
286 kilometers (177 miles), 4 hours (to Lytton)

A long the Way - From Clearwater we follow Highway 5 and the North Thompson River for 115 kilometers (71 miles) south to Kamloops. Here you have a choice. If you want to get back to Vancouver a day early you can continue on Highway 5, from here to Hope known as the Coquihalla Highway. This is a high-speed toll highway that will cut several driving hours from the trip back to Vancouver.

On the other had, if you have another day and wish to see one of the most impressive river canyons and railroad/road engineering projects in the world, head westward from Kamloops on Highway 1. This is our old friend, the Trans-Canada Highway, last seen in Banff National Park. From Kamloops the road travels along Kamloops Lake and then parallel to the Thompson River. When it reaches Cache Creek the highway turns south and soon you are in the Thompson River Canyon.

THOMPSON AND FRASER RIVER CANYONS

On a map the Thompson and Fraser River Canyons appear to be the best route for a railroad or road from the coast at Vancouver to the interior of British Columbia. In fact, the rivers probably are the best route, but they certainly didn't prove to be easy routes. A trip through the canyons is interesting because it allows you to see the difficulties faced over the years

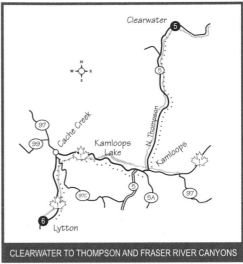

CLEARWATER TO THOMPSON AND FRASER RIVER CANYONS

by the people who needed to pass this way: first the Indians, then the fur traders, then the gold seekers, then the railroads, and finally the Trans-Canada Highway.

Leaving Cache Creek the highway crosses some high dry country and then descends to the level of the Thompson River. In many sections the road is built upon fill right in the river channel. At **Spences Bridge** the highway crosses over the river to the south shore.

The Thompson and the Fraser come together at **Lytton**, you might want to drive down through town to the mouth of the Thompson to see the muddy Fraser and the much clearer Thompson come together. A bridge crosses the Thompson here, you may be tempted to follow the small paved road 69 kilometers (43 miles) north along the east shore of the Fraser River to Lillooet. **Lillooet** now has a population of 2,000 or so but for a very short time during the Cariboo Gold Rush in the early 1860s it was the second-largest town north of San Francisco.

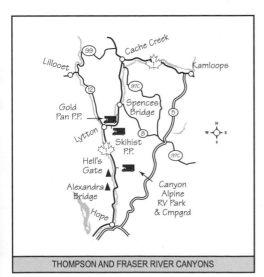

THOMPSON AND FRASER RIVER CANYONS

From Lytton south the highway is in the **Fraser River Canyon**. Notice that there are two sets of railroad tracks in much of the canyon. Eight kilometers (5 miles) south of Lytton there are two railroad bridges where both sets of tracks cross to opposite sides. This seemingly useless exercise was necessary since the first set of tracks had been built along the easiest route by the Canadian Pacific Railroad. When the Canadian Northern built their set of tracks later there was only room on the other side of the river.

Fifty-four kilometers (33 miles) south

of Lytton you will see the upper station of an **aerial tram** on the right side of the highway. You should at least stop and take a look. It is possible to walk down to the river here but the tram is much easier, it runs from April 1 to October 30. Below is **Hell's Gate**, a spot where the river flows so fast that the salmon have to use fishways to get through. Actually, before 1913 the fish could make it on their own, then railroad construction caused a slide that blocked the river to the fish much of the time. The fishways were built several years later to restore the run of salmon up the Fraser. The water level of the Fraser through here varies as much as 30 meters (100 feet) so at higher water levels you can't even see the top of the fishways. You may find it hard to believe but during the construction of the railroad a sternwheeler actually made it up the river through Hell's Gate.

Near Hell's Gate you will pass through 7 tunnels and cross a modern bridge across the river. This modern bridge replaced a much smaller suspension bridge, and that bridge remains, although it is not used at all. The walk from the highway down to the **Alexandra Bridge** is a nice short hike, the trail starts at Alexandra Bridge Provincial Park which is 10.3 kilometers (6.4 miles) south of the Hell's Gate tram station.

Thompson and Fraser River Canyon Campgrounds

You'll find that there is a thin string of campgrounds along the Thompson and Fraser Rivers along this route.

Gold Pan Provincial Park ⊡ ⛺ 🔥   14 sites, open all year - This is a very popular little campground, probably because it is right on the river below the highway where everyone driving by sees it. The campground also attracts fishermen, gold panners, and river rafters. Maneuvering room is tight for big rigs, take a look before you commit yourself. The campground is right off the highway 8 kilometers (5 miles) west of Spences Bridge on Highway 1.

Skihist Provincial Park ⊡ ⛺ ⊞ ⛾ 🔥   56 sites, open May to September - A nice provincial park campground set in pines above the highway in a spectacular section of the Thompson River Canyon. This can be a very warm campground in the middle of the summer. The old Cariboo Wagon Road ran through this park and there are sometimes elk around. The access road up to the campground is 27 kilometers (17 miles) from the bridge at Spences Bridge on Highway 1 and 8 kilometers (5 miles) east of Lytton.

Canyon Alpine RV Park and Campground ⊡ 🚶 ⊞ ⛾ 🐾 🔥 ☰ 🍴 ▦   50490 Trans-Canada Hwy., Box 398, Boston Bar, B.C. V0K 1C0; 604 867-9734 or 800 644-7275 for reservations; 31 sites, open April 15 to October 15 - This is a good campground for big rigs with terraced pull-through sites. It's located 39 km (24 miles) south of Lytton and 5 km (3 miles) north of Boston Bar.

Day 7 - Destination Vancouver
256 kilometers (159 miles), 3 1/2 hours

Once Highway 1 crosses to the west bank of the Fraser River you are in the lower reaches of the canyon. The road remains on the west side for 42 kilometers (26 miles) until it crosses again at Hope.

Just before reaching Hope you have a route choice. If you are in a hurry you can continue on to Hope and then follow Highway 1 back to Vancouver, this is the same highway that you drove when you were heading east on the first day of this tour.

If you have more time you can follow Highway 7 along the north side of the Fraser River. This is a much smaller two-lane highway. You can follow it all the way to Vancouver or cross over the Fraser River to intersect Highway 1 near Agassiz (near Bridal Falls on Hwy. 1) or Mission (near Abbotsford on Hwy. 1).

Information Resources

See our Internet site at www.rollinghomes.com for Internet site addresses.

Destination Okanagan Valley

Minter Gardens, 52892 Bunker Road, Rosedale, B.C.; 888 646-8377

Hope Visitor Info Centre, 919 Water Ave, Box 370, Hope, B.C. V0X 1L0; 604 869-2021

Manning Provincial Park, Box 3, 69 km Hope-Princeton Hwy., Manning Park, BC V0X 1R0; 250 840-8836

Penticton Visitor Info Centre, 888 Westminster Ave West, Penticton, B.C. V2A 8R2; 250 493-4055

Kelowna Visitor Info Centre, 544 Harvey Ave, Kelowna, B.C. V1Y 6C9; 250 861-1515

Destination Revelstoke

Sicamous Visitor Info Centre, 110 Finlayson St, Box 346, Sicamous, B.C. V0E 2V0; 250 836-3313

Revelstoke Visitor Info Centre, 204 Campbell Ave, Box 490, Revelstoke, B.C.; V0E 2S0; 250 837-5345

Revelstoke Railway Museum, P.O. Box 3018, 719 Track Street, Revelstoke, B.C. V0E 2S0; 250 837-6060

Mount Revelstoke and Glacier National Parks, P.O. Box 350, Revelstoke, B.C. V0E 2S0; 250 837-7500

Destination Banff National Park

Yoho National Park, P.O. Box 99, Field, B.C. V0A 1G0; 250 343-6783

Banff National Park: P.O. Box 900, Banff, Alberta T0L 0C0; 403 762-1550

Destination Jasper National Park

Jasper National Park, P.O. Box 10, Jasper, Alberta T0E 1E0; 780 852-6176

Destination Clearwater and Wells Gray Provincial Park

Mt. Robertson Provincial Park: Box 579, Valemount, B.C. V0E 2Z0; 250 566-4325

Clearwater Visitor Info Centre: 425 E. Yellowhead Hwy, Box 1988, RR1, Clearwater, B.C. V0E 1N0; 250 674-2646

Wells Gray Provincial Park: 1210 McGill Rd, Kamloops, B.C. V2C 6N6; 250 851-3000

Destination Thompson and Fraser River Valley

Kamloops Visitor Info Centre, 1290 West Trans Canada Hwy, Kamloops, B.C. V2C 6R3; 250 374-3377

Lytton Visitor Info Centre, 400 Fraser St, Box 460, Lytton, B.C. V0K 1Z0; 250 455-2523

Hell's Gate Airtram, P.O. Box 129, Hope, B.C. V0X 1L0; 604 867-9277

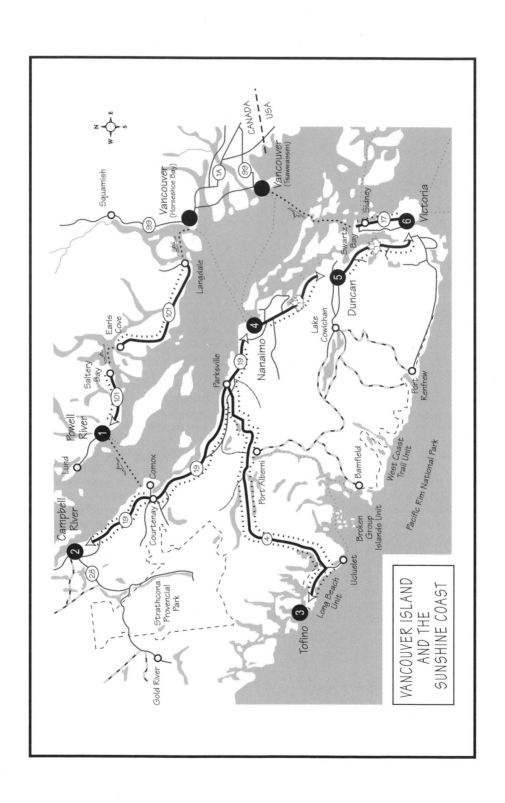

VANCOUVER ISLAND
AND THE
SUNSHINE COAST

Chapter 13

Tour 8

Vancouver Island and the Sunshine Coast

Top Attractions

✦ The Sunshine Coast

✦ Ferry rides up the Sunshine Coast and through the Gulf Islands

✦ Campbell River and great salmon fishing

✦ Pacific Rim National Park

✦ First Nations Culture

✦ Victoria

General Description

One of the most popular destinations in the Pacific Northwest is Vancouver Island. This large island is easily accessible using frequent ferries from near Vancouver on the mainland. On the island you'll find British Columbia's capital, Victoria, as well as remote beaches, northwest Indian culture (called First Nations in Canada), some of the best salmon fishing in the world, and pristine evergreen forests. An added bonus of this tour is the Sunshine Coast which stretches over 100 kilometers (62 miles) north from the city of Vancouver along the mainland and offers surprisingly good weather and warm water because it is in the rain shadow of Vancouver Island's mountains.

The tour starts at the Horseshoe Bay ferry terminal just north of Vancouver. On the first day you take two ferry rides and do some driving on scenic two-lane roads as you travel up the Sunshine Coast to Powell River. Later, when you are ready, you take another ferry across to Vancouver Island. On the Island you visit Campbell River, and then work your way down the island with visits to Tofino, Nanaimo, Duncan, and finally the Victoria area in the south. This circular route ends with another ferry trip through the Gulf Islands to Tsawwassen which is located on the mainland just south of the city of Vancouver.

This is a relaxed tour with relatively short distances between most of your stops. Many days you will have time for a significant amount of sightseeing or just plain enjoying the outdoors. There are also plenty of reasons to expand this tour into a two or three week trip. Total driving distance on this tour is 833 kilometers (516 miles) with 22.5 hours on the road (including ferries).

The Roads and Ferries

The ferries used in this circular tour are all operated by the British Columbia Ferry Corporation, also known as BC Ferries. It is not possible to make reservations for these crossings. Reservations are not usually necessary anyway, however, it is best to avoid travel on weekends during the high season: late May, June, July, August and early September, to avoid long lines. There is a special fare plan for this circle route which is known as the Circlepac and which will net you a discount of about 15%. If your rig is over 7 feet high or 20 feet long you will be paying more than the normal passenger vehicle rate for ferry travel. See the individual route sections for other information about the ferries. Schedule and route information is available at the number given at the end of this chapter.

For the most part the roads traveled on this tour are very good. Few are more than two-lane highways, but they are adequate for all types of RVs and there are no high passes. You will find much more information about the roads in the individual sections of this chapter.

Practical Tips

It is best to make this tour during the summer, say from May to September. The months of April and October are acceptable if you don't mind some rain and have a good warm RV in which to spend the night. You will find that some campgrounds are open year-round, many people love to visit the wild western coast around Tofino just for the winter storms.

It is pretty easy to shorten this loop if you don't have time for the whole thing. One way would be to cut out the Sunshine Coast and Campbell River by taking a ferry directly from Horseshoe Bay to Nanaimo. You could still make the drive out to Tofino (day 3) or skip that too.

DAY 1 - DESTINATION POWELL RIVER
119 kilometers (74 miles) (does not include ferry), 5 hours (does include ferry)

A long the Way - The first segment of today's drive is a 45-minute ferry ride from Horseshoe Bay across Howe Sound to Langdale. There are frequent ferries from Horseshoe Bay (approximately every two hours) so you don't have to worry much about your schedule there, but you should check when you buy your ticket to see when the Earls Cove to Saltery Bay ferry runs. Otherwise you might find yourself waiting for quite a long period at the dock in Earls Cove, particularly if you arrive there in the early afternoon. The travel time given above for this day's drive includes a half-hour for loading and unloading at each of the ferry landings.

When you leave the boat in Langdale you are on the Sunshine Coast proper. Some folks call this area the Lower Coast. Highway 101 runs north near the coast for 79 kilometers (49 miles) through the communities of Gibsons, Roberts Creek, Sechelt, Halfmoon Bay, Madeira Park, and Pender Harbor to Earls Cove.

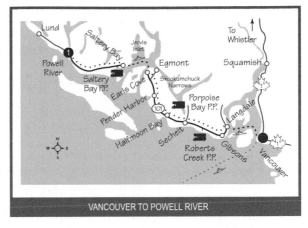

VANCOUVER TO POWELL RIVER

If you decide that you really love the lower Sunshine Coast you will find plenty of campgrounds along the way. There is a good provincial campground set in a cedar grove called Roberts Creek Provincial Park just 15 kilometers (9 miles) north of the Langdale ferry terminal and another larger one called Porpoise Bay Provincial Park about 23 kilometers (14 miles) north of the terminal. There are also a number of commercial campgrounds in the Pender Harbor area.

FERRY ARRIVING AT EARLS COVE

The **Skookumchuck Narrows** are famous world-wide. These are saltwater rapids, much like a river. In the narrows the salt water rushes both north and south, depending upon the tide. You'll want to be on hand when the tide changes at either high or low water so that you can see the flow change directions. You'll find that the best viewing times are easy to find in local papers, at the information centers, and even posted at the trail head. To reach the narrows drive 6 kilometers (4 miles) east on Egmont Road from a point on Hwy. 101 about 1 kilometer (.6 mile) south of the Earls Cove ferry landing. Park along the road in the parking lot and walk down an access road and then along a fine trail for a distance of 4 kilometers (2.5 miles) to the narrows.

The ferry from Earls Cover to Saltery Bay also runs approximately every two hours, but there is a 4-hour gap in the schedule in the afternoon. This run takes about 50 minutes and crosses Jervis Inlet. The coast north from Saltery Bay to Powell River could properly be called the Upper Sunshine Coast but it is so dominated by the town of Powell River that most folks just call it Powell River. The distance from Saltery Bay to Powell River is 27 kilometers (17 miles).

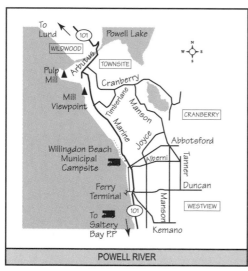

POWELL RIVER

Powell River (population 20,000) was a forestry-dependant town for years, in fact it remains a forestry town since it is home to a huge Pacifica Papers pulp mill. Today, however, tourism is also an important force. Powell River occupies an area offering a full range of outdoor attractions including fishing, kayaking, scuba diving, canoeing, hiking, and golf. The town has all the amenities including good shopping for supplies, restaurants and public transit.

Powell River is actually made up of four communities. The farthest south is **Westview**. This is the first you will see when you arrive from the south, it has the ferry terminal and most of the services. North a few miles but south of the very short river that Powell River is named after is the original town site. It is actually called **Townsite** and is the site of the pulp mill as well as many residences. To the east of Townsite is a suburb built around **Cranberry Lake**, and north of the mouth of the Powell River is **Wildwood**.

While you will probably spend most of your time in Westview, you will find a visit to Townsite interesting. It has actually been designated a Heritage Area by the Canadian government. From the **Mill Viewpoint** you can see the chain of 10 cargo ship hulks that make up the breakwater for the paper mill harbor. **Tours of the mill** are available during the summer and so are tours of the town site. Check with the information centre about both.

There are a wide selection of hiking trails available in the Powell River area. Probably the easiest and most accessible is a short trail north from Willingdon Beach Park along the bed of an old beachfront railroad. You'll find signs identifying different trees and also vintage logging equipment on display from the nearby museum. Another interesting trail is the wheelchair accessible trail circling nearby Inland Lake. For a more challenging trail consider the 165-kilometer (102-mile) Sunshine Coast trail from Sarah Point in the north to Saltery Bay.

You should drive the final 30 kilometers (19 miles) along Highway 101 to **Lund**. This is the northern end of Highway 101 which is said to stretch all the way south to Chile. Lund is a jumping-off point for boating the waters to the north. The historic Lund Hotel makes a good place to catch a meal.

Powell River Campgrounds

🚐 **Willingdon Beach Municipal Campsite** 🔲🔺🔲🔲🔲🔲🔲🔲🔲🔲 6910 Duncan Street, Powell River, B.C. V8A 1V4; 604 485-2242; 70 sites, open all year - A convenient location right next to the beach makes this a fine place to spend the night in Powell River. You can walk in to town for shopping and restaurants. The beach park next door offers a swimming beach and fishing pier. There's also an easy hiking trail leading north from the campground. To reach the campground drive north on Hwy. 101 from the Westview section of Powell River, the campground is on the left at the north edge of the built-up area.

🚐 **Saltery Bay Mermaid Cove Provincial Park** 🔲🔺🔲🔲🔲 800 689-9025 for reservations; 42 sites, open all year - This campground is known as a scuba-diving destination, there is an underwater mermaid statue just off the beach. Drive north on Hwy. 101 from the Saltery Bay ferry terminal, the campground is on the left in 1.5 kilometers (1 mile).

DAY 2 - DESTINATION CAMPBELL RIVER

54 kilometers (33 miles)(does not include ferry), 3.5 hours (including ferry)

Along the Way - The ferry from Powell River to Little River near Comox on Vancouver Island makes the trip only a few times each day. Make sure to check the schedule so that you don't oversleep. The crossing takes about an hour and a half.

From Comox follow Highway 19A north some 45 kilometers (28 miles) to Campbell River. By selecting Hwy. 19A as you near Campbell River you'll come in to town along coast.

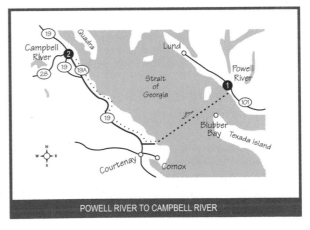

POWELL RIVER TO CAMPBELL RIVER

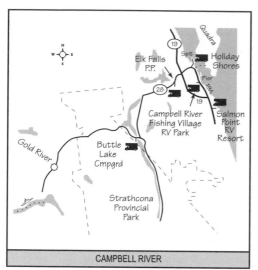

Campbell River (population 30,000) is probably best known as a fishing destination. The town is located at the south end of Discovery Passage at a place where there are extraordinary numbers of bait fish. The bait fish attract salmon year-round. The huge Tyee (large king) salmon are the most-desired prize, but you can also fish for sockeye (red), coho (silver), chum (dog) and pink salmon.

Because Campbell River is a fishing resort town you will find a wide variety of tourist facilities including RV parks, restaurants, and fishing charter operators.

One of the most interesting places to visit in Campbell River is the **Saltwater Fishing Pier**. It is located right next to the downtown boat harbor and juts out into Discovery Passage. Lots of fish are caught here, it's great fun to watch the action.

From Campbell River you can catch a small ferry across Discovery Passage to **Quadra Island**. You'll need to take a vehicle for transportation on the island, it is quite large. There's an excellent First Nations museum here called **Kwagiulth Museum** in Cape Mudge Village south of the ferry landing. There are also **petroglyphs** on display that have been moved here from other locations for protection from vandals.

Highway 28 leads westward from Campbell River through **Strathcona Provincial Park** to Gold River and the west coast of Vancouver Island. There are two large campgrounds in this largest of Vancouver Island's parks suitable for RVs as well as a number of hiking trails, particularly along the side road that leaves Highway 28 near the Buttle Lake Bridge and heads south along the east shore of Buttle Lake. Ninety-two kilometers (57 miles) from Campbell River the road reaches Gold River, a factory town for a pulp mill, and then continues another 14 kilometers (9 miles) to tidewater. From there you can ride the converted minesweeper MV Upchuck III which carries supplies to remote communities along the west coast of the island.

Campbell River Campgrounds

🚐 **Campbell River Fishing Village RV Park** 260 South Island Highway, Campbell River, B.C.   V9W 1A4; 250 287-3630; www.havannah.bc.ca/fishvill; 47 sites, open all year - One of several small RV parks along Hwy. 19A across the highway from the ocean just south of downtown Campbell River. This one rents fishing skiffs and offers guided fishing. A 5-kilometer (3-mile) bike trail runs along the beach across the street and you can easily walk in to town.

🚐 **Holiday Shores RV Park** 3001 Spit Road, Box 274, Campbell River, B.C. V9W 5B1; 250 286-6142 or 888 611-2142 for reservations; 60

sites, open May 1 to October 1 - One of three large RV parks located just outside Campbell River to the north on the Tyee Spit. This one is beachside. Sea planes are based across the road. It's a good big-rig park.

Elks Falls Provincial Park `LOW` `△` `🚐` `🔥` 800 689-9025 for reservations; 122 sites, open all year - This large provincial park campground along the Quinsam River is very popular because it is very near Campbell River, just 6 kilometers (4 miles) to the west off Hwy. 28 to Strathcona Provincial Park. Many sites are right along the river. There are good hiking trails from the campground.

Buttle Lake Provincial Park Campground `LOW` `△` `🔥` `⚮` `🏞` 85 sites, open all year - A large campground in a quiet location along the shore of Buttle Lake in Strathcona Provincial Park. Fishing is good in the lake and there are a number of hiking trails in the vicinity. It is located about 48 kilometers (30 miles) east of Campbell River on Hwy. 28 to Gold River.

Salmon Point RV Resort `MED` `△` `⚡` `🚐` `🚿` `🔌` `⚮` `🚻` `🍴` `⊙` 2176 Salmon Point Rd., Campbell River, B.C. V9H 1E5; 250 923-6605; 139 sites, open all year - A large commercial RV resort about 19 kilometers (12 miles) south of Campbell River offering shaded sites alongside a first-class marina. Some sites are beachside and there is a fine swimming pool with an indoor hot tub as well as an excellent restaurant. The campground is well-signed from Hwy. 19.

DAY 3 - DESTINATION TOFINO
268 kilometers (166 miles), 5 hours

A long the Way - The drive from Campbell River to Tofino takes you south through the Comox Valley region to Qualicum Beach and then all the way across the island to the west coast. While the drive sounds ambitious it really is no problem.

From Campbell River follow Highway 19 south. After 45 kilometers (28 miles) you'll reach Courtenay and drive through an area of strip malls and giant supermarkets. Watch for signs for Highway 19A, it is the road that follows the coast south. A new section of Hwy. 19 passes farther inland and is not as scenic. You'll pass several small seaside towns including Union Bay, Fanny Bay, Bowser, and finally reach Qualicum Beach. This is an attractive stretch of ocean-side country and you might want to watch for a suitable RV park to stop and spend some time. There are many candidates. Just south is Parksville, also with attractive RV campgrounds, we mention two of these as alternatives to staying in Nanaimo on day 4.

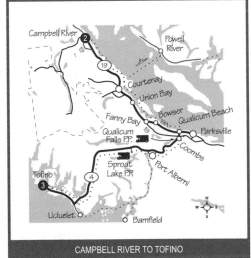

CAMPBELL RIVER TO TOFINO

At Qualicum Beach you will spot Highway 4 heading up the hill to the west toward Port Alberni and eventually Tofino. Turn here and you'll pass through the business district, cross under the inland Highway 19, and then pass the little town of **Coombs**. Pull over and take a look around. You'll probably enjoy visiting the old Coombs General Store, Frontier Town, antique shops, and the Old Country Market. Don't miss the goats on the roof! Heading west from Coombs toward Port Alberni watch for the sign for **Butterfly World**, it's a tropical garden filled with butterflies and birds. Farther west you'll see the signs for **Qualicum Falls Provincial Park**. There's a good campground here as well as hiking paths to see the falls. A little farther west you'll find yourself passing through an area of huge trees, mostly Douglas firs. There's a pull-off parking area here and you can follow trails through **Cathedral Grove in MacMillan Park**.

The road soon rises and passes over low Alberni Summit (375 meters) and then descends to pass through the northern edge of **Port Alberni**. You might consider pausing here, this is the home port for the **MV Lady Rose**. This little ship and another operated by the same company (the MV Frances Barkley) steam down Alberni Inlet and make deliveries to many little towns along the west coast. A day spent riding along is a popular trip. The ships depart from **Alberni Harbor Quay** which has additional attractions including shops, restaurants, and the Forestry Visitors Center.

About 5 kilometers (3 miles) beyond Port Alberni watch for the sign for Sproat Lake Provincial Park. In addition to being a great campground, this lake is the home of two huge **Mars Martin flying boats**. They were built during World War II and today are used as water bombers for fighting forest fires. If they're not in use you'll see them anchored just offshore from the park, really an unusual sight.

About 40 kilometers (25 miles) beyond the park you'll reach 574-meter Sutton Pass and then the road descends steeply and in another 10 kilometers (6 miles) you will reach a T intersection. Ucluelet is to the left (6 kilometers, 4 miles) and Tofino to the right (33 kilometers, 20 miles). Most of the Long Beach section of Pacific Rim National Park is also to the right. For now turn to the right, you can come back and explore Ucluelet later if you desire.

TOFINO AND PACIFIC RIM NATIONAL PARK RESERVE

After you turn north you will almost immediately enter **Pacific Rim National Park Reserve**. There are actually three scattered sections to this park: Long Beach, the West Coast Trail, and the Broken Islands Group. This section, Long Beach, stretches along the coast almost as far as Tofino. Several short roads lead to beach parking lots, overlooks, and trails. There is a use fee for using this park, the parking lots have self-service machines allowing you to buy a ticket allowing you to park for several hours or all day long. The machines accept coins, currency, and credit cards. Note that you do not have to pay a fee to drive through the park, just to park. If it is late you may want to drive on to Tofino and then return to explore the following day.

Almost immediately after entering the park you'll come to the sign pointing right for the Information Centre. Then on the left is the turn for **Wickaninnish Centre** which offers museum-type displays and a restaurant as well as wheelchair-accessible views and trails. The center overlooks Wickaninnish Beach. As you continue to drive north toward Tofino you'll pass turn-offs for the Rainforest Trail, Coombers Beach and Spruce Fringe Trail, Green Point Campground, Long Beach, and Radar Hill.

The section of road through the park is 23 kilometers (14 miles) long. When you leave the park you'll start seeing the outskirts of Tofino. The road passes turnoffs to several resorts, restaurants, and campgrounds and then arrives in little Tofino, the end of the road.

The town of **Tofino** (population 1,100) is quite small and very tourist oriented. You'll find studios, stores, and restaurants in a compact area. Down the hill are three docks: the crab dock, Fisherman's Wharf, and the government wharf. Much of the activity of the town is oriented around **Clayoquot Sound**. There are popular charter trips for fishing, whale watching and sightseeing. One popular destination is **Hot Springs Cove** which of-

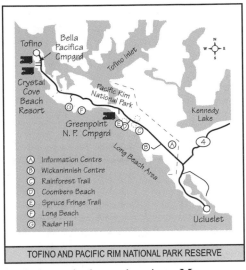

TOFINO AND PACIFIC RIM NATIONAL PARK RESERVE

fers the only hot springs on Vancouver Island. A much shorter hop is to **Meares Island** where you can follow hiking trails through the rain forest. These are also excellent kayaking waters.

The big event of the year in Tofino is the **Pacific Rim Whale Festival** held during the last half of March and first weekend of April. It celebrates the spring gray whale migration.

Tofino and Long Beach Area Campgrounds

🚐 **Crystal Cove Beach Resort** [MED] 🔺 ⛺ 📶 🚻 🚮 🔥 📮 🍳 Box 559, Tofino, B.C. V0R 2Z0; 250 725-4213; www.alberni.net/crystal_cove/; 95 sites, open all year - This resort is located about 2.4 kilometers (1.5 miles) from Tofino next to MacKenzie Beach. There are upscale rental cabins as well as the RV sites. Some large and more expensive sites overlook the water while many others are arranged in a circle and are well-separated by natural growth. All have full hookups. Watch for the campground sign pointed west about 2 kilometers (1.2 miles) outside Tofino on the main highway.

🚐 **Bella Pacifica Campground** [MED] 🔺 ⛺ 📶 🚻 🚮 🔥 🍳 Box 413, Tofino, B.C. V0R 2Z0; 250 725-3400; www.bellapacifica.com; 160 sites, open March 13 to November 12 - This campground is also on Mackenzie beach. There are well-spaced sites with no hookups as well as more crowded sites with hookups overlooking the beach. Watch for the sign for the campground pointed west about 1.6 kilometers (1 mile) outside Tofino on the main road.

🚐 **Greenpoint National Park Campground** [LOW] 🔺 📶 🚻 🔥 800 689-9025 for reservations; 147 sites, open March through mid-October, varies - This is the only campground in the park, it's very popular, you must make reservations during the summer. Some sites overlook the beach. Many are very long and will accommodate large rigs. Try to get one of the front sites overlooking the beach, the ones in back seem overgrown and dark. From the information centre drive north 10 kilometers (6.2 miles), the entrance is on the left.

Day 4 - Destination Nanaimo
215 kilometers (133 miles), 4 hours (to Nanaimo)

Along the Way - To drive to Nanaimo you must retrace your trip westward on Highway 4 as far as Qualicum Beach. You might stop and take a look at Ucluelet which we bypassed on the outbound trip.

Ucluelet is in many ways much like Tofino. While Tofino is the gateway to Clayoquot Sound to the north, Ucluelet is one of several gateways to Barkley Sound to the south. The sound is also accessible by road from Port Alberni and Bamfield. As you drive in to town you can't miss the large ship tied up to the town wharf, this is the *Canadian Princess* which has been converted to a hotel and does not move from the dock. If you drive through town and then take a right on Coast Guard Drive you will find yourself at the light house on **Amphitrite Point** which offers good views of the entrance to Barkley Sound. There are two well-signed campgrounds in Ucluelet that make good alternatives for those listed above for Tofino.

When you have backtracked across the island and again reached the east coast in Qualicum Beach, turn south. Just south of Qualicum Beach is Parksville, which, like Qualicum Beach, has many campgrounds. This is a good place to stay in the Nanaimo area, most of the campgrounds we detail below are in this area, it makes a good base. Highways 19 and 19A merge just south of Parksville, then 16 kilometers (10 miles) south, they split again with the new Highway 19 Nanaimo Parkway (bypass route) being the preferred route to the Nanaimo campground mentioned below.

NANAIMO

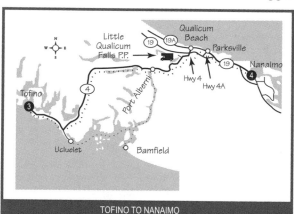

TOFINO TO NANAIMO

Nanaimo (population 80,000) is the second largest city on Vancouver Island and British Columbia's third oldest incorporated town. The early reason for the town's existence was coal, big deposits close to tidewater were the economic driver. Today coal isn't mined here, there is little evidence that it ever was unless you know where to look. Nanaimo has three ferry terminals: north of the central area is Departure Bay with service to Horseshoe Bay on the mainland, south of town is Duke Point with service to Tsawwassen on the mainland, and there is also a small ferry to Gabriola Island. Actually, two even smaller ferries serve Newcastle Island Provincial Park and little Protection Island in the harbor.

The charm of Nanaimo is in its waterfront. There is a **four-kilometer (2.5 mile) walking trail** connecting a chain of parks. Look for **Swy-a-lana Lagoon Park** which is a man-made lagoon designed to attract marine life. Nearby is the pedestrian-only ferry out to **Newcastle Island**, a provincial marine park with a 7.5-kilometer (4.7-mile) trail that circles the island. At the southern end of the waterfront trail you are near the center of the city and several interesting sights. The **Bastion** is a blockhouse built by the Hudson's Bay Company in 1853, now it is the site of the **Bastion Museum** and a daily firing of cannons at noon during the summer. Nearby is the **Nanaimo Museum** with historical displays including a coal mine from the town's early days.

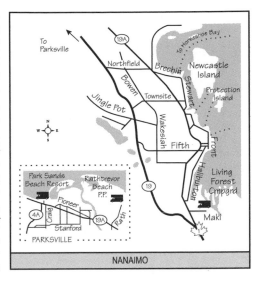

Nanaimo has a huge annual celebration known as the **Marine Festival** during the last half of July. The eagerly anticipated main event is the **World Championship Bathtub Race** between Nanaimo and Vancouver.

Nanaimo Area Campgrounds

🚐 **Park Sands Beach Resort** MED ⛺ 🏕 🔌 🚻 🎣 📶 🖼 📷 105 E. Island Hwy, Box 179, Parksville, B.C. V9P 2G4; 250 248-3171; 99 sites, open Easter to Thanksgiving - This campground is located north of Nanaimo in Parksville. It is one of many there. Many, including this one, are right on the water. The distance from Nanaimo is only 36 kilometers (22 miles). From the intersection of Hwy. 19A and Hwy. 4 along the water in Qualicum Beach drive south for 11.6 kilometers (7.2 miles). You will be in Parksville, the campground is on the left.

🚐 **Rathtrevor Beach Provincial Park** LOW ⛺ 🔌 🚻 🔥 📶 🖼 800 689-9025 for reservations; 175 sites, open all year - Located just south of Parksville, this extremely popular provincial campground is often full during the summer. It's best known for its great beach. On a warm day the incoming tide becomes warm enough for swimming, or at least wading. From the intersection of Hwy. 19A and Hwy. 4 in Qualicum Beach drive south for 14 kilometers (8.9 miles) until you are just south of Parksville. The campground is 2.4 kilometers (1.5 miles) north of the intersection of Hwy. 19 and 19A.

🚐 **Little Qualicum Falls Provincial Park** LOW ⛺ 🚻 🔥 📶 🖼 800 689-9025 for reservations; 91 sites, open all year - Another popular provincial campground in the area. This one is next to Little Qualicum Falls. Swimming is possible in pools in the river or in lakes near the campground. The campground is located inland from Qualicum Beach along Hwy. 4, it is 13 kilometers (8 miles) from the coast.

🚐 **Living Forest Campground** LOW ⛺ 🏕 🔌 🚻 🎣 🔥 📶 🖼 📷 GS 6 Maki Road, Nanaimo, BC V9R 6N7; 250 755-1755; http://www.livingforest.com/; 190 sites, open all year - This is a large campground located about 5 kilometers (3 miles) south of central Nanaimo overlooking the outlet of the Nanaimo River. It's good if you want to be close to town. We prefer the sites overlooking the harbor. Swimming is on the beach below the campground. To reach the campground from the north follow Hwy. 19, the Nanaimo Parkway (bypass route) around the west side of town. At the south end of town take Exit 9 and head back toward Nanaimo on Hwy. 1 Drive two blocks and turn right on Maki. The campground is just ahead.

Day 5 - Destination Duncan and Cowichan Lake
52 kilometers (32 miles), 1 hour (to Duncan)

A long the Way - Duncan lies only an hour's drive south of Nanaimo along what is designated as Highway 1. It's really the same highway that you have been following south along the east side of Vancouver Island, but here it is considered to be the final kilometers of the Trans-Canada Highway that begins in Newfoundland and ends in Victoria.

Before reaching Duncan you will probably want to stop and see **Chemainus**. This town has become famous for the murals painted on the small town's buildings. It seems like everyone stops to take a look around, you might as well too. You'll see the sign taking you east to Chemainus from the highway about 29 kilometers (18 miles) south of Nanaimo. There is quite a bit of parking, even for RVs. Footprints painted on the ground lead you from one mural to the next, and many shops have sprung up to sell you food and souvenirs.

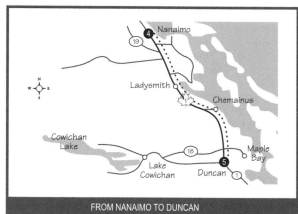

FROM NANAIMO TO DUNCAN

Duncan has yellow footsteps painted on the sidewalks, just like Chemainus. These, however, lead to **totem poles**, not murals. There are about 60 of them. Duncan also is home to the well-known **Cowichan Native Village**. There you'll find a gift shop featuring Cowichan sweaters, the Khowutzun Gallery, and the Longhouse Story Center with a multimedia show of the history of the Cowichan people. There's also a large carving shed and the Bighouse from Expo 86 in Vancouver, it's a replica of a traditional long house. Duncan is also home to the **BC Forest Museum**. The museum has 100 acres of logging displays and a narrow-gauge railway. It is located off Highway 1 just north of Duncan.

Duncan is situated right next to the **Cowichan River** which is 45 kilometers long and leads from Cowichan Lake to tidewater. This is an excellent fishing river, much of it open only to fly fishing. It has steelhead, brown trout and rainbow trout.

There is a paved highway (Highway 18) to **Cowichan Lake** leading west from a point north of Duncan on Highway 1. Twenty-six kilometers (16 miles) up this road you will reach the small community of Lake Cowichan. From here roads follow the north and south shores of the lake, they lead to a web of unpaved logging roads that can take you to Bamfield, Port Renfrew, Carmanah Walbran Provincial Park and Nitinat Lake. These are gravel logging roads with lots of logging truck traffic, before using them check with local information centers to see if they are passable in your rig and to see how much logging traffic you are likely to meet.

Cowichan Lake is one of the largest on Vancouver Island. The southern shore is unusual in that it has much warmer weather than the surrounding region, it has an average maximum temperature of about 75 degrees Fahrenheit. Gordon Bay Provincial Park is a large campground perfectly positioned to take advantage of this fact.

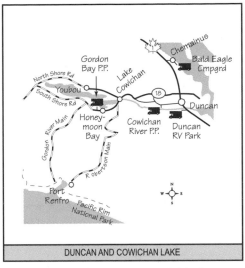

DUNCAN AND COWICHAN LAKE

Duncan Area Campgrounds

Duncan RV Park and Campground 2950 Boys Rd, RR 6, Duncan, B.C. V9L 4T8; 250 748-8511; 96 sites, open all year - This small commercial campground is conveniently located within walking distance of downtown Duncan and the Cowichan Native Village. Heading south from Duncan on Hwy. 1 cross the bridge and take the first right onto Boys Road. Take another right in one block and the campground will be straight ahead.

Bald Eagle Campground 8705 Chemainus Rd, RR 1, Chemainus, B.C. V0R 1K0; 250 246-9457; http://www.cow-net.com/becamp/; 66 sites, open all year - Actually located closer to Chemainus than Duncan, this riverside campground is next to the Chemainus River and offers swimming in the river. Easiest access is from Chemainus. Just drive south on the Chemainus Highway (the main north-south highway through town) for 6 kilometers (4 miles), the campground is on the left.

Cowichan River Provincial Park 800 689-9025 for reservations; 43 sites, open all year - A Provincial Park on the Cowichan River between Duncan and Cowichan Lake. The campground is fairly new with good large sites, it's called Stoltz Pool Campground. From it you have access to several hiking trails, not to mention the river. Access is from Hwy. 18. Watch for the sign for the campground 15 kilometers (9.5 miles) from the Hwy. 18 intersection with Hwy. 1.

Gordon Bay Provincial Park 800 689-9025 for reservations; 130 sites, open all year - This large lakeside provincial campground is on the warm south side of Cowichan Lake and features a swimming beach. To reach it take Hwy. 18 west from a point just north of Duncan, drive 26 kilometers (16 miles) to the town of Lake Cowichan, then another 14 kilometers (9 miles) on South Shore Road.

Day 6 - Destination Victoria
56 kilometers (35 miles), 1 hour

A long the Way - From Duncan it is only a short drive south to Victoria. Twenty-nine kilometers (18 miles) south of Duncan the highway climbs to the **Malahat Summit**, there is a great viewpoint but access from the southbound lanes is limited, you may have to drive another kilometer or so to a good turnaround if you want to stop and enjoy the view.

A few kilometers after the summit viewpoint you pass through **Goldstream Provincial Park**. This park has an excellent campground and is convenient to Victoria. It also has a number of hiking trails through first-growth forest of Douglas fir and cedar as well as waterfalls and look-out points.

Once you pass Goldstream Park you're only a short distance from Victoria and it is time to start watching for the city campgrounds.

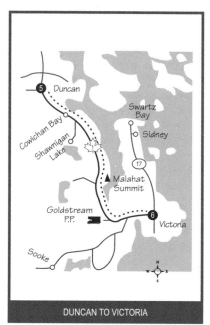

DUNCAN TO VICTORIA

Victoria and the Saanich Peninsula

At the far south end of Vancouver Island the city of Victoria (population 335,000) played many historical roles. Originally the area was a popular First Peoples site, they harvested camas bulbs where Beacon Hill Park is today. In the 1840s the Hudson Bay Company selected a site on the excellent harbor for their western headquarters. Victoria soon became the capital city of the colonies of British Columbia and Vancouver Island. When Vancouver became the terminus for the transcontinental railroad Victoria remained the capital city, but slid into a long period of existence as a quiet tourist attraction and bastion of Britishness. Today the town is rapidly growing but still very pleasant, a great place to live or to visit.

The tourist business in Victoria probably can be dated to the construction of the huge Canadian Pacific Railway **Empress Hotel** in 1908. The hotel remains one of the most popular destinations for the millions of tourists that visit Victoria each year, quite a few on cruise boats from Seattle. Many come for the formal afternoon tea at the hotel. The downtown area, particularly near the hotel, is full of sights and activities for these tourists.

In the immediate vicinity you'll find the following sights, and more. **Red double-decked busses** from London used for tours of the city and the area are popular. At the docks in front of the hotel you can sign up for **whale-watching tours** or catch one of the tiny **harbor ferries**. The **Parliament Buildings** face the hotel across grass lawns, they're lit at night and tours are conducted. The excellent **Royal British Columbia Museum** should not be missed, it has full-sized displays of natural history, cultural history, and the art and culture of the area's First People populations. Other attractions devoted to the daily tourists including **Miniature World, Ann Hathaway's Cottage, the Royal London Wax Museum, Helmcken House, Craigdarroch Castle**, the **Maritime Museum,** the **Crystal Gardens,** and the **Undersea Gardens**.

There are several reasons to get out and away from Victoria. Probably the most popular attraction outside the city is the **Butchart Gardens**. They fill a former limestone quarry on the west side of the Saanich Peninsula. The gardens are one of Victoria's most-visited sights and cover over fifty acres. Nearby are the **Butterfly Gardens** where you'll find thousands of butterflies in an enclosed garden.

For a longer drive you might want to visit **Port Renfrew**. The town is located 104 kilometers (64 miles) from Victoria up the southwest shore of Vancouver Island, Highway 14 is paved for the entire distance. The highway travels past several provincial parks giving access to the beach and from China Beach Provincial Park to Port Renfrew the road is paralleled by the **Juan de Fuca Marine Trail**. Port Renfrew is known as the starting point for the 77-kilometer (48-mile) **West Coast Trail** which leads north along the wild coast to Bamfield. **Botanical Beach** in Port Renfrew is a great tidepool area. It is possible to follow gravel logging roads north from Port Renfrew to **Cowichan Lake**, check road conditions locally before attempting this drive.

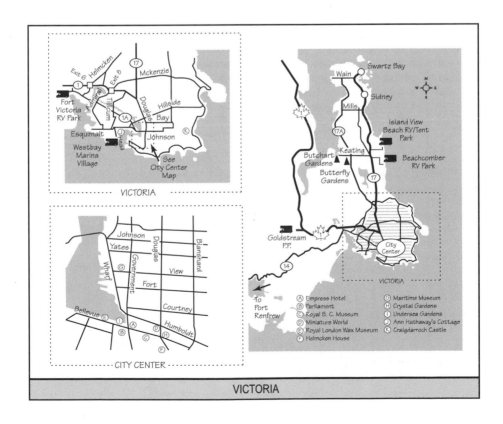

Victoria Area Campgrounds

Fort Victoria RV Park [MED] [symbols] 340 Island Highway 1A, Victoria, BC V9B 1H1; 250 479-8112; http://wwwfortvicrv.com; 300 sites, open all year - This is a very large and well-run campground conveniently located near the freeway where Highway 1 enters Victoria. There is good bus service in to town. It is easily visible from Hwy. 1 as you approach Victoria from the north. Take Exit 8, marked Helmcken Road and follow the signs on a roundabout route about 1.8 kilometers (1.1 miles) to the campground.

Westbay Marine Village [MED] [symbols] 453 Head St., Victoria, B.C., V9A 5S1; 250 385-1831; www.westbay.bc.ca; 61 sites, open all year - This campground sits right on the shore of West Bay, you can look across Victoria's inner harbor at the city. You can also walk along waterfront bike paths right into town, a distance of about 4 kilometers (2.5 miles) or take the bus or the tiny harbor ferryboats. Follow signs from Highway 17 at the Admirals Road exit just west of Victoria, you'll drive south on Admirals Road for 4.5 kilometers (2.8 miles), turn left on Esquimalt Rd. and drive 1.4 kilometers (.9 miles), then turn right on Head and follow signs through the neighborhood to the campground.

Goldstream Provincial Park [LOW] [symbols] 800 689-9025 for reservations; 159 sites, open all year - This is a large provincial park campground conveniently located very near Victoria. The fine hiking trails are a bonus. It's located right off Hwy. 1 as you descend from Malahat Summit into town.

Beachcomber RV Park [MED] [symbols] 3290 Campion Rd., Saanichton, B.C. V8M 1W7; 250 652-3800; www.beachcomberrv.com; 60 sites, open April 16 to October 15 - The campground has a great location right on the beach on the east side of the Saanich Peninsula. For self-contained camping vehicles only. To find it follow Martindale Rd. east from Hwy. 17 between Victoria and Saanich.

Island View Beach RV / Tent Park [MED] [symbols] Homathko Rd (off Island View), Saanichton. B.C. V8M 1W4; 250 652-0548; 50 sites, open April 15 to October 2 - Another campground right on the beach on the east shore of the Saanich Peninsula. Facilities are simple but the setting is nice. Follow Island View Road 3 kilometers (1.9 miles) east from Highway 17, then turn left when you reach the beach.

DAY 7 - DESTINATION VANCOUVER
69 kilometers (43 miles) (does not include ferry), 3.5 hours (including ferry)

The ferry back to Vancouver departs from Swartz Bay at the north end of the Saanich Peninsula. To get there just drive north on Hwy. 17 from Victoria for 32 kilometers (20 miles). Ferries run frequently. They dock at Tsawwassen which is only a half-hour drive south of Vancouver.

Information Resources

See our Internet site at www.rollinghomes.com for Internet site links.

Destination Powell River

BC Ferries, 1112 Fort Street, Victoria, B.C. V8V 4V2; 250 386-3431 and (in Canada only) 888 BC FERRY

Powell River InfoCentre, 4690 Marine Ave., Powell River, B.C. V8A 2L1; 604 485-4701

Destination Campbell River

Campbell River Visitor InfoCentre, 1235 Shoppers Row, Box 400, Campbell River, B.C. V9W 5B6; 250 287-4636

Gold River Visitor InfoCentre (May 15 to September 6), Hwy 28, Box 610, Gold River, B.C. V0P 1G0; 250 283-2418

MV Upchuck III; 250 283-2325

Destination Tofino

Alberni Valley Visitor Info Centre, 2533 Redford St, RR 2, Site 215, Comp 10, Port Alberni, B.C. V9Y 7L6; 250 724-6535

Tofino Visitor Info Centre, Box 249, Tofino, B.C. V0R 2Z0; 250 725-3414

Ucluelet Visitor Info Centre (May to September), Junction Hwy 4, Box 428, Ucluelet, B.C. V0R 3A0; 250 746-4641

MV Lady Rose; 250 723-8313 or 800 663-7192

Destination Nanaimo

Nanaimo Visitor Info Centre, Beban House, 2290 Bowen Rd, Nanaimo, B.C. V9T 3K7; 250 756-0106 or 800 663-7337

Destination Duncan

Duncan Visitor Info Centre (April 15 to October 15), 381A Trans Canada Hwy, Duncan, B.C. V9L 3R5; 250 746-4636

Cowichan Native Village, 200 Cowichan Way Duncan, B.C. V9L 6P4; 250 746-8119

Lake Cowichan Visitor Info Centre (May 24 to September 6), 125 C, South Shore Rd, Box 824, Lake Cowichan, B.C. V0R 2G0; 250 749-3244

Destination Victoria

Victoria Visitor Info Centre, 812 Wharf Street, Victoria, B.C. V8W 1T3; 250 953-2033

BC Ferries, 1112 Fort Street, Victoria, B.C. V8V 4V2; 250 386-3431 and (in Canada only) 888 BC FERRY

INDEX

ABOUT THE AUTHORS

Several years ago Terri and Mike Church decided to do some traveling. Their savings wouldn't cover hotels and restaurants for anything like the length of time they wanted to be on the road. On the other hand living out of a backpack wasn't a particularly attractive idea either. RVs turned out to be the perfect compromise.

In their time on the road the Churches have toured the continental U.S., Europe, Alaska, and Mexico in one type of RV or other. During the course of their travels they noticed that few guidebooks were available with the essential day-to-day information that camping travelers need when they are in unfamiliar surroundings. *Traveler's Guide to European Camping*, *Traveler's Guide to Mexican Camping*, *Traveler's Guide to Alaskan Camping,* and *RV Adventures in the Pacific Northwest* are designed to be the guidebooks that the authors tried to find when they first traveled to these places.

Terri and Mike now have a base of operations in the Seattle, Washington area but they continue to spend at least nine months of each year traveling. The entire first edition of the Europe book and most of the Mexico, Alaska, and Northwest books were written and formatted using laptop computers while on the road.

EUROPE

Traveler's Guide ToEuropean Camping
by Mike & Terri Church
6" x 9" Paperback
448 pages, over 250 maps

ISBN 0-9652968-3-0

D oes the map on the side of your camping rig show you've visited most of the 48 contiguous states, Alaska, or even Mexico? You've shopped the biggest mall in America, wintered in the Florida Keys, camped in the desert outside Quartzsite, Arizona, seen the color in the Northeast in the fall? What next?

If you're looking for a new camping experience, try Europe. ***Traveler's Guide To European Camping*** makes touring the European continent as easy and as affordable as traveling in North America. The guide gives you complete information for planning your trip as well as cost data and specific instructions on how to:

❏ Ship your camping vehicle from North America to Europe.

❏ Buy a camping vehicle in Europe.

❏ Rent a camping vehicle in Europe.

The guide covers almost 250 campgrounds including one in virtually every important European city. Both directions and maps are provided to make finding the campgrounds in these foreign cities as easy as finding those in America. The book features campgrounds in:

*	Paris	*	Munich	*	The Romantic Road
*	London	*	Madrid	*	The Loire Valley
*	Rome	*	Athens	*	The Swiss Alps
*	Lisbon	*	Istanbul	*	The Greek Islands
*	Amsterdam	*	Oslo	*	And Many More!

In addition to planning and campground information, *Traveler's Guide To European Camping* gives you invaluable details about the history and sights you will encounter. This information will help you plan your itinerary and enjoy yourself when you are on the road.

Go for a week, a month, or a year. Europe could fill your vacations or RVing seasons for another ten years!

MEXICO

Traveler's Guide To Mexican Camping
by Mike & Terri Church
6" x 9" Paperback
416 pages, over 200 maps

ISBN 0-9652968-1-4

How would you like to spend your winter camped near crystal-clear blue water on a white sand beach? Mexico has many world–famous beach resorts, and they all have campgrounds. Try Cancun, Acapulco, Ixtapa, Mazatlan, or Puerto Vallarta. If you are looking for a beach, but not a resort town, Mexico has miles and miles of beautiful, empty beaches and many of them also offer camping opportunities.

If beaches aren't your thing, don't despair. The interior of Mexico is full of attractions. Many North Americans are drawn to superior climate and cultural attractions of Guadalajara, Lake Chapala, San Miguel de Allende, Alamos, Guanajuato, and Cuernavaca.

Visit Mexico City, the largest city in the world. Or see the Pre-Columbian Mesoamerican archeological sites scattered throughout the country. There are so many sites you may even discover one yourself!

Traveler's Guide To Mexican Camping will give you all the information you need to cross the border and travel Mexico like a veteran. The book features:

- ❑ Complete descriptions of over 200 campgrounds, accompanied by maps and detailed driving instructions for each campground listed. You'll know the exact location of virtually every campground in Mexico.

- ❑ Coverage of the entire Mexico mainland and the Baja Peninsula.

- ❑ Four possible itineraries including the Baja Peninsula, the Grand Coastal Tour, Colonial Mexico, and Down the West Coast.

- ❑ Border Crossing Information including maps of the major border crossing cities.

- ❑ Descriptions of sights to see and things to do in every city covered by the guide.

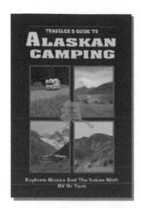

ALASKA

Traveler's Guide To Alaskan Camping
by Mike & Terri Church
6" x 9" Paperback
416 pages, over 100 maps

ISBN 0-9652968-2-2

Alaska, the dream trip of a lifetime! Be prepared for something spectacular. Alaska is one-fifth the size of the entire United States, it has 17 of the 20 highest peaks in the U.S., 33,904 miles of shoreline, and has more active glaciers and ice fields than the rest of the inhabited world.

In addition to some of the most magnificent scenery the world has to offer, Alaska is chock full of an amazing variety of wildlife. You are likely to see bald eagles, Dall sheep, moose, bison, brown bears, caribou, beavers, black bears, a wide variety of marine birds and waterfowl, whales, porpoises, sea lions, sea otters, and even more. Some of these animals may even pay you a visit at your campsite.

Alaska is an outdoor enthusiast's paradise. Fishing, hiking, canoeing, rafting, hunting, and wildlife viewing are only a few of the many activities which will keep you outside during the long summer days.

Traveler's Guide To Alaskan Camping makes this dream trip to Alaska as easy as camping in the "lower 48". It provides details on:

❏ Over 400 campgrounds throughout Alaska and on the roads north in Canada with full campground descriptions and maps showing the exact location of each campground.

❏ Complete coverage of the routes north, including the Alaska Highway, the Cassiar Highway, and the Alaska Marine Highway.

❏ RV rental information for both Alaska and Canada.

❏ Things to do and see throughout your trip, including suggested fishing holes, hiking trails, canoe trips, wildlife-viewing opportunities, and much more. There's even a full chapter on off-road camping trips for those who want to venture away from the beaten path!

ORDER FORM

To order complete the following and send to:

Rolling Homes Press
P.O. Box 2099
Kirkland, WA 98083-2099

Name_____

Address_____

City_____State_____Zip_____

Telephone_____

Description	Qty	Price	Subtotal
Traveler's Guide To Alaskan Camping	____	$19.95	_____
Traveler's Guide To Mexican Camping	____	$19.95	_____
Traveler's Guide To European Camping	____	$19.95	_____
RV Adventures in the Pacific Northwest	____	$14.95	_____
3 Book Set (3 Different Titles) Please List	____	$49.95	_____
4 Book Set (4 Different Titles)	____	$59.95	_____

Method of Payment

❑ Check

❑ Visa

❑ Mastercard

Order total: _____

Shipping: ___4.00 *

Total: _____

Credit Card #   Exp. date
_____

Signature
_____

To order by phone call toll free from the U.S. or Canada 1-888-265-6555
Outside the U.S. or Canada call (425) 822-7846
Have your VISA or MC ready

U.S. Dollars or MC/VISA only for non-U.S. orders

Rolling Homes Press is not responsible for taxes or duty on books shipped
outside the U.S.

*$4 shipping regardless of quantity ordered for all orders sent to the same address

Visit our web site at **www.rollinghomes.com**